T0384056

The Secret of Coaching and Leading by Values

Coaches play a major role in helping people understand their values and the values of their surroundings and helping them make choices and adapt. Sometimes the choice may be to find a situation more in sync with your values. Or it may mean working hard on yourself or in concert with your partner, team, or organization. Whatever we need to do to attain it, a positive fit makes for a happier person, and a happier person will be more successful. This accessible and practical book will help coaches, educators, leaders, and managers understand the philosophy, methodology, and tools that can be used to make a person happier, healthier, and more productive at work and in life in general.

This book compiles short vignettes from over a dozen global academics and celebrated executive coaches, sharing information about aligning values in different settings. Based on years of research and written for readers from all walks of life, you will learn that when you understand your core values, place them on a triaxial template, and align them with your definition of success, everything changes. It will help you come out of your comfort zone in order to embrace the future and enhance the quality of your life. For this, you need a concept, a methodology, and effective tools, all of which are offered in this book.

Rich with practical step-by-step methodologies and tools to facilitate values-led leadership, coaching, and mentoring, this book is essential for any change agent, be it a coach, a leader, an educator, or any person who is interested in learning how to become more effective, improve their practice, and engage in self or professional coaching. At the same time, it will enhance leadership qualities.

Simon L. Dolan is a prolific author with over 75 books published in various languages on themes connected with values, people management, coaching, leadership, consulting, and the future of work. He has more than 40 years of research track teaching at the world's leading business schools in the United States, Canada, and recently Spain (ESADE). He is also the president of Gestion MDS Inc, a Montreal-based consulting firm, and a think tank foundation, "The Global Future of Work," which he recently created.

The Secret of Coaching and Leading by Values

How to Ensure Alignment
and Proper Realignment

Simon L. Dolan

Routledge
Taylor & Francis Group
LONDON AND NEW YORK

First published 2020
by Routledge
2 Park Square, Milton Park, Abingdon, Oxon OX14 4RN

and by Routledge
52 Vanderbilt Avenue, New York, NY 10017

Routledge is an imprint of the Taylor & Francis Group, an informa business

British Library Cataloguing-in-Publication Data
A catalogue record for this book is available from the British Library

Library of Congress Cataloging-in-Publication Data
Names: Dolan, Simon L. (Simon Landau), 1947- author.
Title: The secret of coaching and leading by values: how to ensure
alignment and proper realignment / Simon L. Dolan.
Description: Abingdon, Oxon ; New York, NY: Routledge, 2020. |
Includes index.
Identifiers: LCCN 2020006646 (print) | LCCN 2020006647 (ebook) |
ISBN 9780367456368 (hardback) | ISBN 9781003025146 (ebook)
Subjects: LCSH: Employees–Coaching of. | Executive coaching. |
Personal coaching
Classification: LCC HF5549.5.C53 D65 2020 (print) |
LCC HF5549.5.C53 (ebook) | DDC 658.3/124–dc23
LC record available at https://lccn.loc.gov/2020006646
LC ebook record available at https://lccn.loc.gov/2020006647

ISBN: 978-0-367-45636-8 (hbk)
ISBN: 978-1-003-02514-6 (ebk)

Typeset in Bembo
by Deanta Global Publishing Services, Chennai, India

This book is dedicated to the community of Coaching by Values (CBV) (CoachingxValores in Spanish) and the new emerging community of Leadership by Values (LBV). Since the first edition of CBV was published in 2011 in English, and in 2012 in Spanish, and under the leadership of David Alonso, the community of Coaching by Values has evolved enormously throughout the world, but more specifically in Spain and in the South and Central American continent. The people involved in the community are professionals who have dedicated energy and passion to a divine mission of changing the world and making it a better place to live. I have a deep respect and admiration for these people and gratitude for believing in me. This book has become the Bible (the DNA) for the community, of CBV and LBV, although more products and methodologies are emerging every year and have added significant creative value to my initial thoughts via a process of co-evolution. This book uses the collective experience accumulated both by me and others who have practiced the methodology and tools throughout the globe in the past several years. But I am particularly in debt to my colleague Dr. Salvador Garcia, who has co-developed with me the concept of the triaxial model of values, and who led the writing of the first book on values (in Spanish) in 1997. Thus, I feel in debt to them for the process of co-evolution and wish to dedicate this book to the community leaders, the certified coaches, and the thousands of people like you, who will certainly join us after reading this book.

Contents

Author

Professor Simon L. Dolan is a prolific author who has written over 75 books in multiple languages on various themes connected with values, culture, coaching, work-health, leadership, and, more recently, the future of work. Simon has taught and conducted research at some of the leading global business schools spanning North America, Europe, South America, the Middle East, and Asia. He has published over 150 articles in scientific journals and is a highly sought speaker who has presented over 800 lectures and conferences throughout the globe. Professor Dolan is the co-founder of several organizations of the future, such as the e-Merit Academy and the Global Future of Work Foundation (www.globalfutureofwork). In addition, Professor. Dolan is the co-creator and leader of the "Coaching by Values," and the "Leadership by Values" communities that currently certify professionals and have thousands of followers in all corners of the world. To learn more, visit www.simondolan.com

Contributor (Chapter 7)

David Alonso is the CEO and co-founder of the "coachingxvalores" brand as well as the "Leadershipbyvalues" brand. He graduated in business administration and has a Master's degree in sales and marketing. He has been a professional certified coach (PCC and ICF) since 2009 with over 2000 hours of coaching experience. He is also a certified coach in NLP and the first master trainer in Coaching by Values. He is the creator of the Coaching by Values community, and with his team has certified over 1800 people across the globe, but more specifically in the Spanish-speaking countries. See: www.coachingxvalores.com.

Foreword

Are you wasting your time on value statements?

The corporate credo. Companies have wasted millions of dollars and count-less hours of employees' time agonizing over the wording of statements that are inscribed on plaques and hung on walls. There is a clear assumption that people's behavior will change because the pronouncements on plaques are "inspirational" or certain words "integrate our strategy and values." There is an implicit hope that when people—especially managers—hear great words, they will start to exhibit great behavior.

Sometimes these words morph as people try to keep up with the latest trends in corporate-speak. A company may begin by striving for "customer satisfaction," advance to "total customer satisfaction," and then finally reach the pinnacle of "customer delight."

But this obsession with words belies one very large problem: There is almost no correlation between the words on the wall and the behavior of leaders. Every company wants "integrity," "respect for people," "quality," "customer satisfaction," "innovation," and "return for shareholders." Sometimes compa-nies get creative and toss in something about "community" or "suppliers." But since the big messages are all basically the same, the words quickly lose their real meaning to employees—if they had any in the first place.

Enron is a great example. Before the energy conglomerate's collapse in 2001, I had the opportunity to review Enron's values. I was shown a wonder-ful video on Enron's ethics and integrity. I was greatly impressed by the com-pany's espoused high-minded beliefs and the care that was put into the video. Examples of Enron's good deeds in the community and the professed character of Enron's executives were particularly noteworthy.

It was one of the most smoothly professional presentations on ethics and values that I have ever seen. Clearly, Enron spent a fortune "packaging" these wonderful messages. It didn't really matter. Despite the lofty words, many of Enron's top executives either have been indicted or are in jail.

The situation couldn't be more different at Johnson & Johnson. The phar-maceutical company is famous for its Credo, which was written many years ago and reflected the sincere values of the leaders of the company at that time. The J&J Credo could be considered rather quaint by today's standards. It contains several old-fashioned phrases, such as "must be good citizens—support good works and charities—and bear our fair share of taxes" and "maintain in good order the property that we are privileged to use." It lacks the slick PR packaging that I observed at Enron.

Yet, even with its less-powerful language and seemingly dated presentation, the J&J Credo works—primarily because, over many years, the company's management has taken the values that it offers seriously. J&J executives have consistently challenged themselves and their employees not just to understand the values, but to live them in day-to-day behaviors. When I conducted leadership training for J&J, one of its top executives spent many hours at every class. The executive's task was not to talk about compensation or other perks of J&J management, it was to discuss living the company's values.

A couple of years ago, my partner, Howard Morgan, and I completed a study of more than 11,000 managers in 8 major corporations. (See "Leadership Is a Contact Sport," by Marshall Goldsmith and Howard Morgan, Strategy + Business, Fall 2004.) We looked at the impact of leadership development programs in changing executive behavior. As it turns out, each of the eight companies had different values and different words to describe their ideal leadership behavior. But these differences in words made absolutely no difference in determining the way leaders behaved. One company spent thousands of hours composing just the right words to express its view of how leaders should act—in vain. I am sure that the first draft would have been just as useful.

In many companies, performance appraisal forms seem to undergo the same careful scrutiny as credos. In fact, more effort seems to be put into formulating the perfect words on an appraisal form than managing employee performance itself. I worked with one company that had used at least 15 different performance appraisal forms and was contemplating yet another change because the present sheet "wasn't working"! If changing the words on the page could improve the performance management process, every company's appraisal system would be perfect by now.

Companies that do the best job of living up to their values and developing ethical employees, including managers, recognize that the real cause of success—or failure—is always the people, not the words.

Rather than wasting time on reinventing words about desired leadership behavior, companies should ensure that leaders get (and act upon) feedback from employees—the people who actually observe this behavior. Rather than wasting time on changing performance appraisal forms, leaders need to learn from employees to ensure that they are providing the right coaching.

Ultimately, our actions will say much more to employees, about our values and our leadership skills, than our words ever can. If our actions are wise, no one will care if the words on the wall are not perfect. If our actions are foolish, the wonderful words posted on the wall will only make us look more ridiculous.

I hope that this book on values can serve you, and the leaders you interact with, in committing and governing in congruence with your statements. In this book, we find information on the importance of values, on how they can be audited, measured, and placed in a hierarchy. The book also offers some useful tools enabling reflection and development of a strategy for succeeding in the life of business and in the business of life. I applaud this creative and educational initiative.

Dr. Marshall Goldsmith
Consultant
Co-founder of Marshall Goldsmith Partners
Consulting

Dr. Marshall Goldsmith, UCLA, PhD, and co-founder of the Marshall Goldsmith Partners Consulting, is a world-renowned consultant who turns already successful leaders into even better leaders. *The London Times* named him "one of the 50 greatest management thinkers who still live and influence leaders today." He has published more than 23 literary works and books, many of which have become bestsellers, and he is one of the few consultants who has advised more than 100 CEOs of some of the largest companies. He is a member of many NGOs and is hyper-solicited as a global speaker. To learn more about his works, see www.MarshalGoldsmithlibrary.com. He can be reached via email at Marshall@2MarshallGoldsmith.com.

Preface

What's new in this book?

When I wrote *Coaching by Values* and published it in 2011, I had never dreamed that it would become an established school of thought within the coaching community. However, to my surprise and great pleasure, the impact of the first version was massive. A lot of things have happened since 2011. We are in a constant state of coevolution; this coevolution came about because the book has been translated into many languages including Hebrew, Arabic, Portuguese, French, Italian, and I, myself, have traveled hectically to spread the message. In parallel, a true community of Coaching by Values (www.coachingxvalores.com) has evolved in Spain and the Iberoamerican continent under the leadership of David Alonso and Laura Moncho. The community is doing a lot of things.

In addition to using the massive digital media to spread the message, the community has entered into an agreement with prestigious organizations such as the ICF (International Coaching Federation) and the AECOP (Spanish Executive Coaching Association) to prepare various certification programs for coaches, leaders, and other professionals. Today, we have trained and certified thousands of people, coaches, leaders, and educators all over the world. They have been certified to adhere to our code of conduct, and we guarantee that they possess a good knowledge base and a relatively high level of competence to practice coaching by values and/or to be familiar with our recently released APPs in "Leadership by Values" (see www.leadershipbyvalues.com). I continue to receive messages from people who have been trained (and certified) by our master-expert coaches, telling me that their lives have changed (for the better), and they thank me for developing the concept, methodology, and, especially, the tools that help them, as they use them to train and provide services to others with a view to enhancing life and well-being.

Thus, this type of very positive feedback fueled my body and soul and gave me the energy to do more, to create more tools and to refine the ones already in use. Many more activities and certifications and innovations are planned for the next few years. This new book already includes more information, more ideas, and an expanded methodology, with the aim of helping professionals accomplish the not-so-easy role of becoming an effective coach and/or an effective leader.

In this book, I (along with my star alliance partners, and selected world-renowned experts who have been invited to add their opinion or share their practice) try to deliver the message in a much more complete manner. The ideas are parsimonious (it seems simple), but always keep in mind that many years of research are embedded in the messages. In addition, given the development of the Web, the Internet, and the latest technologies, I have tried to take advantage of the suggestions and comments of members of our community, so that the text is complete and up to date.

For years I have been saying that *Coaching and Leading by Values* is based on my 40 years or more of research. Being trained in science, I don't like to use just empty words; I like to echo my messages with research-based evidence that supports my claims and arguments. I have spent years validating the ideas, methodologies, and tools put forward in this book. Obviously, I am not claiming that this is a purely scientific book. Nonetheless, much of the content is based on rigorous research and has been completed recently using the experiences shared by followers of the methodology. Therefore, in this book, I continue to mix science and practice.

This book includes several innovations compared to my previously published books. The most important thing is that my collaboration with some world leaders and coaches I've met in my role as an executive coach, academic, or consultant has convinced me that we need to write an entire chapter dedicated to those who want to help leaders do a better job by becoming executive coaches. This topic is also related to my recent book in Spanish titled: *Leading, managing and Coaching by values: the 10 commandments of managing people in the XXI century* (self-published by "Circulo Rojo," 2018 and Amazon). However, this new chapter is aimed at not only professional coaches, but also at leaders who want to have a basic understanding of how to coach and mentor their teams with a focus on values. The other innovation is a chapter where we share practical applications of the methodology of coaching by values. This chapter was written by my partner, the corresponding director of the leadership and coaching by values communities, David Alonso. David, along with Laura Moncho, has trained and certified thousands of coaches and has accumulated unique practical no-nonsense experience, and thus I have asked him and Laura to share their wisdom with the readers of this book.

I am privileged to have eminent experts contributing to this book through short vignettes in various chapters. You will meet and get to know them as you move from one chapter to the other. They have been listed in alphabetical order of their first name in the Acknowledgment section of this book. I am indebted to Dr. Marshall Goldsmith, who was kind enough to step into the shoes of the late Sir John Whitmore, who had promised to write the foreword to this book but unfortunately passed away in 2018. Marshall is perhaps the best-known global executive coach currently. He has coached and trained the leaders and the executives of the world's most famous and well-known companies; hundreds or perhaps thousands of people attended his webinars, workshops, and speeches. Some of his books are bestsellers and have a substantial impact on how we understand today's leadership. I am fortunate to have him as a collaborator in this book, and I am very grateful.

So, what was my main dilemma in the preparation of this book? My earlier writing, such as *Coaching by Values* (2011) and other related books, enjoyed huge success and I was afraid to add content that will dilute the former message. In addition to sales, news, and citations on social networks, the old books were reviewed by independent experts, and received extraordinary evaluations and praise. Here is a short excerpt of what reviewers say about the *Coaching by Values* book. If you wish to read the complete review, I suggest that you log on to www.forewordreviews.com/reviews/coaching-by-values/ (reviewed by Barry Silverstein-Clarion).

> In recent years, coaching has grown in importance (and popularity) in many areas of life. This widespread interest in coaching makes Simon Dolan's *Coaching by Values* particularly relevant. Dolan, who has extensive coaching experience in business, approaches the topic with a scientific eye, referencing numerous sources to first offer a comprehensive overview of coaching in general and then define and detail the concept of coaching by values Written with a sense of passion and purpose about a meaningful and important topic, Coaching by Values is not a breezy business book. It will take work on the part of the reader to fully comprehend the depth of Dolan's discussion and to understand how best to apply his methodology. The reader who works through this book should be better off for the effort.

And here is another review, by the late Professor Ruth Alas, published in the book review section of *Cross Cultural Management: An International Journal*, in 2013:

> The value of this book lies in the applicability of the concept of coaching by values in organizations. In addition to the theoretical aspects of coaching and values, practical tools are also presented to the reader. It provides the tools and guidelines for self-coaching and coaching others followed by examples of implementation. The book suits both academicians through assisting research and practitioners through serving as a practical guide. Since the two fields overlap, the book fits perfectly in the libraries of both academic and organizational institutions.
>
> The real treat for consultants, however, lies in the fourth chapter, entitled "CBV Methodologies and tools for everyone." The 34 pages appear more like a manual than academic reading. Detailed guidelines are given on how to implement the 7-step process of coaching by values. Some steps include 8 sub steps, described in detail as well. In the conclusion the author

highlights the need to be creative and imaginative within these steps, and the importance of developing a personalized approach.

To conclude, by addressing real human needs, this book conveys meaning and value at both the individual and organizational levels and is good value for money. It contains the convincing story of how implementing coaching by values can help to enhance the well-being of the individual and the working environments in organizations. The final sub-chapter "Values in the New Age" invites readers to consider new global needs and new paradigms. In Estonia we have a saying—"Several heads are better than one head." From this we can conclude that thinking together about critical issues for our common future in a global world will help to create something for the common good.

Similar reviews hailing the book were published in Blue Ink, Amazon, Google books, and other outlets. And finally, I can't resist mentioning an interview that is still available on the Internet with Pep Guardiola (the legendary football coach) of Futbol Club Barcelona, then Bayern Munich, currently with Manchester City. When asked what were the books that impressed him, his list included my book *Coaching by Values*.[1]

In short, once you have a good product, you don't want to change it completely. So in this book I have opted to update, fine tune, clarify, reduce redundancies, improve the quality of graphics (figures and tables), add two new chapters (one on leadership and executive coaching and the other on applications of the methodology), and expand the chapter on the future, speculating about new paradigms in the field of values and in the field of leadership and coaching. This is all linked to my previous work as the future of work chair at ESADE Business School in Barcelona, and my current position as the President of the Global Future of Work Foundation (see GFWF, www.globalfutureofwork.com).

I would like to take this opportunity and thank some of the people who have helped me develop and promote the concept of Coaching and Leading by Values. David Alonso is the leader and promoter of the values concept. He has created communities that attempt to make the world a better place to be via values of the Spanish-speaking readers of this book. He has the vision and the entrepreneurship skills to develop the community with its different offerings and products. Please visit the website at www.coachingxvalores.com and judge for yourself. He also wrote the final chapter in this book sharing practical experiences. Laura Moncho is the co-president and current director of the various certification programs in the Iberoamerican world. David and Noelia Alonso are also the current directors of the Leadership by Values training and certifications (www.leadershipbyvalues.com). I also wish to thank Mr. Isidro Fainé, the former president of CaixaBank and current president of the CaixaBank Foundation, for all his support and encouragement and for his generosity in writing the preface to two of my recent books in Spanish: *Liderazgo, Dirección y Coaching por Valores: los 10 mandamientos para gestionar personas en el siglo XXI* (2018) and *Más Coaching por Valores* (2019).

My brother Avishai Landau lives in Israel and manages the Israeli Center for Values (see www.values-center.co.il). Avishai is also the co-developer of the main tool that coaches and leaders use, which we have labeled *The Value of Values*™. Today he is helping me develop several new tools that will be available soon and especially the new game/tool to identify and manage the stress of our life. We tentatively labeled this new tool *The Stress Map*.

In addition, I am blessed to have a list of certified contributors and coaches who broadcast the message across continents and in several languages: Avi Liran in Singapore (and Asia), Phil Harrell in Australia, and Martine Guidoni and Adnane Belout, who were involved in the French-speaking countries (in the future we hope to engage Veronique Barlange); and Paola Valeri in Italy; Misael Enoch in Puerto Rico; Daniela Vatti in Argentina; Patricia Franco in Peru; Marie De Lemus in Guatemala; Kristine Kawamura, Bonnie Richley, and Tony Lingham in the United States; Anat Garti in Israel; and Ani Páez in Spain. As the community expands, I imagine that, in the next edition of this book, we will add many more people, countries, and languages to the list. My apologies if I have forgotten anyone.

As a result of all this evolution, we have created a new concept, a methodology, and the tools required to help organizations diagnose and train leaders who must cope with the challenges posed by the chaotic world in which we live today. We labeled this new concept *Leadershipbyvalues*™ and it is available for use online—it is a 100% web-based assessment tool. If you want to know more, please visit www.leadershipbyvalues.com.

While we are producing this book, the world is on hold as we are all suffering and fighting the terrible CORONA Virus. Nobody can ignore the fear (life and death) that accompanies us for months, and the emotions of uncertainty about life and work in the future. Thus, we have decided at the last minute to add a postscript containing an article published at the *European Business Review* where many of the concepts discussed in this book are described in reference to the COVID19 pandemic.

I would never have completed this second edition without the help of my lady. Adela is my partner in life and has freed me from thousands of chores and has provided an environment that facilitated the calm, reflection, and meditation that allowed me to think and write. Thank you, Adela, for being there and stepping in to encourage and motivate whenever necessary.

Simon L. Dolan
www.simondolan.com and www.globalfutureofwork.com
President of the Global Future of Work Foundation
Barcelona and Montreal, Spring-Summer 2020

Note

1 See: www.sport.es/es/noticias/barca/la-biblioteca-del-despacho-de-guardiola-1226 051 (checked on February 1, 2019 and site was active).

Acknowledgments

This book contains short inserts from the following world leading experts and coaches:

Alessandro de Vita Zublena—Master coach in "PNL" (Swiss)

Anat Garti—Master trainer in Coaching and Leading by Values (CLBV) and a specialist in "Family coaching & education" (Israel)

Ani Paez—Master coach in CBV and a specialist in "Educating by values" (Spain)

Avi Liran—Master trainer in delivering happiness, Master coach CLBV (Singapore)

Avishai Landau—Master coach and trainer in leading, managing, and coaching by values—CLBV (Israel)

Bill Phillips—Trainer and Master coach in "PNL" (UK)

Bonnie Richly—Professor, consultant, and co-author of "Managing by Values" (USA)

Dave Ulrich—Professor, consultant with RBL, and Master coach in executive coaching and HRM (USA)

David Caruso—Trainer and master coach and co-developer of the methodology of Emotional Intelligence (USA)

Kristine Kawamura—Trainer and master coach in "Affection, Care and Values" (USA)

Michael Arloski—Trainer and master coach in "well-being" (USA)

Michele Hunt—Consultant and aster coach in "executive coaching" (USA)

Nacho Plans—Master coach and strategic consultant in culture transformation (Spain)

Phil Harrel—Trainer and master coach in leading, managing, and coaching by values—CLBV (Australia)

Richard Barrett—Writer, trainer, founder, and president of the "Barrett Value Academy" (UK)

Salvador García—Professor, consultant, co-author of "Managing by Values" and author of "The intelligence of Values" (Spain)

Tony Lingham—Professor, consultant master coach in CLBV and a specialist in high-performance team coaching (USA)

Introduction

A short voyage into the history of Coaching and Leading by Values

"Coaching by Values" (*CBV*), "Managing by Values" (*MBV*), "Leading by Values" (*LBV*), and "Coaching and Leading by Values" (*CLBV*) were born many years ago. In fact, humans have been using them ever since we first attempted to organize work. Only recently, however, has the significance of values been part of the global discussion on coaching, leading, and managing. As a part of my contribution to this conversation, I crafted the formal methodologies for "Managing by Values" (*MBV*) with Salvador Garcia in the late 1990s (in Spanish) and then with Salvador Garcia and Bonnie Richley in the early 2000s, "Coaching by Values" (*CBV*) in the middle of the 2000s, and "Leading by Values" (*LBV*) with David Alonso, which is still being developed these days. I created them after a series of internal debates based on my academic work, my experiences as a professional consultant, and the evolution of my personal life.

In the 1970s, I experienced a "management reality shock" that forced me to rethink the basic paradigms underlying most methods of dealing with and managing people in organizational and nonorganizational contexts. While completing my doctoral work in Minnesota, I was at the Mayo Clinic and the University of Minnesota Hospital conducting a small-scale qualitative study of patients who had survived their first heart attack. I discovered that more than 90% of these patients attributed their condition to stress at work. At about the same time, I noticed the constant push of senior managers in organizations to increase productivity without taking larger issues into consideration. They completely ignored such critical questions as: Why do we work? What is the purpose of our firm/organization? Are profits and power the supreme objective whereby all means justify ends?

This led me to see the essential paradox of modern societies: We have better hygiene conditions and medical care, better working conditions, and more means to provide care and enjoy leisure, but many of us kill ourselves trying to achieve or conform to unrealistic goals. Today people are not only killed by physical guns but also (and likely more often) by psychological ones: the threat of losing one's job (or partner), the pressure to perform at superhuman levels at work for prolonged periods, and so on. I realized that we were witnessing the emergence of a new type of toxicity. It has no color and no odor but causes tremendous suffering and illness, and at times it even leads to death.

I started to question deeper issues of life and death and the meaning of life (work life and personal life) in general. I also began to search for a new definition of success. I was convinced that in any organizational or social context (e.g., partner, family, community, and the like), success had to include the well-being and prosperity of both the organization and the individuals who make it up. To begin to examine this two-dimensional (organization and individual) approach to success, I developed a four-quadrant model (see Figure I.1).

Quadrant *A* represents a win–win situation. Clearly the most problematic situation is quadrant *D*, where not only does a person perform poorly, but his or her health becomes affected as well. Quadrants *B* and *C* are also problematic zones in which either individual health or organizational health is affected. The question that this simple two-dimensional model of success suggested to me was: Can we create a culture in which people's well-being is not endangered (or is just minimally affected) or is even enhanced and in which their performance contributes to the organization's well-being?

I believed the answer was yes; it must be possible for people to perform well while keeping their personal mental and physical health intact. In fact, I hypothesized, this could lead to even better performance and make for a healthier and more robust organization. I thought long and hard about this and realized that a journey toward enhanced well-being would begin with values. And thus, this simple model became the foundation for "Coaching and Leading by Values," methods, tools, and techniques that can be used by professional coaches and for self-coaching and self leadership assessment in organizations and in life.

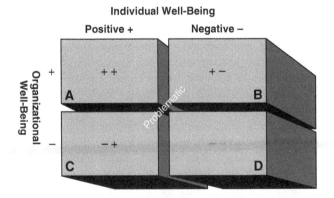

Figure I.I   A two-dimensional definition of success. Source: Dolan S. L., Arsenault A. (1980) Stress, santé et rendement au travail. Monographie #5, Université de Montréal. Used with the authors' permission.

Values are predispositions to our behavior; they are associated with beliefs and norms. I recognized that if we can understand our values, organize them in a coherent logic (a logic that makes sense to us), and align them with our goals (life, work, family, and so on), we can get closer to that state of utopia known as optimal well-being. To begin to create a model for this, I had to better understand the multidimensional core element that is represented by the construct of value(s).

A value is a belief, standard, mission, or principle that has worth and is useful.[1] Values are deeply held beliefs regarding what is good, correct, and appropriate. They help us determine how we should be and act if we are to be of worth to ourselves and useful to society. Values can range from the commonplace, such as the belief in hard work and punctuality, to the more psychological, such as self-reliance, concern for others, and harmony of purpose. Once we identify the values that are meaningful to us, we can develop strategies for implementing them. But toward what goal? What exactly is "optimal well-being"? Naturally, it varies from person to person, organization to organization, and culture to culture. But to create models flexible enough and specific enough to help people attain the state as they see it, I had to get more clarity about its universal elements. To arrive at a new definition, I needed to know more. I had to go beyond a general understanding of "well-being" and happiness by starting at the beginning.

Philosophers and social researchers have defined happiness and well-being in a variety of ways. The largest divide is between the hedonic view, which emphasizes pleasant feelings and avoidance of pain, and the eudemonic view, which emphasizes doing what is virtuous, morally right, true to one's self, meaningful, and growth-producing. The hedonic approach focuses on one's subjective well-being, which is usually seen as having two correlated components: (a) one's judgment of life satisfaction—overall or in specific domains such as relationships, health, work, and leisure—and (b) having a preponderance of positive feelings and relatively few negative feelings. In contrast, the eudemonic approach focuses on self-validation and self-actualization, and it suggests that the key to a happy or good life is to do what is right and virtuous, grow and pursue important or self-concordant goals, and develop and use one's skills and talents, regardless of how one may actually *feel* at any point in time.[2] I decided to take an eclectic approach in developing "*Coaching by Values*," an approach that would combine both.

And finally, "*Coaching by Values*" had to be a dynamic concept and a methodology susceptible to growth, able to change as the world is in constant change while staying true to its core. It has grown and evolved dramatically in the past several years, based on the feedback of thousands of practitioners and academics. I am sure that in the future it will evolve further (in chapter 6 I look at some possibilities for this, particularly, adding a spiritual dimension, and catering to the new generation—"generation Y"). But underlying this concept and this book is my belief that values are the most fundamental element of our road to success in the life of the business and the business of life.

Through self-coaching, or in dialogue with a professionally trained coach, you can improve the alignment of your values with your goals and achieve a more meaningful life and enhanced happiness. When your vision of reality finally matches reality itself, your actions will consistently produce the best possible results. This isn't just an individual journey; it involves all humankind. Social creations like democracy, human rights, global sustainability, and the right to food, education, partnership, and care are developments in the ongoing process of values clarification.

Coaching by Values is not just another fancy gadget or chimerical technique. In its application both to the individual and to larger cultures or contexts, it requires serious thought and mindful action. It gets to the heart of what it means to have a good life and a creative, robust, and versatile organization. It is integral to the entrepreneurial spirit and leadership necessary to imaginatively tackle the challenges confronting the world today. In the twenty-first century—at least at this point—no one can claim that there is not an oversupply of true entrepreneurs and true leaders either in our organizations or among other organizations.

Today, almost 40 years since I experienced the "management reality shock," things have not changed. We hear reports of epidemic proportions of suicides among professional employees of the giant French company *France Telecom* and of a wave of suicides of Chinese laborers who were stuck with repetitive, routine, and boring jobs. At a recent Davos meeting (World Economic Forum 2019) it was emphasized that, due to mental health issues, every 40 seconds a person commits suicide. According to the World Health Organization, depression and anxiety disorders cost the global economy $1 trillion every year in lost productivity. Yet the same study also suggested that every dollar invested in scaling up treatment for depression and anxiety—the two most common mental health conditions—can generate a return of $4 in terms of improved well-being and increased ability to work.[3] We are living in a twilight period in which people are experiencing a growing sense of futility and numbness in every sphere of life, not just at work, but in the family, in politics, and in economics. We see our environment decaying—or being destroyed—around us. We are facing constant chaos. Things are changing sporadically and unexpectedly at an ever-increasing pace, as can be evidenced in the coronavirus pandemic situation that is occurring now while I am reviewing this book.

I cannot provide any guarantees, and it may not be the last word, because there is no last word, but the content of this book addresses real human needs, it has real meaning, and it makes sense at both the individual and organizational levels. If you use the methods I've developed to audit, sort, and prioritize your values, align them with your goals, and follow them with concrete actions, embodying them in the smallest details of your life and work, the result will most likely be a more fulfilling and harmonious life, which in turn generates an inner satisfaction that increases your physical and mental well-being and energizes your state of mind. This is my definition of success.

I wish to conclude this journey by paraphrasing something I wrote in the preface of the 2011 version of *Coaching by Values*, which goes like this:

Values are words embedded with significant meaning,
So, when they are sorted, and translated into concrete behavior aligned with your goals/objectives
And, shared with people whom you care (work, family, friends),
They become a tool for a very powerful guide to:

Success in the life of business

and

the business of life

I hope that you will enjoy reading and learning from this book as much as I had when I wrote it. Remember that it is all about values. It can serve for auto-coaching or self-coaching as well as a model and a tool to be used by leaders and professional coaches.

Notes

1 As we will see later in the book, values, beliefs, and norms are not the same in terms of their etiology, i.e., there is a sequential development within each person and within societies from beliefs to values, which are then expressed on a social level as norms.
2 For an excellent review on happiness at work, see Fisher, C. D. (2010). Happiness at work. *International Journal of Management Reviews, 12*, 384–412. And for life happiness, I really recommend Ben-Shahar, T. (2007). *Happier: Learn the Secrets to Daily Joy and Lasting Fulfillment.* McGraw-Hill, and Ben-Shahar, T. (2018). *Short Cuts to Happiness: Life-Changing Lessons from My Barber.* The Experiment.
3 www.who.int/mental_health/in_the_workplace/en/

Chapter 1

A coaching kaleidoscope

1.1 Everyone can be a coach

Everyone can develop a personal life and find or create a work situation imbued with creativity, innovation, and playfulness. Everyone can find relative happiness, despite the dour predictions of politicians and pundits. And anyone can be a coach. You may be a professional coach, or perhaps you are a manager who is eager to engage employees. Maybe you just want to improve your own life or your spouse's. Maybe you want to help your colleagues—or your group or team—define goals and move toward their fulfillment effectively and efficiently.

In this chapter, I will present an overview of the types of coaching available and the primary schools of thought in the field. I will explore what it means to be a coach—and how coaching is different from mentoring, training, and counseling.

But primarily, this book is about values; it is about life values, work values, community values, world values, and all the values that power our lives and our organizations. It is also about value alignment. And in chapters 3, 4, and 5, I'll introduce you to a way of thinking about values and present a framework, a methodology, and tools for value reengineering—Coaching by Values.

1.2 What is coaching?

Coaching is the art of bringing out the greatness in people in a way that honors the integrity of the human spirit. It is both an innate human capacity and a teachable skill.

Coaching is not a new discipline that has suddenly been invented. It is probably as old as the first Stone Age spear-throwing competition and has always been a natural part of life for people everywhere. It is used by millions of great parents who love their children unconditionally, believe in them, and put their own needs aside to nurture their potential and encourage them to be great. It is used by thousands of great business leaders who try to develop their people, not by abusing their power, but by believing in them, challenging them, supporting them, giving them more positive than negative feedback, and making sure they take care of themselves.

The term *coach* originated in the sports field in the late 1880s and became a well-known sports profession that's taken many different forms over the years. Even today, the term *coaching* often produces a mental image of a football or basketball coach. Depending on what the coach actually does, this analogy may or may not be adequate. The head coach is in fact usually a general manager or chief executive officer responsible for running an entire program. The image of a quarterback coach or an offensive line coach who enables others to play through teaching is somewhat more accurate.

The first use of the term *coach* to mean an instructor or a trainer arose around 1830 at Oxford University as slang for a tutor who "carries" a student through an exam, but only in the past −20 years or so has an individual been able to purchase coaching services outside the sports or performance arena. The evolution of coaching has been influenced and enhanced by many other fields of study including personal development, adult education, psychology (sports, clinical, developmental, organizational, social, and industrial), and other organizational or leadership theories and practices.

In its modern application—as a new way of working with people within different contexts—coaching is a relatively new discipline. Although its emergence as a popular profession is unclear, according to some sources, it began in the United States in the late 1980s. Only a decade or two after its quick rise to popularity, however, the practice (at least in terms of application to management) appeared to fall into disuse for a time. These were the days of the full-blooded management-training programs and marathon groups.

The current field of coaching is the result of the convergence of several developmental strands dating back as far as the 1940s. Only in recent times has it been recognized as a field with a largely cohesive set of principles, knowledge, and skills. Since the mid-1990s, it has coalesced into a more independent discipline. The proliferation of coach-training schools—close to 100 in the United States alone—and the establishment of the International Coach Federation[1] (ICF) have led to a dramatic increase in the number of professional coaches worldwide. The ICF, one of the largest nonprofit professional coach associations, has more than 35,000 members spanning many chapters in 123 countries. Members in ICF hold one of three credentials: Associate Certified Coaches, Professional Certified Coaches or Master

Certified Coaches (MCC). It has drafted a set of core competencies for coaching that are now recognized as the fundamental competencies for this profession globally.

According to British sources, the most important developments in the profession of coaching, especially in the business world, include the following:

- Tim Gallwey's 1974 book *The Inner Game of Tennis* proposed a novel, psychological approach; he claimed that as well as being prepared physically and technically, a player must be prepared psychologically to attain peak performance. Gallwey, a tennis coach, observed that the opponent in one's head is greater than the one on the other side of the net.[2] From this observation, he pioneered the facilitative approach to sports coaching, a discipline that had previously been solely a skills-based learning experience with a master in the sport.
- In 1992, Sir John Whitmore, a motor racing champion, published *Coaching for Performance* in which he developed one of the most influential models of coaching, the GROW model (Goal, Reality, Options, Will). He has since become a guru in the business world and has continued to refine his model. The latest version of the GROW model appeared in the fifth edition of *Coaching for Performance*, published in 2017.[3]
- In the 1990s, the Western world went into recession, and corporate downsizing became the rage. It may have seemed good in theory, but did not take into account human needs. This left managers and leaders in highly stressed environments without support, increasing the need for individuals and organizations to continuously develop. This need for performance maximization contributed to the upsurge in coaching.
- When businesses first began to rely on coaches, they were brought in as often for poor performers as for high performers (often to deal with performance issues when the manager did not want the hassle or conflict). Now, however, the vast majority of coaching is aimed at high-level performers rather than remedial cases. Coaching today is for the high performer, top talent, and those leading an organization.

What is the process of coaching all about?

Coaching is for people looking to work actively toward making tangible changes. The process of coaching refers to the activity of the coach in developing the coachee's abilities, especially those required for making the sought-after change(s).

Coaching tends to focus on an existing problem that an individual wishes to resolve (or move away from) or on a specific outcome that the individual wishes to achieve (or move toward). In both cases, the coach aims to stimulate the coachee to uncover innate knowledge and/or skills so he or she can achieve a sustainable result. Coaches will normally make sure the specific learning can be successfully reapplied by the coachee to other problems in the future. The structure and methodologies of coaching are numerous, as we will see later, but all coaching approaches have one unifying feature: *They are predominantly facilitating in style*; that is, the coach mostly asks questions and challenges the coachee to learn from his/her own inner skills. The coaching process is underpinned by the coach's established trust in the coachee.

It is important to note here that—despite their focus on questioning and dependence on trust—coaching is not therapy, and coaches are not therapists; psychological intervention is outside the scope of the coach's tasking. The problems and outcomes that coaches address are rooted in current contexts with aims for the future; they do not have emotional etiology or baggage from the past—in other words, the coachee has the resources he/she needs to make reasonable progress at the time he/she seeks coaching. As Vicki Brock said in her 2008 doctoral dissertation on the history of coaching,[4] "Most definitions [of coaching] assume an absence of serious mental health problems in the client and that coaching's purpose is to affect some kind of change using similar knowledge, skills, and techniques."

During the process of coaching, a coach may find that a coachee is so unfamiliar, inexperienced, or ignorant of an area that requires sharp focus if the coachee is to achieve his or her stated aim(s) that the coach will need to impart knowledge and examples to the coachee. So, there may be an education component in which new skills or information are shared, but a coach always returns to the facilitation style.

Even though the practices and professional disciplines of coaching are diverse, the effects of the coach's questioning on the coachee are consistent and almost universally observed along a continuum of levels of challenges— regardless of the specific coaching approach: At the lowest level, questions excite intellectual processes in the coachee, and the coachee is observed to be alert and to respond quickly. When questions are more demanding (for example, "Imagine what it might be like to be the person you are experiencing relationship difficulties with"), the coachee will be observed to be actively alert, thinking and leaving pauses between some responses. The highest levels of challenges cause the coachee to access deeper structures in his or her experience than those accessible by a rapid, intellectual recall. This more in-depth information may include feelings (emotions), pictures, auditory experiences, and metaphors.

Coaching is most often performed on a one-to-one, face-to-face basis, but it may involve telephone or web-based sessions. Sometimes it is conducted totally via phone or web-based interaction. The coach may assign homework to be done between sessions as a way of beginning to help a client integrate changes into daily realities.

Some coaches are wholly coachee-centered and responsive to the coachee's objectives and needs. Other coaches set up a program or "learning journey" that the coachee must follow over a specified period of time. Some coaches or coach-training schools prescribe a certain number of models or a "toolkit" to guide the coach. There are also many generic coaching pathways to help coaches know where they are in a coaching process; these are used by both independent coaches and training schools (including academic and commercial schools and those affiliated with associations). Multiple coach-training schools and programs are available, allowing for many options (and sometimes causing confusion) when an individual decides to gain "certification" or a "credential" to apply to the coaching industry.

Core competencies for coaches

Regardless of his or her approach, a professional coach must have the following core competencies:[5]

- **Knowledge:** Knows the background of coaching and can distinguish coaching from counseling, therapy, training, and consulting; has familiarity with the specialist vocabulary of coaching; and knows the criteria for testing both process and outcome goals.
- **Relationship skills:** Builds a relationship of respect and trust with the coachee; works so the coachee is accountable for the coaching process and the tasks he or she agrees to in that process; and creates an equal, synergistic partnership with the coachee.
- **Listening skills:** Fully attentive during the coaching process; able to listen and provide support to the coachee's self-expression; focuses on the coachee's agenda and not his or her own; and finally, is in touch with and pays attention to his intuition.
- **Self-management skills:** Keeps his or her own perspective and does not become enmeshed in the coachee's emotions; evaluates and distinguishes the different messages the coachee gives; is sensitive to and calibrates the coachee's nonverbal signals. "Calibration" is more critical in some coaching schools of thought (such as NLP) than in others, as we will see later.
- **Inquiry and questions:** Helps the coachee define the present situation in detail; asks powerful questions that provoke insight, discovery, and action; uses different perspectives to reframe and clarify the coachee's experience; supports the coachee's growing self-awareness; and finally, makes the coachee aware of incongruence between his or her thoughts, emotions, and actions.
- **Feedback skills:** Shows the coachee areas of strength and elicits and supports his or her inner resources; shows the coachee where habits are holding her back and supports any change she wants to make; celebrates the coachee's successes.

- **Goals, values, and beliefs:** Works with the coachee to overcome limiting beliefs; explores the coachee's values and helps coachee become aware of them; does not impose his or her own values; works with the coachee to clarify his goals and check that they are congruent with his values; clearly requests actions that will lead the coachee toward his or her goals.[6]
- **Designing actions and tasks skills:** Creates opportunities for ongoing learning for the coachee; gives appropriate tasks for the coachee to challenge him or her and move her forward toward her goals; helps the coachee to develop an appropriate, measurable action plan with target dates; provides challenges to take the coachee beyond her perceived limitations; and finally, holds the coachee accountable for the mutually agreed tasks and actions.

Differences between coaching and mentoring, managing, and training

Advocates of coaching claim that the role of coaches and the processes they employ are very different from those used in consulting and other helping professions. Although there is some overlap between coaching and mentoring, coaches are supposed to help clients build skills, while mentors shape mental attitudes. Moreover, while instructors and teachers train for immediate tasks, coaches are supposed to accompany achievements. Here is an encapsulation of the responsibilities of managers, trainers, and mentors:

- Managers need to ensure that people do what they know how to do.
- Trainers need to teach people to do what they don't know how to do.
- Mentors need to show people how the people who are good at doing something do it.

Coaches seem to be none of the above. They are supposed to help people identify the skills and capabilities that are within them (inner skills) and enable them to use these to the best of their abilities, increasing the individual's independence and reducing reliance.

However, as we will see later, increasingly companies are expecting their managers to have some coaching skills that they can use to guide their employees and help them realize their potential.

The principal differences between mentoring and coaching are found primarily in the areas of focus, role, relationship, source of influence, and arena, as listed in Table 1.1.

A nice way to distinguish between coaching and mentoring has been provided in a site labeled: NHS Education for Scotland and is provided in Table 1.2. It is helpful to understand these differences because although many of the processes are similar, they are generally delivered by individuals with different qualifications and different relationships with their clients.

Table 1.1 Differences between Mentoring and Coaching in Work Context

	Mentor	Coach
Focus	Individual	Performance
Role	Facilitator with no agenda	Specific agenda
Relationship	Self-reflecting	Perks (come with the job)
Source of influence	Perceived value	Position
Arena	Life	Task related

Source: Adapted from: www.coachingandmentoring.com/Articles/mentoring.html

Table 1.2 Key Differences between Mentoring and Coaching

Coaching	Mentoring
Coaching aims to develop the coachee's potential. The focus is on development/enhancing performance. Aimed at specific present-moment work-related issues, and career transitions.	The focus is on developing the mentee professionally, career development, and managing transitions. Takes a broader view of the person. Mentor can open doors to activities and opportunities.
The coach and the client are equals working in partnership. The coach does not require direct experience of the client's role.	A mentor has more experience than a client, and shares it with a more junior or an inexperienced employee.
Coaching is essentially non-directive; though this is not a hard and fast rule.	Mentoring is typically more directive, sharing experiences, offering advice.
The coach/coachee ratio of speaking is roughly 20:80.	The mentor/mentee ratio of speaking is roughly 40:60.
At a transactional level, coaching enables the client to incorporate skills into their leadership/management repertoire. Coachees develop their self-awareness and awareness of their impact on others. Coach can sometimes enable the client to achieve transformational behavioral and attitudinal change.	Enhances the client's technical and business-related skills. Develops the mentee professionally.
Structured meetings of variable length every month or so. Relatively short term.	Can last for a long period.
Meet in the client's organizations or a neutral place.	Can be informal and meetings can take place as and when the mentee needs some advice, guidance, or support.

1.3 Types of coaching

Having glimpsed the complexity and diversity of the professional disciplines, methodologies, and theories that have helped shape coaching, it is clear to me that there is no one single definition of coaching. Consequently, I titled this chapter "A coaching kaleidoscope" because of this variety of focuses, approaches, and paradigms involved in the coaching process. I also found useful a classification offered by Hawkins & Smith (2006), who have developed a continuum of coaching that has four distinct types of focuses: skills, performance, development, and transformation (see Figure 1.1).

Having outlined the basic coaching focus and process and the competencies an effective coach must have, I'll present—at the risk of leaving out some important facets of the discipline—a few of the major types of coaching, each of which has its own paradigms, gurus, and leaders. In the next section ("Principal Schools of Thought in Coaching"), we will turn to principal schools of thought in the coaching field.

By "types of coaching," I'm referring to the environments in which coaching takes place and the types of clients involved. "Business coaching" takes place within an organizational context and may involve an individual, a team (e.g., a department or a group working together on a project), or the organization (e.g., a small business or nonprofit). "Executive coaching" focuses on an individual executive in a business setting. Over the years, I noted that executive coaching is really expanding and most solicited, so I have decided to add an entire chapter (the next one—chapter 2) to describe it and connect it to our value model. But there is also, obviously, "Life coaching," which is a one-to-one relationship with a client regarding personal goals. "Family coaching" is coaching within the family; it may involve a couple, parents, teens, or other family members.

Business coaching

Business coaching is always conducted within the constraints placed on the individual or group by the organizational context. Interestingly, a good business coach need not have specific business expertise and experience in the same field as the person receiving the coaching to provide a quality business coaching service. Business coaches often help businesses grow by creating and following a structured, strategic plan to achieve agreed-upon goals. However, coaches are not consultants; business analysis is outside the realm of their activities, although some coaches may have a background in this field.

Coaching is not a practice restricted to external experts or providers. Many organizations expect their senior leaders and middle managers to coach their team members toward higher levels of performance, increased job satisfaction, personal growth, and career development. These organizations back up their expectations with training in coaching skills, access to feedback tools, and/

HAWKINS (2006) GOES ON TO DESCRIBE A USEFUL CONTINUUM OF
COACHING THAT DISTINGUISHES FOUR TYPES OF COACHING BY
THEIR MAIN FOCUS. THESE ARE:

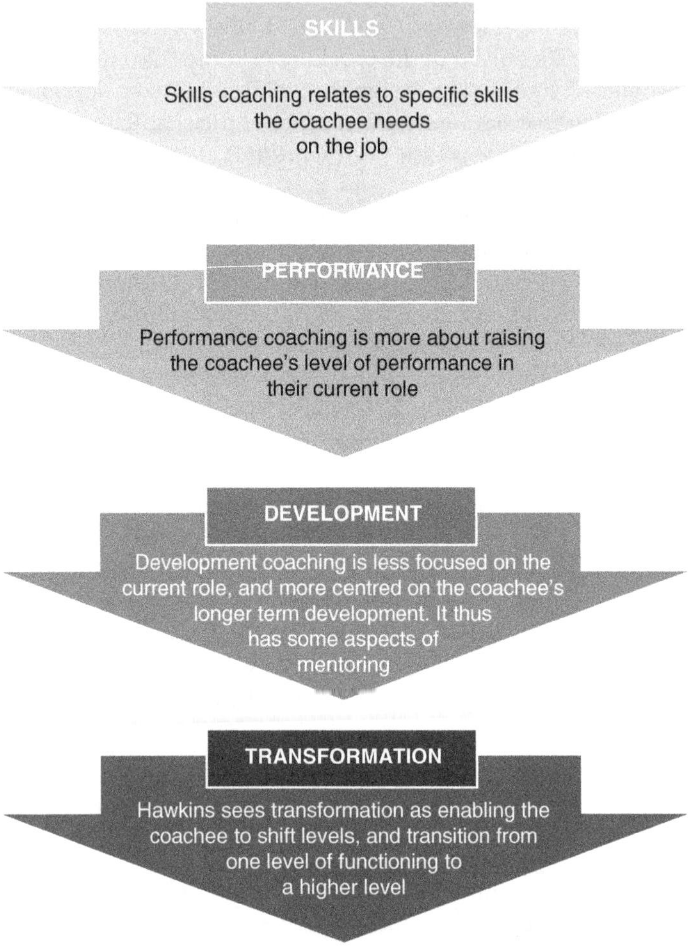

SKILLS

Skills coaching relates to specific skills
the coachee needs
on the job

PERFORMANCE

Performance coaching is more about raising
the coachee's level of performance in
their current role

DEVELOPMENT

Development coaching is less focused on the
current role, and more centred on the coachee's
longer term development. It thus
has some aspects of
mentoring

TRANSFORMATION

Hawkins sees transformation as enabling the
coachee to shift levels, and transition from
one level of functioning to
a higher level

Figure 1.1 Hawkins & Smith type of coaching in their corresponding focus. Source: Hawkins P., Smith N., (2006) *Coaching, Mentoring and Organizational Consultancy.* Open University, McGraw Hill. Found in: www.central.knowledge.scot.nhs.uk/ CoachMentor/assets/4_similarities-and-differences between-coaching-and-mentoring.pdf

or descriptions of specific coaching behaviors in their leadership competency models. In many organizations, human resource managers are gaining expertise either in coaching or in selecting and subcontracting business coaches for their top talents.

Executive coaching

This is a special case within the business coaching model. Executive coaching is the one-to-one relationship between a coach and a client based on the intrapersonal goals of the client within the organizational context.

Whereas coaching was once viewed by many as a tool to help correct underperformance, today, as I mentioned earlier, it is becoming much more widely used to support top producers. In fact, in a 2004 survey by Right Management Consultants (Philadelphia), 86% of companies said they used coaching to sharpen the skills of individuals who have been identified as future organizational leaders.

Although both the organization and the executive must be committed to coaching for it to be successful, the idea of engaging a coach can originate either from human resources and leadership-development professionals or from the executives themselves. In the past, it more often came from the organizational side. But given the growing track record of coaching as a tool for fast movers, more executives are choosing coaching as a proactive component of their professional life.[7]

Many approaches and models are used for executive coaching. According to the Linkages Best Practices in Coaching Survey, which included participants from 19 countries, the majority of organizations that use coaching use it for developing leaders with one or a combination of the following models or concepts: 360° feedback (62%), action learning (48%), supervisor interview (48%), peer interview (40%), behavior modeling (35%), Appreciative Inquiry (32%), and shadowing (29%).[8] We will look at some of these in the next chapter.

Life coaching

Life coaching, or personal coaching, is a future-focused practice designed to help clients determine and achieve personal goals. It has its roots in executive coaching, which itself drew on techniques developed in management consulting and leadership training. Life coaching also draws inspiration from disciplines including sociology, psychology, positive adult development, mentoring, career counseling, and other types of counseling. An individual coach may employ such techniques as values assessment, behavior modification, behavior modeling, goal setting, and others.

The process of life coaching is accomplished by first gaining a thorough understanding of an individual's personal traits, needs, and wants, then developing an understanding of the goal(s) or aim(s) to be achieved, and finally formulating action plans, review processes, and measurable outcomes. Goals may be in almost any realm of life, including personal, business, educational, relationship, and health.

Some people trace the origin of life coaching to Thomas Leonard, a former financial planner who came on the coaching scene in about 1988 from the business world. While working for Werner Erhard, he began doing life planning work on the side, creating a course titled "Life Creates Your Life." With others, he assembled some basic ideas about life planning, applied to the knowledge derived from the business and financial arenas, and launched the industry we now call life, or personal, coaching. He organized his concepts into a curriculum for training coaches that could be implemented around the world via telephone. He also set up his own company and founded a coaching university (www.coachu.com).

Between 1998 and his sudden death at 47 in 2003, Leonard authored six coaching-related books: *Working Wisdom, The Portable Coach, Becoming a Coach, Simply Brilliant, The Coaching Forms Book,* and *The Distinctionary.* He is widely credited with having codified, popularized, and globalized the coaching discipline. Interestingly, while he was collaborating with thousands of people, he held within the broader vision of these efforts a vision of himself as a highly impactful leader and as one who was competitive with others doing similar things; he was intensely competitive and intensely collaborative at the same time.

Psychology and life coaching may seem—at first glance—to be pretty much the same thing. However, while psychology helps you understand your life better and uncover why you do the things you do, life coaching is more like your cheerleader along the way, using common sense tools to guide you forward. Life coaching can be therapeutic, but like other forms of coaching, it isn't therapy Table 1.3 shows the distinctions that Leonard and others have made between coaching and therapy.

Table *1.3* Differences between Coaching and Therapy

Coaching is about ...	Therapy is about ...
Achievement	Healing
Action	Understanding
Change or transformation	Change
Momentum	Safety
Intuition	Feelings
Joy	Happiness
Performance	Progress
Synchronicity	Timing
Attraction	Protecting
Creating	Resolving

In sum, the primary functions of a life coach are to aid individuals in the achievement of their goals, aims, and aspirations and to help individuals, couples, and groups achieve lasting joy and synchronicity.

Family, couples, and parents coaching

Like all coaching disciplines, family coaching is forward-moving and action-based. It is focused on creating strong family ties and explores ways coachees can deal effectively with issues and flourish as a family "team." Family coaches may be part of parent coaching or teen coaching (a discipline that is becoming increasingly popular), or they may fall under a variety of other areas of coaching.

As we know, all parents face challenges as they raise their children to adulthood. Parenting involves highs and lows, laughter and joy and excitement, as well as trials, difficulties, and exhaustion. The knowledgeable, objective voice of a parent coach can be helpful and supportive in this parenting process. Parent and family coaching explore innovative and learning-based approaches for raising children, becoming effective parents, and creating healthier, happier families.

The focus in couples coaching is on growth, going beyond where the couple is now, and bringing into their life the qualities they want. They may be looking for:

- intimacy and passion
- harmony
- increased care and affection
- clear decisions about contentious topics
- a shared vision of life together

In couples coaching, the process starts with understanding the couple's hopes, dreams, and aspirations for a love relationship. Then the coach attempts to zoom in on individual aspects of these and create a positive tension for change, which leads to experimentation. Sometimes this involves learning new communication skills. But the principal focus is on using the partners' inner skills to help each one see himself or herself through new eyes and to reorient them to what registers as love, enabling their relationship to make a major shift.

What's is on the horizon for the profession of a coach?

Since my involvement with the Global Future of Work Foundation (www.globalfutureofwork.com), we are accumulating data that enables us to make some predictions about the future of some professions, the disappearance of others, and the emergence of new ones. Our experience in the field of coaching has led us to make the following observations:

- The number of new professional coaches will increase as the profession is still in the growth period. However, it will level off over time, as many coaches will be unprepared to compete with the increased competition.
- Coaching will no longer be considered exotic or just for the rich and famous. It's becoming almost as common as personal training today. Many people will have a positive experience and will see the benefits of coaching from childhood onward.
- Advanced technologies will provide coaches with excellent options to serve their customers internationally, while local services requiring face-to-face connections remain important. Actually, we predict a hybrid model of coaching delivery for which technology will enable us to integrate online with offline. Most coaching in corporate settings is likely to be done through computers, smartphones, and other mobile devices.
- Professional coaching will be regulated in some countries, and others will follow. These regulations will require coach-specific training, certification and/or university qualifications, as well as compliance with standardized codes of ethics as requirements for coaches who coach for a fee.
- Coach training will be done through tele-seminars, webinars, or other online methods. Many private coaching schools will close, leaving mostly the training to credible associations (i.e., ICF) or aligned with universities. Coach training will be conducted through multimedia distance education and less through live training at universities and hotel conference rooms. As universities try to take on the work of educating coaches, the cost of training coaches will be skyrocketing.
- Consumers will generally be aware of the horror stories of poorly pre- pared coaches and know that they should not seek help from uncertified coaches. There will be no single dominant certification center, as many will exist at the same time. True, this will lead to greater confusion among those who hire coaches, as well as those who want to become coaches. Nonetheless, newer coaches will have titles, certifications, and/or certifi- cates related to the coaching of reputable schools and universities for their rigor and code of ethics. The oldest coaches, those with years of coaching experience, but not possessing certifications and titles, will survive only if they have an excellent reputation as effective coaches.

What does all this mean for people who want to practice coaching in the future? Well, the future looks extremely bright for talented coaches. If you plan to be a professional coach and want to get paid well, do whatever it takes to distinguish yourself as one of the best. That includes training, certifications, and evidence-based coaching skills with a clear methodology and good tools. Consider getting more from a certification of good thematic coaching, as that may soon be a requirement to practice coaching in the place where you live. In addition, it will help you stay up to date with important trends, earn higher fees, and help you stay in business if regulatory kicks in.

1.4 Principal schools of thought in coaching

There are numerous schools of thought in coaching (only some of which I'll present here). The variety and sheer number may seem overwhelming if you're new to the field, but the existence of all these models and theories opens a world of opportunities. They provide an abundance of tools, techniques, methodologies, and models you can put into action. They offer a wealth of information, views, and knowledge that can increase your understanding and hone your ability to think critically and discriminatingly. They may even challenge your assumptions—such as those you may have about the boundary between action and thought—but in rising to these challenges, and in being attentive to your reactions to them, you will become more self-aware and more aware of the people and world around you, more ready to facilitate an effective coaching process.

1.4.1 John Whitmore and the GROW model

The GROW model (or process) is a technique for problem solving or goal setting. It was developed in the UK by Sir John Whitmore and his colleagues and used extensively in the corporate coaching market in the late 1980s and 1990s. It was a pioneer model in coaching, and it still has impact today. GROW is very well known in the business arena, but it also has many applications in everyday life. A value of GROW is that it provides an effective, structured methodology that simultaneously helps set goals and solve problems. According to Whitmore, it can be used by anyone and does not require special training. It is easy to understand, straightforward, and very thorough. In addition, it can be applied effectively to a variety of issues.

The version of the GROW model in Figure 1.2 is a modification of Whitmore's original. It ascribes two different meanings to the O, it is a bit different from the original way Whitmore envisioned it. There are other versions of the model as well, with various views of the stages (see Figure 1.3 for which the drawing I developed is closer to the original of Whitmore model).

Like many simple methods, GROW provides users an opportunity to apply a great deal of skill and knowledge at each stage, but the basic process remains the same. There are numerous questions the coach may use at any point, and part of the coach's skill is knowing which questions to use and how much detail to uncover.

GROW was developed from the Inner Game theory that Timothy Gallwey[9] crafted after noticing that even though he could often see what tennis players were doing incorrectly, simply telling them what they should be doing did not bring about lasting change.

Gallwey's theory is often illustrated by the example of a player who does not keep his or her eye on the ball. To try to correct this, most coaches would give instructions like, "Keep your eye on the ball." The problem with this

Goal	This is the end point, where the client wants to be. The goal has to be defined in such a way that it is very clear to the client when they have achieved it.
Reality	This is how far the client is away from their goal. If the client were to look at all the steps they need to take in order to achieve the goal, the Reality would be the number of those steps they have completed so far.
Obstacles	There will be Obstacles stopping the client getting from where they are now to where they want to go. If there were no Obstacles the client would already have reached their goal.
Options	Once Obstacles have been identified the client needs to find ways of dealing with them if they are to make progress. These are the Options.
Way Forward	The Options then need to be converted into action steps which will take the client to their goal. These are the Way Forward.

Figure 1.2 A GROW model of coaching. Note: This version was available in 2011 and thus cited in my book. Apparently it was removed and is no longer available on the net. I still like it. The original was found in: http://en.wikipedia.org/wiki/GROW_model, accessed March 28, 2011.

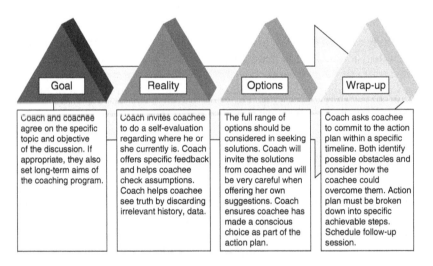

Figure 1.3 Whitmore's GROW model of coaching.

sort of instruction is that a player would be able to follow it for a short while but would be unable to keep it in the front of his mind in the long term. As a result, progress was slow. Coaches and players grew increasingly frustrated at this laggardly progress, but no one had a better system of coaching. One day, instead of instructing a player to "keep his eye on the ball," Gallwey asked him to say "bounce" out loud when the ball bounced and "hit" when he hit it. The player started to improve without a lot of effort because he was keeping his eye on the ball—without needing to maintain a voice in his head saying, "Keep your eye on the ball." Instead, he was playing a simple game while playing tennis. Once Gallwey saw how play could be improved in this way, he stopped giving generalized instructions and started asking questions that would help players discover for themselves what worked and what needed to be changed. This was the birth of the Inner Game.

A useful analogy to the GROW model is the plan you might make for an important journey. First, you start with a map; with this, you help your team members decide where they are going (their Goal) and establish where they currently are (their Current Reality). Then you explore various ways of making the journey (the Options). In the final step, establishing the Will, you ensure that your team members are committed to making the journey and are prepared for the conditions and obstacles they may meet along the way (Figure 1.4).

The GROW model is deservedly one of the best known and most widely used coaching models. It provides a simple yet powerful framework for navigating a route through a coaching session and for finding your way when lost.

While GROW is a helpful model/technique, in his later writings, speeches, and conferences, Whitmore insisted that the role of a coach is to help the coachee unlock his or her potential and that this involves more than just using tools such as GROW. The key to unlocking potential is the coach's ability to be aware—that is, the coach must be able to acquire a basic understanding of the organization (or environment) in question, be able to gather facts and information, and be able to determine the relevance of these by considering the organizational dynamics. In addition, because coaching deals with human nature, knowledge of some of the basic tenets of psychology on the part of the coach is important.

One of Whitmore's central precepts is responsibility. An acceptance of responsibility leads to commitment, which optimizes performance. He emphasizes the need to move away from a "blame culture" in which responsibility is constantly shifted onto someone else. According to Whitmore, the job of a manager can be simplified into two central tasks: get the job done and grow

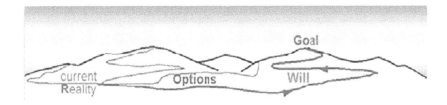

Figure 1.4 A schema of Whitmore GROW model.

the staff. If you apply the principles of coaching to the job, both of those tasks can be accomplished simultaneously.

The GROW model can be used as a self-coaching tool for improving your performance and developing a road map to your personal success. Identify specific goals you wish to achieve; assess your current situation; list your options; make choices (narrow and prioritize your goals); and finally, take steps toward your specific goals and define a time frame.

Next, let's examine two brief ways to use the GROW model. The first is a three-minute speed-coaching session with a coach and an overweight teenager. The second is a self-coaching exercise.

CLBV Reflection ♣ ♠ ♥

Speed coaching using the GROW model

Coach: What area would you like to discuss?

Teenager: I'd like to do some more exercise. (THEME OF COACHING)

Coach: And what would you like out of the coaching session? (QUESTION TO ESTABLISH THE GOAL)

Teenager: I'd like to commit to taking some regular exercise.

Coach: Where are you now when it comes to exercise? (REALITY QUESTION)

Teenager: I'm not exercising as regularly as I'd like.

Coach: So if you'd like to commit to regular exercise (THE GOAL OF THE SESSION), what are your options?

Teenager: I was given a fancy heart rate wrist monitor; I could learn how to use it. I could get my old bike serviced. I could try a bit of running as well. I could find an event in the future that I could aim for.

Coach: Of all these options, which are you most committed to? (NARROWING DOWN THE OPTIONS)

Teenager: I'd like to use my new heart monitor while I am biking. I was told that I can improve my heart-rate functioning and at the same time reduce my weight. There's a safe 30-km trail in the city that goes around and inside the parks; I think I'd like it.

Coach: So what will you do between now and the next time we talk? (FURTHER NARROWING DOWN TO SPECIFIC OBJECTIVES)

Teenager: I'll call a friend who has a similar overweight problem and ask him to join me at least three times a week doing the trail. If he doesn't come with me, I'll do the trail myself. The first time I'll try a 10-km stretch (and watch my heart-rate monitor before and after); the second time I'll bike for 20 km (and also watch my monitor); and the third time I'll try to do the entire 30-km trail (probably during the weekend). I'll also weigh myself today and next week before we meet again.

Coach: Are you sure your objectives are realistic? Will you complete them with or without a friend? (REFLECTIVE QUESTIONS TO ENSURE THE GOALS ARE REALISTIC)

Teenager: I am committed to up to 20 km with or without a friend. Depending on the experience, I may commit to the 30 km alone, but if I find that too difficult, I'll stop at around 20 km.

Coach: OK. I think that I understand your plans and your commitments. I will see you next week, and we will discuss the accomplishments of the objectives and fine-tune your goals. (WRAP-UP)

Teenager: See you next week.

CLBV Reflection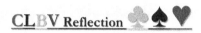

Self-coaching: using the GROW model on yourself

Whether you've begun to go through the GROW self-coaching steps I mentioned above and are trying to choose among a few possible goals, or already have a goal in mind, you can use this GROW exercise. Simply choose one goal and ask yourself these four questions:

1. Why?

_____

_____

_____

_____

_____

2. Why not?

_____

_____

_____

_____

_____

3. Why not me?

_____

_____

_____

_____

_____

4. Why not now?

_____

_____

_____

_____

_____

Note: As I was preparing this book, the bad news has arrived about the death of John Whitmore. I had the honor to be with him a couple of times in London, and have been inspired and pushed to write my first coaching by values book back in 2011. John is considered to be one of the fathers and founders of modern coaching. His figure will be kept forever in my memory. In 2018, I edited a book, written by 17 certified coaches by values which was labeled: _Values: The Compass for People and Organizations of the Future_ (2018), which was dedicated to the memory of John Whitmore. The book is available (in Spanish only): www.amazon.es/Valores-brújula-personas-organizacio nes-futuro/dp/8417479066

1.4.2 Laura Whitworth and others: The Co-Active Coaching model

The central principle of Co-Active Coaching, developed by Laura Whitworth and colleagues,[10] is that both parties actively collaborate in the coaching partnership. It is based on the following four fundamental principles:

- The client is naturally resourceful and capable of finding the answers to her challenges herself.
- The agenda comes from the client and is the key focus of the coaching relationship.

- The coaching addresses the client as a whole person.
- The coaching relationship is a "designed alliance" for promoting action and learning, in which the client, and not the coach, is ultimately in control.

This model concentrates on the development of specific coaching skills and techniques rather than on the content or structure of a coaching session.

The purpose of the Co-Active Coach is to meet clients' needs and help them achieve the results they want. The client's agenda is at the very center of this model. Whitworth and her colleagues highlight three important elements of this:

- fulfillment (achieving success and reaching client's full potential)
- balance (addressing all aspects of the client's life)
- process (focusing on the means as well as the end result)

Based on the above, the authors propose five key coaching skills: listening, intuition, curiosity, action learning, and self-management. The Co-Active Coaching model is graphically represented in Figure 1.5.

An inquiry, which is the basis of the Co-Active Coaching, is a powerful question that is not meant to be answered immediately, but instead, offers the coachee an opportunity for reflection, discovery, and learning. The power questions, or inquiries, below were adapted from *Co-Active Coaching*, by Whitworth et al.

Figure 1.5 The Co-Active Coaching model. Source: Adapted from Donnan, S. (2007, May) Appreciative inquiry and co-active coaching. *AI Practitioner.* p. 37.

CLBV Reflection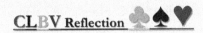

Sample co-active coaching power questions

- What do I want?
- What am I tolerating?
- Where am I not being realistic/practical?
- Where is my attention?
- What is the difference between a wish and a goal?
- If my whole attention is focused on producing the result, what will I have to give up?
- What is working for me?
- What will it take to keep me on track?
- What am I willing/unwilling to change?
- What am I settling for?
- What is it to be creative/passionate/focused/a leader?
- What is it to speak/act from my heart?
- What does it mean to be proactive/centered/optimistic?
- What is present when I am at my best?
- What motivates me?
- What am I resisting?
- If I were at my best, what would I do right now?
- What are my assumptions (about life, work, family, etc.)?
- Where do I limit myself?
- Where do I hold back?
- What are my expectations for this project (or life, family, work—area under consideration)?
- How can I make this easy?
- Whom can I get to play with me on this project?
- What have I learned about myself (by contemplating these questions and throughout the project)?

Advocates of Co-Active Coaching describe the process as "a thought clarification process." Two of its underlying assumptions distinguish it from other coaching schools of thought. The first is that no other person can ever know enough about you to decide for you more effectively than you can decide for yourself. Based on this assumption, most people's primary need is not the advice or direction of others; it is clarifying one's own thinking. So the

Co-Active Coaching process facilitates your clarifying your own thinking. Co-Active Coaching's second underlying assumption is that people are intrinsically creative, resourceful, and whole. Coaching is a way for you to discover, with the aid of a trained coach, what you value, what you need, and what you want out of your life.

This form of coaching is called "co-active" because it is a customized designed alliance between a coach and a client to maximize the benefit of coaching to each client. A good historical example of Co-Active Coaching is that of Socrates. Whenever a student came to him with a question, he would "answer" with a question—and continue doing this until, eventually, the student discovered the answer himself.

1.4.3 Bandler, Grinder, and colleagues: The Neuro-linguistic programming (NLP) coaching method[11]

Neuro-linguistic programming as a study of human functioning has, since its inception in the early 1970s, permeated virtually every field of human endeavor, particularly in relation to communication, influence, and change in the business world. Dr. John Grinder, co-originator of NLP with Dr. Richard Bandler, describes NLP most simply as "the modeling of excellent behavior/genius."

Historical background

According to Grinder, Bandler and their colleague Frank Pucelik had been having fun mimicking the behavior of recently deceased Fritz Perls (the cofounder of the Gestalt school of thought in psychology) in evening Gestalt classes with students when they noticed that they and the students were achieving remarkable therapeutic results by playing at "being" Fritz Perls. Thinking that Perls's use of language, among other things, might be at the center of their apparent success, Bandler invited Grinder, who was an assistant professor of linguistics at the University of California, Santa Cruz, to sit in on the classes and help them make sense of what was happening.

Grinder decided that because Bandler and Pucelik had modeled Perls by pure mimicry without understanding what they were doing, he would model them in the same way by running parallel classes with other students until he could reproduce their results. He and Bandler then stepped back to analyze the process, identifying and encoding the patterns of behavior and language use that seemed to yield these results. They taught these encoded patterns to others and noticed that their model enabled naïve subjects consistently to reproduce Perles's unique talent.

At about this time, Bandler assisted at a workshop delivered by Virginia Satir, a leading family therapist considered a genius in her field. Bandler noticed that she employed a number of questions and language patterns that were almost identical to those of Perls, and she agreed to allow Bandler and Grinder to model her work over a period of months. This modeling work, and the addition of language patterns inspired by Noam Chomsky's pioneering work in transformational grammar, led to their development of the meta-model for language and its publication in their 1975 book *The Structure of Magic*.

They were later introduced to the psychiatrist Milton Erickson by Gregory Bateson. Bateson was so impressed by their modeling process that he thought at last someone might be able to reveal the secrets of Erickson's genius with hypnosis and trances—after many prominent specialists he had sent to study Erickson over the years had failed. Based on their encoding of Erickson's very unusual language and nonverbal behavior, and in particular what he revealed about workings of the unconscious, they presented to the world a new, explicit, and teachable model not only of genius and its practical acquisition but of the interplay of human neurology, language, and behavioral functioning (programming). A series of new discoveries followed from these observations as Grinder and Bandler coded and published descriptions of their experiences. Here are two of these discoveries:

- the matching of people's unconscious choice of predicates to thinking modes (seeing, hearing, and feeling) and the cues offered by corresponding eye movements
- the structuring of memories in the characteristics of internal pictures, sound, and sensation (sub modalities) and the ways that these modes of cognition not only were implicated in the structure of clients' difficulties, but could be manipulated in ways that helped clients to "reprogram" themselves to achieve more desired and healthy responses

The patterns that Grinder and Bandler encoded were originally intended to be therapy, and at the core of these originally therapeutically directed procedures and patterns are modes of calibrating unconscious physiological responses, establishing and maintaining rapport, and leading clients' attention so they can achieve more choice (see footnote 15 for more on calibration). These include communication skills that have since become ubiquitous, such as matching and mirroring and the use of "specifying" and "influencing language." NLP experts claim that such skills were not explicitly available before they were modeled and coded by Grinder and Bandler. They suggest that practitioners of NLP, rather than learning fixed sets of useful questions to ask, learn to recognize the underlying syntactic structures of the client's language and to apply these patterns of language to constructing questions and challenges based on what that specific client has just said or done.

The purpose of their original meta-model, they say, was not to help the coach (or therapist) gather information or understanding, but rather to help the client expand his or her restricted model of the world and from that develop a set of possible solutions. This gives a very different meaning to accessing inner resources from those implied in other coaching methods, in which the client is guided to formulate her or his own solutions.

The discovery of mirror neurons

The now-ubiquitous matching and mirroring mentioned above were patterns of functioning detected and explicated by Bandler and Grinder in the early 1970s. They were at the heart of their modeling process, which leads to the unconscious uptake of excellent performance, and were proposed as effective ways to achieve significant relationships of rapport. In the mid-1990s, researchers in neuroscience[12] discovered what are now called "mirror neurons." These are apparently the neurological mechanisms responsible for what Grinder and Bandler had observed and coded 20 years earlier.

The finding of mirror neurons was hailed by world-renowned neuroscientist V.S. Ramachandran in 2000 as the single most important unpublicized story of the decade. He believes that "mirror neurons will do for psychology what DNA did for biology."[13] Mirror neurons were first discovered in monkeys and are now known to exist in humans, in much more complex configurations, and with more highly sophisticated capacities.[14] Grinder claims,

> It seems inevitable that our work in NLP discovering/creating patterning that works (using direct experience and calibration primarily) will continue to run some decades in advance of the discovery of the underlying mechanisms that are the neurological correlates. How is that possible? We simply experiment and use consequences and calibration[15] as tools to guide us.

The New Code of NLP

Grinder and Bandler parted company at the end of the 1970s. After this, Grinder recognized what he considers a series of "flaws" in their original encoding. Apart from noticing that several patterns could be reduced and made more elegant, he realized that the amount of information gathering (verbal eliciting of internal processes, values, and beliefs) in the original encoding:

1. created the problem of the coach's being obliged to interpret meaning via his or her own internal representations, due to lack of precision inherent in the semantic functioning of words
2. meant the client had to reveal the content of sometimes deeply private experiences (failing to respect the client's absolute confidentiality)
3. demanded mostly processing and behavior change from the client's conscious attention, when it was obvious from experience that changes were both accepted or generated and subsequently executed by unconscious processes

The use of terms such as *conscious* and *unconscious* is considered metaphorical in NLP, in the sense that a separate "mind" in a body is not a tangible neurological function (Descarte's error). This can be imagined as a continuum of attention from that which is immediately noticeable to that which lies outside immediate attention, such as the sensation of toes on the reader's left foot right now or examples of subtle changes in the appearance of an individual as she processes her experiences (e.g., elements of mirroring, breathing, gestures noted in rapport building). Adherents of NLP describe the further reaches of the continuum of the unconscious as the total functioning of autonomic and endocrine systems, body chemistry, metabolism, and the like being conducted on "automatic pilot" and normally outside conscious manipulation.

In their book *Whispering in the Wind*, Carmen Bostic St Clair and Grinder suggest that learning how to create a "partnership" with the unconscious allows the use of *yes* and *no* signaling systems (involuntarily felt physiological changes in the body) to access new choices of response to challenging and unpredictable circumstances.[16] These signals tend to elicit a "wow!" response from individuals when they first encounter them. Gregory Bateson said that the logic of the unconscious process is profoundly different from the logic of the conscious process, and the collision of these two processes is the basis of creativity and art.

Grinder further observed that many of the people he and Bandler had trained often worked effectively with clients but demonstrated little evidence of having worked on themselves. He now insists that congruency within the coach is a prerequisite for high-quality, respectful, and effective change-work.

These observations prompted him to re-code many of the original patterns and to supersede several of them with the designed (rather than modeled) processes of the New Code. What most people in the world know as NLP is what the New Code people now call the "Classic Code" of NLP. With Bostic, Grinder has continued to develop and elaborate procedures that assign choice and execution of change to the client's unconscious. Rather than changes of behavior, or of beliefs and values, New Code processes are directed at choice of and access to physiological "states." Beliefs and ineffective behaviors need not be directly addressed but are simply handled through the use of the high-performance states generated by New Code games and activities. These high-performance states are then associated with the context selected by the client.

New Code Change Format in action

Example one, general manager of a banking group:

> *A General Manager of a banking group had a fear of giving performance feedback to a colleague. As he prepared for a meeting, he would perspire, experience stomach cramps and find it difficult to breathe because of pressure in his chest. During the meeting, he would struggle with discussing performance improvements, because his colleague was a sensitive person and the GM was afraid of hurting him. After his*

coach took him through the New Code Change Format, playing "The Alphabet Game," the GM confessed he was skeptical that this could help him.

After the next meeting with his colleague, however, the GM reported that during the meeting he became aware he had not experienced his usual symptoms while preparing for it. He also noticed he was hearing himself speak in a relaxed, informal way, even using language and expressions not typical of him. No sweating, no cramps, no sign of labored breathing. In addition, his colleague noted how different he seemed and how much he had enjoyed and found useful their feedback discussion.

The General Manager reported how deeply surprised and gratified he was that such a big change could be achieved in just one game.

Example two, a motorbike racer:

A well-known motorbike racer had a problem when faced with fleeting opportunities to overtake a rider in the narrow space on the inside of bends on the racetrack. Despite all his efforts to overcome his hesitation at making this complex and dangerous maneuver, he continued to unconsciously brake at the critical moment. When coached through the New Code Change Format, he expressed disbelief that a simple game could possibly help him.

During his next race, he passed the then-leading rider in the race on the inside of a tight bend without braking and improved his own position in the race, coming in third. He reported his amazement, adding that now of overtaking, he had no conscious perception of what he was doing. He only became aware of it as he came out of the bend.

BOX 1.1 COACHING WITH NEW CODE NLP

Bill Phillips and Alessandro de Vita Zublena

For NLP coaches, all learning in the context of coaching is experiential. What is important is noticing what works and giving freedom and choice to their clients in contexts where they normally have no choice or choices which are not satisfactory to the client. The coach's purpose is to elicit, define, refine, challenge, and facilitate the client's expression of goals and intentions. This is contained in a process that includes gaining rapport, establishing frameworks and contracting, eliciting information, creating action plans, getting commitment, and following up. Understanding the problem is not an essential element in the successful change process. In fact, it can be quite dangerous for the coach to attempt to understand a client's problem because it can lead to projection, misunderstanding, and especially unethical practices of imposing the coach's own perception, beliefs, and values on the client.

The problem is not the problem. The problem is the state in which the client approaches the context in which the problem resides. So, what is needed in order to jump into a successful change process? There is absolutely no need for concern about the problem. Instead, explicit and precise information about the context and a set of manipulations, in the most positive and ethical sense, are required to create a high-performance state in the client, and to ensure that when a client next enters the context in which the problem exists, he or she innovates from a high-performance state.

The New Code approach to coaching emphasizes the importance of state over behavior change (this is illustrated below). As in some other coaching methods outlined in this chapter, clients are helped to experience and identify sensory evidence of achieving their intentions through a structured guidance process. This allows a contract to be made between the coach and the client, and facilitates subsequent evaluation of results, especially with corporate clients, regarding specific objectives and outcomes.

The New Code Change Format is a powerful, simple, and effective way to help a client create "generative change" in a particular class of circumstances. Four key steps are:

1. The client identifies a context or situation that he or she wishes to experience differently and is helped to "see and hear" representations of himself, performing as he currently would in this chosen situation. The client imagines this as if he were watching himself on film just a few feet away.

2. Once the client reports an adequate representation both verbally and nonverbally (the latter verified through calibration by the coach), he steps into and experiences directly "being in" the representation without attempting to change anything. When effective, a clear shift in physiology is observed (calibrated) by the coach. This is the physiology of the client's present state.

3. After the client steps away from the spot and shakes off its related physiological sensations, the coach guides him through a New Code game designed to produce a shift in state that will enable the client to respond in a new and effective way in the given context through the development of a high-performance state. The effect of playing the game is that the client reaches a point where he stops trying to correct little faults

and enters what might be termed a state of "flow" (similar to an athlete's being "in the zone").

4. When the client begins to exhibit this "zone" or "flow" physiology, identified by the coach, the client is invited to step immediately back into his original imaged context. What the coach expects to calibrate now is that this new state becomes associated with the context in which the client wanted a difference. The coach is also verifying that there is no trace of the original physiology associated with the client's former state. There is no discussion or analysis with the client of the new experience because that can undermine success through conscious interference and limit the generalization of the new choices in the client's experience. The net effect is that the next time the client experiences the context, instead of his old reaction, some new and more appropriate responses will arise borne out of an unconscious recognition of the surroundings and an immediate and unconscious reactivation of the high-performance state.

The unrehearsed and effective result of this format gives meaning to the term *generative change*. The specific shift in state is unconsciously prompted and gives rise to not only appropriate choices, but often quite novel and surprising ones (see "New Code Formation in Action" examples in this chapter). Such responses cannot be rehearsed because the specific events in the given context inevitably are unpredictable. The key word is *appropriate*.

When a person has only one way to respond in a given context, he or she could well be characterized as an unhappy robot. If, with the help of her coach, she examines possibilities and rehearses new skills or behaviors, then as long as the expected happens (almost never), she may be said to be a happy robot; she has access to more than one reaction. The weakness of this approach shows up when the unexpected, the unpredictable, happens. The client cannot find an adequate response because she has rehearsed only behavioral change. The spontaneous creation of an appropriate response in the face of the unexpected is evidence of generative change. The client's system has learned how to learn. This was achieved by working with states rather than with behaviors or beliefs and values and is a key differentiator for coaching with New Code NLP.

According to New Code NLP specialists, changes in state can and do alter what is attended to (perceived, the movement of attention) and thus give rise to altered internal "models of the world" and the choices implied by such a radical shift. They insist that their purpose is not to teach an unhappy robot on how to become a happy robot. Their goal is to create a person who, on the spot, on his or her feet, can generate creative and successful behavior from a high-performance state without needing to know at any point what specific behavior will occur.

Bill Phillips is a Management Consultant, adept at analyzing and interpreting complex situations, building networks and relationships and facilitating agreement. For the past 18 years Bill has consulted both nationally and internationally with organizations including the United Nations High Commissioner for Refugees (UNHCR), other parts of the UN and the International Federation of Red Cross and Red Crescent Societies (IFRC). Bill is a Founder Member of the International Trainers' Academy of NLP (ITA) (for more: www.nlpacademy.co.uk /trainers/profile/bill_phillips/)

Alessandro de Vita Zublena was born in Val d'Aosta (Italy). He is an Executive Coach and psychologist specializing in change management, with an MA in Counseling Psychology in 1993, a Certification as Master Practitioner in neuro linguistic programming in 1997, a Trainer Certification in NLP from John Grinder (Co-creator of NLP) and Carmen Bostic St. Clair (Co-developer of New Code NLP) in 2005, a New Code Trainer Certification in NLP in 2006 (Grinder-Bostic St Clair) and a Certification as International NLP Coach in 2007 (Grinder-Bostic St. Clair). For more, see: www.mycoachingpartners.com/en/page/33/alessan dro-de-vita-zublena

Note: Following a lengthy correspondence I had with John Grinder back in 2011 he has asked two disciples, Bill and Alessandro, to prepare this insertion. I am grateful to all three of them.

The New Code Change Format Phillips and Zublena describe in "Coaching with New Code NLP" is just one of many procedures NLP coaches employ to assist coachees with changing states. A key characteristic it shares with most other New Code processes is an emphasis on the coach's functioning content-free. Here, a question immediately presents itself: How does the coach know what is going on if the only information available is likely to be changes in the client's appearance? New Code coaches and practitioners are, they say, trained to refine their skills in calibrating—skills such as differentiating between the conscious and the unconscious external cues—beyond those normally developed in Classic Code NLP.[17]

Yet most coaches know that clients will frequently insist on telling their story and want their coaches to show they can, and do, listen. The focus of a New Code coach, however, is said to be on detecting the patterns, tonal emphases, and indicators of how a client constructs his or her inner reality, and not on understanding the content and meaning of the story. The New Code term for this is "listening off the top." Staying with the process of their clients' experiences is the most respectful way to assist them, allowing coaches to avoid imposing their own perceptual filters, values, and beliefs.

In addition, they believe that those working as coaches who fail to make the distinction between process and content are quite dangerous. They are dangerous, New Code advocates say, because, without a clear operational appreciation of the process/content distinction, these coaches will, even with the best of intentions, impose their own perceptions, beliefs, and values on their clients without even realizing what they are doing. This makes them doubly dangerous: They are imposing, and yet are totally unaware of it.

Some New Code core principles

In Part III, chapter 2 of *Whispering in the Wind* (p. 317), Bostic and Grinder explain the distinction they make between first- and second-order change. The New Code NLP Coach selects interventions based on these principles. If the client has goals to change addictions, physical symptoms, or behaviors with significant secondary gains or payoffs, the coach will select processes working with the (usually) unconsciously held intention of the unwanted experiences (second-order processes). Clients' unconscious responses to these interventions are always bounded by the requirement that they satisfy the intention, making them appropriate and ecological, and more likely to be lasting changes. Many of the Classic Code processes that function at the first order of change, such as anchoring techniques, have been prone to reversion over time.

However, all NLP patterns, both New and Classic Code, share certain essential qualities:

> All patterns and formats in NLP (Classic and New Code) are nothing more than instructions to the agent of change where to fix his/her attention and where to direct the attention of the client. The NLP Coach has a clear representation of patterning in the change work, e.g. a description of the pattern, the consequences of the use of the pattern and the selection criteria, meaning the identification of the conditions or contexts in which the selection and application of the pattern is appropriate.
>
> (*Whispering in the Wind*, p. 314)

A further key feature of the NLP Coach's approach modeled originally from Milton Erickson is tasking. In this, the client is given homework designed to provide counter examples of limiting behaviors or convictions. In one light-hearted example, Grinder tasked a young man who had difficulty approaching relationships with women to conduct what appeared to be a legitimate and serious marketing survey in a high-class women's underwear store. Grinder set this up in agreement with the store and a manufacturing supplier. It resulted not only in a successful survey but, more important, in the client's happy report of dates with two different women.

Guiding their clients to self-sufficiency and independence through the accessing of high-performance states and discovering and exercising the ability to induce change within themselves (i.e., the clients) are core principles for New Code NLP coaches. Bostic and Grinder assert that when a coach successfully, consistently, and reliably practices self-application of NLP patterning, he or she knows the difference between process and content and is therefore able to recognize and use the multitude of unconscious signals that clients offer. Coaches do not become archaeological investigators of the past, focusing attention on what happened in the past and how to go from there to the future the client wishes for; rather, they know how to elicit a context and generate a state in which the client becomes competent and independent. For these coaches, the change process is never finished; each successful change opens the door to a new set of possibilities. Coaches working with the New Code of NLP continue to experiment, to learn, and to develop further patterning in the art of coaching.

A final note about NLP

Although the bulk of the section on NLP was written by current colleagues of John Grinder's (i.e., Bill Phillips and Alessandro de Vita Zublena), it is important to mention the work Richard Bandler has done in this field since he and Grinder parted ways. Bandler has developed new processes deriving from the original NLP, most notably, Design Human Engineering (DHE) and Neuro-Hypnotic Repatterning (NHR). Both methods employ a variety of communication and persuasion skills and use self-hypnosis to excite motivation and produce change. Like all his work, they are about personal freedom. The common denominator is communication. As Bandler put it, "Language is communication and it is all hypnosis; this is how language works."

When creating NHR, he wanted to get people out of the "personal jails" they build for themselves so they could have greater freedom. He observed that people were not having enough fun. It is not that people are not capable of it; they are just not using their neurology in a way that produces pleasure. Neuro-Hypnotic Repatterning uses very deep trance tools to make very pervasive changes across a wide range of behaviors and teaches people to spend more time practicing feeling good than feeling bad. NHR takes people beyond communication skills and beyond persuasion and enables them to use their brain chemistry and neurology to bring about changes in beliefs, thoughts, and feelings. According to Bandler, NHR moves people swiftly, painlessly, and with laughter into better ways of being.

NHR uses the hypnotic process to restructure experiences that people have at the neurological and chemical level. Instead of teaching people to lead with their minds, NHR teaches them to lead with their feelings. They learn to saturate their neurons with the chemicals that make them feel good. Bandler insists that "if you get your whole body in the right state," you can do almost anything. NHR helps a client get her body to this state, by enabling her to redesign the way she connects with herself—physically, mentally, and to some extent, spiritually. NHR makes changes using some principles from time, memory processing, feelings, and language.

Even though Bandler and Grinder stopped collaborating decades ago, they both still work in the field they co-founded, albeit with marked differences in how each evolves that field. NHR and DHE are Bandler's rightful applications of NLP. Bandler continues to refine and develop competence in the way the nervous system stores and processes experience and memories in the subcomponents of seeing, hearing, and feeling, referred to as "sub modalities," and to manipulate (in the most positive sense) those mechanisms through trance and hypnosis to help clients have more choice.

Grinder and Bostic have gone back to much of the original encoding and patterning of NLP, and refined, simplified, or re-coded the way NLP change-work is done. They give much greater importance to congruence in the practitioner, to respecting clients' privacy by not engaging in exploration of reasons and meanings, and to working with clients' unconscious reactions, observed through heightened calibration of signals that are beyond clients' awareness. Their work is based on the concept that the deepest changes are affected by satisfying unconsciously held intentions rather than by manipulating behavioral outputs.

1.4.4 Emotional intelligence as a coaching tool

Emotional intelligence (EI) comprises all the non-IQ areas of human intelligence. Often called people skills, street smarts, common sense, or savvy, this wide array of capabilities is emerging as the most important set of competencies in business. These personal and social, managerial and leadership, skills are increasingly recognized as the core of what separates star performers from the rest of the pack.

Peter Salovey of Yale and John D. Mayer of the University of New Hampshire defined the term *emotional intelligence* in a groundbreaking 1990 article in the journal *Imagination, Cognition, and Personality* as "the subset of social intelligence that involves *the ability to monitor one's own and others' feelings and emotions, to discriminate among them, and to use this information to guide one's thinking and actions.*"[18] Since then, many have researched EI and written about what it is, how it works, and what people can do to improve one's EQ (the measurement of one's EI; often the terms are used interchangeably). This has had an important impact on the coaching profession, with Daniel Goleman's 1995 book *Emotional Intelligence: Why It Can Matter More Than IQ*, as well as an updated ten-year anniversary book published in 2005, becoming essential reading.[19] Many coaches incorporate EI concepts, techniques, and tools into their work.

Emotional intelligence is, in fact, relevant to all of us, because it encompasses the most important skills we use every day, skills that determine how well we know ourselves, how well we deal with everything that happens to us, and how well we deal with others. And whether we know it or not, these skills are vital to our success.

The available evidence shows that an individual cannot achieve extraordinary levels of success without a high level of competency in the core EI areas (see Figure 1.6 for core EI competencies). The professional landscape is littered with bright, would-be leaders with great technical skills who failed because of their lack of self-knowledge, self-control, or confidence, or because of their inability to understand others and build trusting, empowering, mutually beneficial, and productive relationships with their constituents.[20]

Practicing (or being coached) to increase emotional intelligence, an individual needs to:

- know oneself by enhancing emotional literacy and recognizing patterns
- choose oneself by applying consequential thinking, navigating emotions, engaging intrinsic motivation, and exercising optimism
- give oneself by increasing empathy and pursuing noble goals

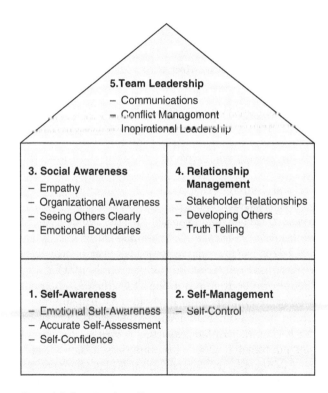

Figure 1.6 Emotional intelligence competencies.

Some people can practice EI without a coach, but for others a coach can be instrumental. A coach can be an objective observer who can help clients focus on their fundamental beliefs and assessments, change their behavior, and improve their decision making in those aspects of EI where they are most deficient (Figure 1.6).

ESADE Business School (where I taught between 2002 and 2017) used a LEAD program with all MBA students. Their EI competencies were assessed, and they were assigned a coach for the duration of the program. I have seen individuals make tremendous progress in improving their EQs when working with a coach. Emotional intelligence is combining the head and the heart, and a coach can help make the combination work. The LEAD program at ESADE was based on the concepts developed by Goleman and Boyatzis and in my opinion played an important role in the school's ranking as one of the top 20 MBA programs in the world.[21]

However, EI as a method and model of coaching can be problematic, and I'd advise you to do more homework before venturing into this area—whether you are looking for a coach who claims to be an expert in this field or you are simply looking for an EI tool or method to incorporate into your work or life. Many of the mass-marketed "emotional intelligence" training courses discuss "self-awareness," "resilience," and "authenticity" under the heading "emotional skills." Clearly these concepts are not emotions. They are personality characteristics that may or may not have an impact on how an individual deals with his or her emotions.

Because coaching works in the domain of emotions, it is imperative that all coaches have clear definitions of emotions and clear boundaries when working with them. Coaches who work with EI must know what constitutes negative and positive emotional states, be able to distinguish between the two, and possess a finely honed understanding of which aspects of emotions a coach can work with effectively. Naturally, coaches who do not have a background in the behavioral sciences are hesitant, sometimes apprehensive, about working with a coachee's emotions.

CLBV Reflection ♣ ♠ ♥

Emotional intelligence quiz*

Complete this if you are in a management position and responsible for others in your organization.

Circle the Yes or No for each statement. Think of your usual behavior, not the occasional exceptions. Be very honest in your responses.

1.	I am aware of how I respond in crisis situations.	Yes	No
2.	My workplace behavior is consistent with my core values.	Yes	No
3.	I have examined and am clear about my core values.	Yes	No
4.	I can articulate my core values with my staff, colleagues, and bosses.	Yes	No
5.	My management style is flexible enough to be functional.	Yes	No
6.	I am proud of the way I handle myself with the most difficult staff.	Yes	No
7.	I clearly communicate my ideas to the highest levels of management.	Yes	No
8.	I consciously draw from many different leadership styles and approaches, based on the situation.	Yes	No
9.	I understand the different drivers, both personal and professional, that dictate my staff's actions.	Yes	No
10.	My approach to motivation is highly individualized, based on the unique needs of the individual.	Yes	No
11.	I am clear about how politics impact activity in this organization.	Yes	No
12.	I know my staff's strengths and weaknesses.	Yes	No
13.	I find ways to maneuver around obstacles.	Yes	No
14.	My successes are not achieved in isolation; they are the result of concerted, coordinated, collaborative activities.	Yes	No
15.	I encourage my staff to communicate with and assist other departments.	Yes	No
16.	I regularly reach out for help from my peers.	Yes	No

Each of these statements corresponds to a competency in one of the first four quadrants in Figure 1.6. Total the number of Yes answers for each statement:

Self-awareness	Questions 1, 2, 3, 4	_____
Self-management	Questions 5, 6, 7, 8	_____
Social awareness	Questions 9, 10, 11, 12	_____
Relationship management	Questions 13, 14, 15, 16	_____

After analyzing your answers, assess yourself and look for developmental opportunities. Alone or with the help of a coach, you can plot a course for growth based on building or strengthening your competencies in a selected area or areas.

★Note: This quiz has been developed for demonstration only; it has not been tested or validated. Also, it is an exercise in progress and does not yet test competencies in all five quadrants of Figure 1.6.

BOX 1.2 ASSESSING AND COACHING EMOTIONAL INTELLIGENCE WITH THE MAYER–SALOVEY–CARUSO EMOTIONAL INTELLIGENCE TEST

by David R. Caruso

Michael was an executive coaching client who worked for the New York City office of a major investment bank. After one very difficult quarter with his team, his managerial duties were removed, and he returned to the trading desk full-time. Even though this was technically a demotion, top management saw Michael as technically skilled and high potential and the bank did not want to lose him to a competitor. As a result, the VP of his group went to HR to see what could be done to help Michael. The head of HR referred Michael for executive coaching, but cited fairly vague issues, such as "Michael did not play office politics well" and that it might be an "EQ problem."

The vague referral question was not helpful, nor was the initial interview with Michael, who was not sure why he was there. In fact, he mentioned that he saw himself as having "high EQ." One of the many challenges facing coaches is that "EQ" or emotional intelligence has come to mean very different things. Most approaches and assessments of EQ rely on self-report and are measuring traditional personality traits such as optimism or assertiveness (see Mayer, Caruso & Salovey, 2016[22] for an overview). Certainly, these traits are important, but they have been studied, measured, and coached for decades. Emotional intelligence (EI) should be something new and different and it should be and can be defined as an intelligence and should be and can be objectively measured. In this case study, we focus on what is sometimes called the "ability model of emotional intelligence," which was first proposed by Peter Salovey and Jack Mayer in 1990[23] and was the basis of the popularization of "EQ." Since that time, the concept has been stretched quite a bit. In the ability model approach, EI is a standard intelligence and is related to other kinds of intelligence. It consists of a set of hard skills including the ability to accurately perceive emotions in self and others, to match emotions to the task to be more effective, and to match emotions of others to emotionally connect, to understand the underlying meaning and trajectory of emotions, and to effectively manage emotions in self and others. The four abilities are sometimes labeled Perceive, Facilitate, Understand, and Manage emotions. More recently, we have labeled these Map, Match, Meaning, and

Move emotions to refer to a four-step problem-solving approach and to aid recall[24]. Map refers to a 2 × 2 map or grid to help people plot or map their current mood or emotion.

Match means to match mood to the task and to match others' moods to create an emotional connection. Meaning is detecting the meaning of emotions and feelings and how they might change. Finally, we decided to label the fourth ability Move because it takes thought and action to simply maintain an existing mood let alone change it.

As part of the executive coaching process, Michael took several assessments, including an ability-based measure of emotional intelligence, the Mayer–Salovey–Caruso Emotional Intelligence Test (MSCEIT) and a standard personality assessment. Personality self-assessment revealed that Michael viewed himself as a "people person" with excellent social skills and a high level of optimism. These assessment data aligned with his view of himself as having "high EQ." However, his results on the MSCEIT suggested otherwise. The MSCEIT measures a person's actual emotional intelligence abilities in an objective manner rather than relying upon a person's self-assessment. Instead of asking the client to rate their ability to read others' emotions ("I am good at reading people"), the MSCEIT displays a photograph of a person's face and the test taker indicates how much of several emotions are expressed in that face. There are better and worse answers for each of the 141 questions. The MSCEIT yields a total score as well as scores for four related abilities: accurately perceiving emotions, matching mood to the task, understanding the meaning of emotions, and effectively managing emotions in self and others. It is common for people to be poor estimators of their emotional intelligence, and the more one overestimates their EI, the less interested they are in developing their EI skills[25]. Michael's overall score was 93, on the low end of the competent range on the MSCEIT, with a Scatter Score of 116, suggesting that his total score might not be a good overall estimate of his emotional intelligence and that his results were complicated. (MSCEIT scores have a mean of 100 and a standard deviation of 15.) A high scatter score meant that it was important to look at the four abilities of emotional intelligence in greater detail. His score for "reading people" was his lowest score (in the Consider Developing range, or 82). The other scores were higher: Matching Mood to Task (Using Emotions) was 111 (Skilled), Understanding was 114 (Skilled), and Managing was 91 (on the low end of the Competent range). The results suggested that he may initially misread people but was able to connect with others emotionally and to "get" the underlying causes of emotions. The emotions he took on (Using Emotions) could, at times, overwhelm him since his ability to integrate and manage those emotions was lower (Manage).

Given the resistance many clients have regarding MSCEIT feedback when they score lower than expected, it is critical for the test administrator to limit the client's "escape routes" (Sheldon, Dunning & Ames, 2014). Following a structured process where the EI model and assessment are explained in detail and using the language of hypothesis testing (e.g., "Someone with this score on Perceiving Emotions may at times not accurately 'read' others. Has that ever happened to you"?) blocks access to the major escape route and is also a way to treat the client respectfully. The process of giving feedback on the MSCEIT is also an example of the ability model of EI in action as the test administrator uses the four skills (reading the client, initially matching the client mood and then changing it to enhance openness, predicting how they might react, and managing their own and the client's emotions) in real time and points this out to the client.

In Michael's case, initial misreading of his clients' and team members' moods and emotions gave him inaccurate data, and so his empathy and understanding skills were hobbled as he reacted to those bad data and was therefore perceived as a bit "off." In explaining the test results, the coach asked questions such as "have you ever misread people?" and "what would happen if he misread people?". Most professionals find it difficult to say something is impossible or to claim that one has never misread another person, and Michael did indicate that some outcomes of meetings had surprised him. Michael was generally open and receptive to the feedback and was able to provide specific behaviors and examples to illustrate his scores.

Only recently have there been studies to indicate EI itself can be increased. Either way, instead of focusing on increasing one's EI, an effective EI coach teaches remedial or compensatory strategies. We use an analogy with clients to explain this process: someone with low spatial intelligence will easily get lost when heading to a new destination but rather than trying to increase their spatial intelligence we provide them with a GPS. The result? They don't get lost anymore (unless the battery dies, or the satellites go down). With EI, we provide clients with a "GPS for emotions," and the client's MSCEIT results allow us to focus on the most impactful remedial strategies. For Michael, the remedial strategies focused on the initial read of people. Instead of asking the typical "How are you?" question which usually garners non-specific replies such as "fine," "okay," or even "great" we taught him to use targeted, closed-ended questions and to follow-up. Rather than ask "what did you think of that meeting?" he was coached to ask questions such as "what 2 things would you have done differently if you were running the meeting?" or "how would you evaluate the meeting from 1 to 10?" and if the answer was under 10, to follow-up with "what would get it to 10?" when the real evaluation of the meeting would be shared. He also began to model greater transparency with the "how are you?" question. Michael stopped saying "how are you?" as a greeting and instead, when asked, would pause for a moment and provide a more honest answer. In meetings, he would sometimes provide an answer other than "great" and indicate how he was really feeling. In one meeting, a planning session for a pitch to a new client, he noted that he was a bit anxious about the upcoming meeting and unsure of their approach. This openness, unexpected but not unwelcome, allowed other team members to share their concerns, and the result was they went back through the pitch and addressed concerns everyone had but no one had voiced previously.

Because Michael had been identified as high potential, the VP of the division was looking for behavioral markers of Michael's growth and development. And, after a few months, she saw them given Michael's focus on changing some of his behaviors and how they were verbalized. Eventually, he was promoted again and did well in the role. Michael was still Michael—he did not accurately read people—but when he was in a difficult situation, he had compensatory strategies to rely upon to get accurate emotional data about the situation. His other EI skills then kicked in, allowing him to succeed in this competitive, people-intensive role. A good coaching plan should be based on good data about a client, and assessing a client's emotional intelligence in an objective manner with MSCEIT can provide good, and accurate, data.

David R. Caruso, PhD, is a co-author of the Mayer–Salovey–Caruso Emotional Intelligence Test, *The Emotionally Intelligent Manager* (with Peter Salovey) and *A Leader's Guide to Solving Challenges with Emotional Intelligence* (with Lisa T. Rees). He is a research affiliate at the Yale Center for Emotional Intelligence and conducts training and consulting on emotional intelligence for organizations. Disclosure: Caruso receives royalties on sales of these products. E-mail: david@eiskills.com.

1.4.5 *Appreciative Inquiry (AI) coaching: concept and methodology*

David Cooperrider and Suresh Srivastva developed Appreciative Inquiry (often known as AI) in the 1980s as a variation of action research. This theory contends that organizations, and other systems, do not present a problem to be solved but a miracle to be embraced. An organization that looks for problems will keep finding them, and an organization that appreciates what is best in itself will discover more and more that is good. From these discoveries, it can build a new future in which the best becomes more common. AI uses a way of asking questions and envisioning the future that fosters positive relationships and goodness in a person, a situation, or an organization and that enhances a system's capacity for collaboration and change. AI's four-process cycle consists of discover, dream, design, and destiny (or deliver).[26]

Appreciative Inquiry (AI) is also distinct from other coaching schools of thought in the emphasis it puts on the system. It has been defined as the study of what gives life to human systems when they are at their best. Its advocates describe the AI Coaching process as a "co-creative partnership" between the client, the coach, and the relevant social system (e.g., organization, team, family). Often the process is used with a group within a system, such as a team in an organization or several members of a family, but it can be used with an individual.

So Appreciative Inquiry is both a specific methodology and a perspective. To further understand this, we need only look at the two words that make it up:

- *Appreciative* has two meanings: to look for the best/acknowledge the best (in something) and to increase (something) in value, such as when a stock or real estate appreciates.
- *Inquiry* means to seek understanding using a process based on provocative questions.

In an AI Coaching session, the coach asks provocative questions to draw out powerful success stories and identify the factors that are already working well within a human system. This understanding becomes the basis for helping the clients bring into being what they want more of (which is dramatically different from the usual cultural focus on reducing what they want less of).

The specific methodology of Appreciative Inquiry provides the tools to do this, involving both left and right brains and exploring the past, present, and future. It consists of five main phases (the four-process cycle mentioned earlier and an introductory interview):

- **Affirmative Topic Choice:** The coach conducts an interview using several provocative questions; from the clients' responses, the coach and the clients choose several themes as the focal points for the rest of the inquiry process.

- **Discover:** Provocative questions are explored regarding each of the Affirmative Topics, and, from the clients' responses, the coach and the clients again choose several themes. These themes reflect the system's central success factors—its best strengths, talents, assets, values, and ideals—and are known as its positive core.
- **Dream:** Clients use creative processes to verbally and/or experientially explore what the future might be like if the positive core were more thoroughly enacted throughout the system and to examine, looking back from that vantage point, what must have happened to bring it to such an optimal state.
- **Design:** The system is organized into architecture and preferences are chosen for each element of that structure that will enable further enactment of the positive core and lessons from the Dream phase throughout the system. Clients may also develop "Provocative Propositions," by putting in writing broad goals or ideas to help encourage the organization to move in the direction of optimization.
- **Destiny:** Concrete plans are made and supporting resources put in place for enacting the chosen preferences in the service of amplifying the positive core and making the clients' dreams a reality. This step involves both the system and the clients.

In the following excerpt from their article "Appreciative Inquiry in Coaching,"[27] Barbara Sloan and Trudy Canine emphasize the significance of the system and highlight the AI principles that are brought to bear on the AI Coaching experience:

AI Coaching is highly effective for a variety of specific coaching purposes, including leadership, transition, development, working relationships, and life planning. The principles of AI influence all stages of AI Coaching, from the initial contact through the final follow-up sessions. The phases of AI guide the general sequence of activities. Both the principles and phases provide guidance in the improvisational dance of the coaching process.

The following describes the impact of the principles of Appreciative Inquiry in AI Coaching, adding Wholeness to the well-recognized five principles— Constructionist, Positive, Anticipatory, Simultaneity, and Poetic.

- **Constructionist principle:** The principle of Social Construction recognizes that meaning is made, and futures are created through conversations; that our perceptions of reality itself are the product of these conversations; and that our perceived reality defines what we see or do not see (Discover Phase). The stories that are told and retold both formally and informally create and perpetuate the reality of our perceptions. These stories have the power to limit our options as well as to expand the possibilities we can imagine and create. Social construction is happening all the time, everywhere. In organizations, we refer to the socially constructed environment and belief system as the organization's culture. In AI Coaching, we intentionally engage the social system in support of the desired outcomes of the coaching. We use a wide-angle lens, if you will, to engage significant others in conversations.

- **Positive principle:** At any moment we can choose to focus on deficits or strengths. From the first contact, including a request for coaching and what might be considered a contracting (Define Phase) conversation, AI Coaching unabashedly focuses on the positives and the strengths, even in the midst of challenges or "problems" that may have led to the request for coaching. Recognizing that each conversation has the capacity to either further cement existing perceptions or open awareness to strengths and new possibilities, each interaction in AI Coaching is guided by the appreciative principle. Since "we find what we look for," the AI Coach looks for what is appreciative.
- **Anticipatory principle:** We create what we imagine. As the saying goes: "If you're going to have a fantasy, why not go first class?" AI Coaching enables the client to create her/his first-class fantasy (Dream Phase), with the support of others whose input and support are important to the client's future. To quote Peter Drucker, great "guru" of the management sciences, "The best way to predict the future is to create it!"
- **Principle of simultaneity:** Change begins with the first question we ask. So AI Coaching begins by asking questions about the best of times and wishes for the future, even in the face of the habitual inclination in our culture to focus on what's wrong and what's missing—to focus on problems. As Barbara Carpenter, a psychotherapist, says, "It's a new now!" And it is in every moment that we are changing and influencing change. AI Coaching is mindful that moment to moment, in every question we ask or statement we make, we are creating the future for good or ill.
- **Poetic principle:** With the daily demands for productivity in life and work, the poetic, the artistic, the inspirational can easily be lost. In AI Coaching, we begin by asking for stories rather than for lists or ideas. Thus, the poetic principle seeks to give voice to the poetic impulse, to illuminate aspirations and dreams, and to create opportunities for deeper connections between people—all toward the creation of a valued, shared future.
- **Principle of wholeness:** Wholeness acknowledges interconnectedness rather than divisions. Wholeness has a permeable or flexible boundary and is defined and redefined by the focus on inquiry. So, in AI Coaching, a client may engage his/her manager and his/her

staff in inquiry, later expanding this to include colleagues and clients. By engaging the most appropriate and most whole group of people (rather than a sample) in generative conversations, AI Coaching creates widely shared awareness and appreciation of differing views, shared dreams for the future, and greater support for meaningful change.

Now that you have a general understanding of AI, why don't you try the following AI exercise? This will work with any team or group, even if you are not a professional coach. It is also effective if you train coaches.

CLBV Reflection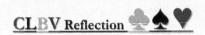

Working with AI: A powerful example

Ask participants to give you the absolute worst, most horrible, difficult, hopeless problem they can think of, anywhere in life or work. Often, they come up with things like HIV/AIDS, urban violence, corruption, civil war.

Next do a quick "problem tree" analysis of root causes and their impacts/fruits. Ask the participants about the chances to solve the problem, and at the same time, ask them to draw a face that represents their feelings about these chances. You will normally get a miserable sad face with tears.

Ask the participants to "flip this into an opportunity": "What does the opposite look like?" Defining the problem as its opposite may take a while (in my experience up to an hour). After they've done this, ask the participants to come up with an action plan and personal commitments. This is very often full of energy and fun. Sometimes participants may even choose to create skits and dances. At this moment, do a quick "opportunity tree analysis" and ask for new pictures of faces reflecting how the participants feel about it all. You may get (as expected, of course) lots of smiling, happy faces and great optimism.

Then say, "OK, what happened here? Did the problem go away? Did the world change during the last 60 minutes?" This opens a lively discussion on the heart of AI, how changing our language, our questions, changes reality, and people understand that we have the power to change the world through the questions we ask, through the approach we take. This will lead them into taking their organizational "problems," issues, hang-ups, headaches, and hopeless situations and building an AI environment around them. Exercises like this are often eye-openers. AI is powerful stuff.

1.4.6 Fernando Flores and collaborators: Ontological coaching model

Ontological coaching is an eclectic approach. It borrows concepts from PNL, from emotional intelligence, and from the biology of cognition (specifically from the work of the holistic living-system scientist, Humberto Maturana).[28] In their book *Understanding Computers and Cognition*, Fernando Flores, a key figure in the development of the ontological approach, and Terry Winograd pulled together the ideas of Maturana with those of philosopher John Searle and came up with the concept of an organization as a "network of commitments." Flores says that in developing the framework for ontological coaching, while he and his colleagues brought together Searle's notions of the philosophy of language and Mantura's ideas about perception, cognition, language, and communication, he was also influenced by the existential philosophy of Martin Heidegger.[29]

Ontology is the study of being, and ontological coaching focuses on all aspects of communication (which are essential aspects of one's "way of being") as a means of producing major shifts in perception and behavior. An individual's way of being can be thought of as the internal reality he or she lives in, which includes—and this is especially important—the relationship the person has with herself. According to Flores and his colleagues,[30] an individual's understanding of the external world and the ways in which he or she participates in it derive from this internal reality.

Ontological coaching is based on the power of language, moods, and conversations to effect behavioral and cultural transformation. The role of an ontological coach is not to tell the client how to be or behave, but rather to help the client to achieve what he or she desires. Ontological coaching is not based on a script the coach has learned in advance. It is about enabling people to better serve themselves, to expand their possibilities, and to increase their capacity to learn, to act more effectively, and to better design their own future. It is more an art than a science.

Way of being, as proponents of ontological coaching define it, is a dynamic interplay between three spheres of human existence: language; moods and emotions; physiology and body posture. A person's way of being shapes his or her performance and effectiveness. Figure 1.7 shows us graphically how these

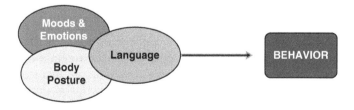

Figure 1.7 The three components of the ontology approach to coaching.

three areas are interconnected and that changes made in these areas will result in changes in behavior.

Language

The ontological coaching methodology is based on an understanding of language and communication developed in the latter part of the twentieth century. The essence of this understanding is: (a) language consists of both listening and speaking, and (b) language is fundamental in creating reality. Language produces outcomes and generates realities. People act from what reality is for them. Effective behavior depends strongly on people's use of language (including listening). The ways in which people do or do not use language shape what they do and how well they do it.

Included in this methodology is an interpretation of and a detailed model of the process of listening. This model provides a deeper and more effective way to listen that enhances communication and relationships. Listening is regarded as a crucial factor in communication and as essential for establishing trust and rapport. Listening is a core business process.

Speaking is also a key business process. This methodology contains six precise linguistic tools (called "basic linguistic acts") that humans use in everyday conversations to create reality and get things done. Typically, people are not aware of how they use and misuse these linguistic tools. Gaining an awareness of how to use them enables people to intentionally produce more effective ways of conversing, relating, and performing in workplace settings.

Stories and narratives are often silent, invisible, and in the background of everyday conversations. They reflect the deep culture of organizations and can be major barriers to change. They provide powerful contexts of meaning, shaping what people see as possible and not possible for an individual, a team, or the organization. The culture—and the shadowy stories that reproduce and reinforce it—can be a limiting horizon or a flexible sense of the possible that encourages improvement throughout the system. A key part of using the ontological methodology is uncovering destructive narratives and developing powerful and empowering narratives.

Moods and emotions

Traditional organizations ignore human emotions. However, the renewed focus on humanity in organizations requires an understanding of human emotions. To energize employees is to harness emotion. Negative emotions have a negative effect on people and on profit; good emotions are fuel that drives productivity, quality, and customer satisfaction. An individual is always in some mood or emotion. Moods and emotions permeate and influence everything people do and as such, they constitute a core business process.

The ontological coaching methodology contains tools for recognizing, managing, and shifting moods and emotions. The power of moods and emotions is that they always predispose people toward certain behaviors and away from others. Speaking, listening, and engaging in conversations are indispensable forms of human behavior. The effectiveness with which people speak and listen cannot be separated from moods and emotions.

Unfortunately, until very recently, moods and emotions have not been seen as an area of learning crucial to performance improvement. They are an integral part of using language for effective communication in leadership, management, coaching, and team building. In short, they form a crucial dimension of morale and organizational performance. Tools in this methodology include those that teach people:

- how to distinguish between moods and emotions
- how to recognize and use six basic moods of life as a deeper level of emotional intelligence, and how they impact on morale and performance
- how to shift from negative moods to positive moods
- how to use moods and emotions to have more effective and influential communication that builds relationships and long-term collaboration
- how to engage in constructive emotional leadership

Physiology and body posture

This would seem to be an unlikely area of attention in the context of organizational performance and improvement. Like moods and emotions, the body has largely been ignored as a key area affecting individual and organizational performance. The importance of the body can be expressed in the following way: "Our way of being is embodied."

The body is always present in how people listen to each other and speak with each other. Speaking is not limited to the vocal cords; it is generated from the entire body. (Actors and singers know this well.) An individual's posture consists of subtle configurations of muscles and skeleton that have been learned throughout life. In many subtle and powerful ways, posture can keep people trapped in negative moods and negatively impact listening and speaking. Conversely, posture can engender good moods and positively affect listening and speaking.

Specific tools that are part of this aspect of the methodology help people learn:

- how to use the body to get into more constructive and productive moods
- how small shifts in body posture can generate a more positive outlook and produce more effective communication

So, proponents of ontological coaching assert that organizations and individuals who engage in an ontological coaching relationship can expect to experience different perspectives on personal challenges and opportunities, enhanced thinking and decision-making skills, improved interpersonal effectiveness, and increased confidence in carrying out their chosen work or life roles.

1.4.7 Wellness coaching

Wellness coaching is a fast-growing industry. Wellness coaches appeal to the current consumer desire for a holistic-and-customized approach to health. They are trained professionals who help clients find ways to pursue healthier lifestyles. They are available to both individuals and to employees—or departments—of an organization.[31]

A wellness coach is not the same as a personal trainer, who primarily develops individualized exercise programs. A wellness coach can work with clients to help them change any of the aspects of their lives that are the unhealthiest, including dietary habits, exercise, and smoking, among others. A good coach won't simply tell a client to drop some behaviors or engage in others. He or she will work with a client to figure out how present life contributes to negative behaviors and to determine what can be done to make behavior change easier. The coach will then create a customized program that addresses diet, fitness, and emotional well-being. Most wellness coaching models that I am aware of require an HRA (health risk assessment), a PHA (personal health assessment), or an ORA (organizational risk assessment). Each of these not only produces a data set that can be mined to determine program success but also gives the wellness coach a feel for the client's background.

Individual wellness coaching

Despite the significant advances in medical science, many people are still unhealthy. They are overweight, stressed, or indulging in unhealthy behaviors like smoking and excessive alcohol and drug use. Time spent in a doctor's office is usually minimal, and doctors' schedules are so packed that they may address the issue of wellness simply by imploring a patient to live in more intelligent ways or delivering a sound lecture on the evils of certain behaviors. This does not often succeed in producing the desired change. But suggesting a patient get wellness coaching might be.

In the best sense, wellness coaching creates a relationship between coach and client. The coach looks holistically at the person's life prior to helping him or her evolve ideas for changing it. The number of visits and the amount of time this could take vary, depending on each coach's preferences and the client's individual needs.

Corporate wellness coaching

In organizational wellness, the focus can be on the individual worker (here is where the coach can play a major role) or on units of the organization in which an epidemiological assessment shows a high level of risk. The latter is normally handled by HR experts or organizational consultants who may propose changes in working conditions or other types of remedies. Approaches to wellness vary greatly. Some programs are oriented to "employees at risk" and others are preventive in nature and focus on enhancing well-being.

One of the trendiest wellness programs is the so-called *Mindfulness*, which means maintaining a moment-by-moment awareness of our thoughts, feelings, bodily sensations, and surrounding environment, through a gentle, nurturing lens. Mindfulness also involves acceptance, meaning that we pay attention to our thoughts and feelings without judging them—without believing, for instance, that there's a "right" or "wrong" way to think or feel in a given moment. When we practice mindfulness, our thoughts tune into what we're sensing in the present moment rather than rehashing the past or imagining the future.

Though it has its roots in Buddhist meditation, a secular practice of mindfulness has entered the general coaching mainstream in recent years, in part through the work of Jon Kabat-Zinn and his Mindfulness-Based Stress Reduction (MBSR) program, which he launched at the University of Massachusetts Medical School in 1979.[32] Since that time, thousands of studies have documented the physical and mental health benefits of mindfulness in general.

But, remember that wellness coaching covers a wide range of activities (personal and organizational), and coaches need to be well trained. As opposed to other coaches, wellness coaches normally require a background in medicine, in psychology, and in spiritual knowledge as well as in coaching.

Figure 1.8 describes the overall content of what is, or should be, addressed during wellness coaching. The goals of the wellness coaching process are the

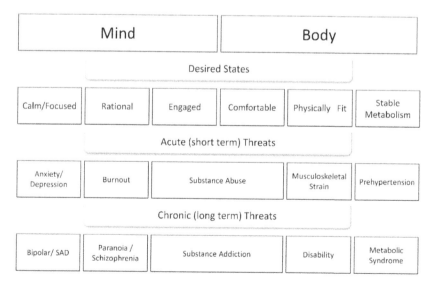

Figure 1.8 What should be included in wellness coaching?

"Desired States" in the graphic. This exhibit is hypothetical but is offered as a reference for you the reader if you wish to be trained well in the field of wellness coaching.

BOX 1.3 WELLNESS COACHING AND VALUES

Michael Arloski, PhD, PCC, CWP

The field of wellness and health promotion has evolved over the last 30 years to show us that lifestyle is the key determinant for the health of a population and that we need to do much more than simply educate to see behavioral change. The paradigm shift has been toward the individualization of wellness and lasting behavioral change, seeking to reach each person not just with better information, but with working alliances that can help them achieve lasting lifestyle improvement. Those allies accompany the person through the behavioral change process instead of just pointing them in the right direction and encouraging them to succeed alone. We have discovered that the more these allies shift from a medical prescriptive approach, or an educational approach, toward adopting a coach approach, the more they see actual behavioral change.

Wellness coaching is fast becoming a service offered by corporate wellness programs, disease management companies, employee assistance programs, health insurance companies, and employee wellness programs based in hospitals, educational institutions, and various organizations. Dee Edington, from the University of Michigan's Health Management Research Center, and a pioneer in the field of health risk assessment, has recently made a case for wellness coaching in his new book *Zero Trends: Health as a Serious Economic Strategy*. He shows us that wellness coaches can not only help those who are at high risk, but help "keep the healthy people, healthy," which he states is the best long-range economic and health strategy.

Wellness coaching methodology is very client-centered. Coaches help their clients to (a) take inventory of their health and wellness, then (b) get clear about their own vision of what living a healthy and well life looks like (a well-life vision). Addressing the disparity or gap between where the client is now (current health status) and where they want to be (vision) helps the client to (c) form a wellness plan made up of areas they want to focus on to improve their lifestyle. That wellness plan has action steps co-created by both the client and the coach. The coach is then able to help the client to (d) be accountable to themselves and gain the support they need to succeed both within the coaching relationship and throughout the rest of their life. Working through both internal and external barriers to change, the coaching ally helps the client to (e) succeed in achieving effective, measurable outcomes that improve their lives. As you can see, wellness coaching is not simply a process of goal setting; it is whole-life planning, and at the heart of it are the client's values.

The values and beliefs the client holds about themselves and the world around them drive their attitudes and behavior. The effective wellness coach honors the client's values and helps them examine and clarify their value base. The coach approach maximizes motivation by having the client set the agenda for change and co-create the wellness plan with the coach, rather than pushing a pre-packaged "how-to-be-well" program for the client to follow. The client's values are foundational to all of the choices and all the prioritization that takes place.

Wellness coaches begin by honoring what is. They honor the client's values and do not attempt to replace them with their own. A real valuable process the coach offers, however, is to help the client to (a) clarify what their values really are and to (b) examine how self-enhancing (and health-enhancing) or self-defeating their values are. They also can help their clients to (c) gain insight into ways that they are living which are incongruent with their values and hence are a source of tremendous stress and conflict. For example, a client may have grown up valuing self-sufficiency to such a degree that they are unwilling to ask for or receive the help they need. Without social support their efforts at changing behavior perpetually fail. The coach does not identify this self-defeating behavior and label it as such, but instead asks the client to examine how holding such a strong value works for them in some ways, but may be working against them when it comes to improving their quality of life and their health.

Exploring and examining such lifestyle-related values can be challenging for both the coach and the client. Our ways of living are often based on values learned and adopted from our familial, cultural, and religious backgrounds. These values are then expressed in the norms of our peers. Peer health norms are widely known to be powerful influences on our health choices. It can be very difficult to be the only family member working at improving her diet. Being surrounded by friends whose style of recreation is always sedentary can make adopting physically active pursuits challenging. At the same time, it is often peers who can provide the support clients need to achieve success at lifestyle improvement. If a client's family members or co-workers encourage and praise health-enhancing behaviors—such as being more physically active, eating in a healthy way, and not smoking—the client will find it much easier to adopt those behaviors. Wellness coaches can help their clients expand their peer groups, learn to ask for the help they need, and develop strategies for dealing with negative peer health norms.

Wellness coaching clients often find that the process of self-assessment/ self-exploration, clarifying a well-life vision, and co-creating a behaviorally based wellness plan is in fact a gigantic values clarification exercise! When coaches ask, "What do you really want?" the client has to connect with values at a core level. When coaches help people remember how truly free they are to make their own choices, they examine automatic default behaviors and either embrace or reject them. Throughout this process of change, the client enjoys the support of a real ally who expresses genuine caring and compassion.

The values that the wellness coach expresses are found not in clinical or health professional recommendations or prescriptions, nor are they found in mere coaching techniques. They are found in the ways of being that make them effective coaches. Effective coaches value the same things that psychologist Carl Rogers found long ago to be the keys to effective therapy, what he called "the facilitative conditions of therapy" and we can just as easily call "the facilitative conditions of coaching." Empathy, warmth, unconditional positive regard, and being genuine enhance the coaching relationship and allow the client to grow. Providing these conditions is done not by practicing techniques but rather by holding such values and living them. The best coaches develop the ability not only to hold such values but to express them in the coaching sessions with their clients. When clients experience deeper levels of acceptance, honesty, trust, compassion, and safety, they are free to explore their own values and ways of living with more openness and candor.

A web of values is interlaced throughout the wellness coaching process. The values of the client, the values in the client's environment, and the values of the coach affect the process of working toward lifestyle improvement. By including values in the coaching process in a very conscious way, we can enhance the probability of successfully achieving lasting lifestyle change.

Michael Arloski, PhD, PCC, CWP, is a licensed psychologist, professional certified coach, and certified wellness practitioner. He is CEO of Real Balance Global Wellness Services, in Colorado (www.realbalance.com). Over 2,000 wellness coaches have been trained by his company worldwide. Dr. Arloski is the author of numerous wellness publications, including *Wellness Coaching for Lasting Lifestyle Change* (Duluth MN: Whole Person Associates), the leading book in the wellness coaching field. For more: https://realbalance.com/about-dr-arloski

DELIVERING DELIGHT:

A new angle to train leaders and transform the firms' culture positively

Avi Zvi Liran

Laugh often, long and loud. Laugh until you gasp for breath. (George Carlin)

Humor helps enhance well-being through two paths:

Happiness—humor helps enhance well-being by creating positive emotion. Humor typically increases positivity and decreases negativity. Moreover, the act of creating something humorous can help people cope with pain, stress, and adversity. (As an aside, when people tell me about their bad day, I often say, "Sometimes you're the hammer, and sometimes you're the nail." It often gets a laugh and reminds people that not every day will be like that.)

Relationships—humor enhances well-being by enhancing how people get along. Humor helps smooth interpersonal and cultural exchanges by reducing conflict.

In many parts of the world, positive psychology associations often discuss the relationships between humor, positivism, and enhanced well-being. In one experiment reported recently, researchers developed an exercise called "three good things." The idea is to write down every day three good things that happened to you. Research showed that people who are asked to practice this exercise for one week report greater happiness levels up to six months afterwards. The experiment was extended by others who put a humorous twist by asking people to write down "three funny things" from their experience. Results, compared to a control group, showed that they did indeed show significantly higher happiness three months after the exercise and significantly lower depressive symptoms at one month, three months, and six months afterwards. Other compelling evidence comes from researchers such as Robert Provine (University of Maryland), who describes laughter as a "social Glue" that brings people together. He is the author of such books as *Laughter: A Scientific Investigation* and *Curios Behavior: Yawning, Laughing, Hiccupping, and Beyond*. Martin Seligman, author of "Authentic Happiness" and "Flourish," considered to be the father of positive psychology, seems to agree, saying that "laughter tunes the group," thereby helping to strengthen the cooperation that underpins much of the cultural evolution of man.

It seems that laughter is a powerful antidote to stress, pain, and conflict. Nothing works faster or more dependably to bring your mind and body back into balance than a good laugh. Humor lightens your burdens, inspires hope, connects you to others, and keeps you grounded, focused, and alert. It also helps you release anger and forgive sooner.

So, can you teach yourself to laugh more often, or can you train leaders to build a culture of positive and laughing environment? We in delivering delight think so. An essential ingredient for developing a sense of humor is to learn not to take everything too seriously and laugh at mistakes and foibles. As much as we'd like to believe otherwise, we all do foolish things from time to time. Instead of feeling embarrassed or defensive, embrace imperfections. While some events in life are clearly sad and not opportunities for laughter, most don't carry an overwhelming sense of either sadness or delight. They fall into the gray zone of ordinary life—learning and practicing the other choices with a focus on laughing will make a big difference.

We are attempting to convince organizations to create the position of Chief Delight Officer (CDO), who will be an incurable optimist fascinated by the power of positivity, as well as having the ability to transform people's lives and experiences through his words and tones. That's why this officer should devote his time and energy to teach and inspire, helping leaders and organizations to delight people.

In the past several years I have traveled across Asia-Pacific and Europe, sharing this thought-provoking idea, mimicking laughter and producing instant spontaneous delight, inspiring audiences of all backgrounds, from Fortune 500 leaders to students, community leaders to service frontlines to consider it seriously. After all, passion lies in sparking others and tweaking their inner delight and leading with their values so they can convert employees and customers into ardent fans and reach a higher purpose.

In sum, I am a firm believer in the concept of "edutainment," which has led me to create the "*Delivering Delight* and *Leading with Values*" consulting firm. Although on the surface the activities and methods to delight seem light or perhaps just an entertainment, there is widespread support and scientific evidence that humor is good for all employees' physical health. Naturally, the research also shows that laughter brings people together and strengthens relationships, which is a key to sustainable performance at work settings and an antidote to retain talented employees.

Avi Zvi Liran is currently based in Singapore. He is the CEO and CDO (Chief Delight Officer) of *Delivering Delight* and *Leading with Values*. His most recent articles have been featured in *Business Times* and *European Business Review*. He has co-published two papers with Simon Dolan on the fallacy of corporate ethics. When he's not inspiring anyone, you can find him shooting hoops with his youth basketball team or challenging random service staff to delight their customers. For more information see: www.deliveringdelight.com

1.5 On coaches, professionalism, and professional associations

Today, anyone can call himself or herself a coach. There are no rules, regulations, laws, restrictions, or enforced codes. Personal coaching produced a startling number of successes in its early years. Since then many people have jumped on the bandwagon to take advantage of the good name that these successes created. Now, these people, all calling themselves coaches, offer a myriad of different coaching methods, styles, philosophies, structures, ethics, backgrounds, niches, and purposes.

The coaching community itself is confused about what constitutes coaching and how to determine what the coaching process is. Vicki Brock pointed this out in her 2008 doctoral dissertation on the history of coaching,[33] "Inside the field there is much divergent thinking of what coaching is and whose approach is best. Outside the field there is even more confusion among clients and the public about what makes up coaching." This is compounded by the existence of "many definitions of coaching, some of which contradict each other, are based on and influenced by practitioners' backgrounds, theories, and models."

Government bodies have not found it necessary to provide a regulatory standard for coaching, nor does any state body govern the education or training standard for the coaching industry; the title "coach" can be used by any service provider. Critics charge that life coaching is akin to psychotherapy without restrictions, oversight, or regulation. The state legislature of Colorado, after holding a hearing on such concerns, disagreed, asserting that coaching is unlike therapy because it does not focus on examining or diagnosing the past. Instead coaching focuses on effecting change in a client's current and future behavior. Additionally, life coaching does not include diagnosing mental illness or dysfunction.

Sociologists many years ago developed criteria for assessing professionals. Some of these are a common body of knowledge, a minimum requirement (and testing or certification) to enter the profession and a clear code of ethics. Those who criticize "coaching" as a profession claim that as of today coaches do not meet any of these criteria (as distinguished from medical doctors or psychologists, for example).

The International Coaching Federation (ICF) has created a code of ethics—and does certify coaches—but does not have the capacity to enforce its code or follow up on its certification (by, for instance, requiring recertification after a period of time or insisting continuing education be a basis for keeping one's certification). Only a small segment of the coaches worldwide even bother to become members of the ICF. Moreover, the public at large isn't aware of its existence. Likewise, the International Coaching Community (ICC), which claims to be the largest such organization in the world (13,000 coaches in 67 countries), has developed a code of standards and ethics but admittedly cannot enforce it. The ICC's code comprises four sections: Professional Conduct at Large, Conflicts of Interest, Professional Conduct with Clients, and Confidentiality/Privacy. I hope—and it's safe to say that many, if not most, professional coaches share my hope—that in the future governments will step in and create some order in the field.

1.6 Selecting your coaching model

How do you select *your model* of coaching (whether you are a professional coach or not) when so many models are available?

We have seen that the coaching discipline integrates several fields of knowledge, each having its own schools of thought, models, and theories. This may seem confusing, even daunting, but it opens a world of opportunities. If you learn about different models—mining their unique elements while noticing what they have in common—you can incorporate aspects of them into your coaching approach to craft a flexible methodology that will work for you.

Creating an *entire* model from scratch is extremely difficult but being locked into one model can severely limit you. The fluid, shifting, and various natures of the circumstances you will encounter while coaching will frequently leave you stumped if you are wedded to a single model, a single way of doing things. But it is important that you remain mindful of the essential elements that effective coaching approaches share. To be successful, a coaching process must be based on these three pillars:

• the establishment of a relationship built on trust, genuine communication, and confidentiality

- the formulation of client-based, agreed-upon goals and expectations
- a deep questioning and learning dynamic in relation to clients' goals

In addition, a coaching process needs to have models and methods that address the following areas:[34]

Advanced communication model—for a focused conversation: Coaching is a *highly focused conversation*, a specialized communication that gets to the heart of things as a client explores dreams, hopes, and values. An advanced model for communication is essential to quickly and incisively getting to the core issues. Otherwise, the coaching degenerates into "a nice chat."

Reflexivity model—for facilitating emotional intelligence: Coaching involves and facilitates a client's *stepping back to the thoughts in the back of the mind*. Bringing out the reflexive thinking of the self-dialogue that goes on simultaneously in the back of one's mind is an important element in getting to the crux of things in the coaching process.

The kind of consciousness that humans have is very special. Its self-reflexive consciousness. This speaks about the human ability to think-about-our-thinking, to feel-about-our-feelings, and to respond to our responses. A professional coach will have studied the principles of meta-cognition and use a meta-cognitive reflexivity model for efficiently and effectively facilitating this degree of awareness.

Generative change model—for facilitating change: Coaching first and foremost deals with performance change (a change in one's quality and level of performance), but it does not stop there. A coach also works with developmental change—for example, the changes necessary when a client needs to evolve his or her sense of identity, beliefs, and values. Nor does it stop there. An even higher level of change is transformational change. This speaks about changing one's direction, purpose, mission, and vision. These multidimensional levels of change indicate the generative change of coaching and call for a model of generative change so that a coach can determine the level of change a client is seeking and how to facilitate it.

Most coaching change models come from therapy change models rather than change models specifically designed for the healthy self-actualizing person, a person who embraces change rather than fighting it. In fact, this is one of the two key differences between generative change and the remedial change of therapy. In therapeutic models of change, clients are expected to resist and relapse. This is not so in a generative model of change. If a coach is a change agent, he or she will obviously have to know how to dance with the mechanisms of change for a healthy person who simply wants to unleash more of his or her potential and will work from a coaching change model that specifically deals with this kind of change.

Implementation model—for measuring change: Coaching, while a conversation, is not merely about talking; the bottom line of coaching is *doing*. An effective coach is able to bring about change by enabling and empowering a client to actually incorporate the change and embody it in his or her physiology. In this way the coach facilitates implementation of the great ideas, visions, and values talked about in the coaching session. Coaching is ultimately about actualizing potentials and visions. It is about executing the co-created action plans and following through to ensure the client makes them real (i.e., realizes them in his or her life).

An effective coach needs several models for implementing ideas and visions. At the most fundamental level, there needs to be a personal implementation model that empowers the client to *embody* the changes so that they become part of his or her way of being in the world. Next, there needs to be a way to mark and measure the change, a way to benchmark even intangible and conceptual principles so that one can know that all the talk during the coaching sessions actually makes a difference. This requires an explicit implementation model for measuring change.

Systems model—for systemic change: The process has to be systemic in nature because coaching works with the whole person, the mind-body-and-emotion within many systems—relational, family, work, cultural, and organizational, among others. A coach has to be able to think, speak, and work systemically with clients. To that end, an effective coach needs a systemic model that enables him or her to see and work with multiple systems simultaneously. This is critical for ecological reasons and it is crucial to effectiveness

To work systemically is to energize the person's mind-body-and-emotion system so that what is imagined and envisioned becomes a congruent change fully aligned within all the contexts and relationships of life.

Self-actualization model—for unleashing potential: Coaching depends on a unique form of psychology—not on abnormal psychology, which deals with neurosis and psychosis, and not even on normal psychology, which deals with the average. It deals with a healthy person who is self-actualizing to become his or her best. It deals with the psychology of the person seeking excellence. The kind of human psychology an effective coach uses works to unleash potentials so that a client will activate his or her best and experience peak performance.

This kind of psychology is self-actualization psychology as pioneered by Abraham Maslow (we will discuss his hierarchy of needs theory in the next chapter) and others, as part of the Human Relations Movement. Given this psychology informs most coaching, the professional coach will work from the current self-actualizing models in the field.

1.7 Conclusion

In this chapter, I offered an overview of the coaching discipline—presenting several coaching types, approaches, and models. This review wasn't meant to be exhaustive, but rather to be a jumping-off point for your own research. Looking at these coaching approaches and briefly at the standards and guidelines created by international coaching federations gave us a basic understanding of the competencies that all effective coaches must have and the features that successful coaching processes share.

But there is a key point that I haven't yet addressed—a question each individual needs to ask before choosing an approach: Do I want to apply the model to myself or to others whom I would like to help?

As I said earlier, with few exceptions all people can be coaches, at least to themselves and to their immediate families, friends, and colleagues at work. But some methods and tools require more training than others. While I have been trained in hypnotherapy, I use the technique only for self-hypnosis or with my family, my relatives, and my children. I don't think I am qualified to use hypnotherapy as a professional. Coaching models vary in terms of their assumptions, complexities, and readiness for use. Not all can be picked up and followed step-by-step or simply imposed as is on a situation. Here are some thoughts about coaching models that I find helpful:

- They serve only as tools for coaches.
- They are limited by cultural factors that influence coaching beliefs and practices (both for the coaches and for the coachees).
- There is no one model that is the best, nor is there one right way to coach.
- Remember: Coaches learn, and coaching models evolve.
- Start from where you are and where you feel comfortable.

What lies ahead in coaching? I think one of the best ways of looking at the future is to quote one of the founders of this profession, John Whitmore. Whitmore says[35]:

> The coaching profession faces many challenges and huge opportunities, and a great responsibility. It has grown from personal coaching to group coaching. From a cottage industry to a workplace profession; can it now shed the inevitable self-limiting beliefs of an expanding role to become a global force to serve humanity on a big scale and on the front line? What coaching has to offer is the means to construct exactly what is most needed all over this time, the individual and collective responsibility essential for the survival of life as we know it.

Another approach to coaching: In the remainder of the book, I will present another approach to coaching, one that is based on values. My experience has shown that focusing on values offers a parsimonious, simple, and easy-to-follow framework that produces deep, lasting, and generative change.

The Coaching by Values model is based on three fundamental principles: (a) a presentation of a distinct concept that explains why values should be the cornerstone of a coaching effort, specifically when the coach attempts to bring about positive changes in the coachee's life (be it at work or in other settings); (b) a clear description of the process and methodology for applying the CBV model; and (c) concrete practical tools that enable the coach to get results efficiently and effectively.

If you are open to these ideas and think you'll benefit from CBV, please read on. I will present it in detail, so don't worry if this is unfamiliar territory. But remember the importance of the sequence. Please do not jump ahead before you really understand the foundations. After explaining the logic, I will provide you with a step-by-step methodology for applying it. I will not deceive you and leave you with only the theory. My proposed method also involves performing steps within a specific sequence, but within that sequence there is room for great creativity. So, let's begin the "voyage."

In the next chapter, I will show just how powerful words are as we explore the concepts "values" and "value." In chapter 3, I'll introduce you to the 3Es triaxial model that is the basis of the CBV methodology. In chapter 4, I will go step-by-step through the CBV method, applying it to both personal and work situations. In chapter 5, I will take the risk of looking at the future—of values, of CBV, and of the world. But now, let us begin the Coaching by Values journey.

CLBV Reflection ♣ ♠ ♥

Think of the key message(s) you retained after reading this chapter. Then complete the following sentences:

The principal points I liked in this chapter include

1. _____
2. _____
3. _____

The principal points that I did not like or disagreed with in this chapter include

1. _____
2. _____
3. _____

This part is to be completed only if you are already a professional coach:
After reading this chapter, I am more convinced that (select only one and explain)

a. The coaching method(s)/philosophy I use really works and I do not need to broaden it because

_____

_____

_____

b. The coaching method(s)/philosophy I use works relatively well, but I am willing to incorporate complementary approaches because

_____

_____

_____

c. Wow!!! I realize how incomplete my method(s)/philosophy is. I am willing to search for better or complementary methods, because

_____

_____

_____

Notes

1 Davison, M., & Gasiorowski, F. (2006). The trend of coaching: Adler, the literature, and marketplace would agree. *Journal of Individual Psychology, 62,* 188–201.
2 Gallwey, W. T. (1974). *The Inner Game of Tennis* (1st ed.). Random House.
3 Whitmore, J. (2017). *Coaching for Performance Fifth Edition: The Principles and Practice of Coaching and Leadership. Updated 25th Anniversary Edition.* Nicholas Brealey.
4 Brock, V. (2008). *Grounded Theory of the Roots and Emergence of Coaching* (Unpublished doctoral dissertation), p. 13. International University of Professional Studies, Maui, Hawaii. Recent update can be found on her website: "Coaching History" http://vik-kibrock.com/coaching-history/
5 I have modified these from the ICF (International Coach Federation) list as presented in: Davison, M., & Gasiorowski, F. (2006). The trend of coaching: Adler, the literature, and marketplace would agree. *Journal of Individual Psychology, 62,* 188–201.
6 All competencies are important. However, I believe that in relative terms, the most important competencies are those of identifying values, analyzing incongruence between values and goals, and steering or aligning respective behaviors. In later chapters, I will explain "Coaching by Values," which focuses and expands on these.
7 For more information, see Michelman, P. (2005). What an executive coach can do for you? Harvard Working Knowledge Archive (http://hbswk.hbs.edu/archive/4853.html).

8 Morgan, H., Harkins, P., & Goldsmith, M. (Eds.) (2005). *The Art and Practice of Leadership Coaching*. Wiley.

9 Gallwey, W. T. (1974). *The Inner Game of Tennis* (1st ed.). Random House.

10 Whitworth, L., Kimsey-House, H., Kimsey-House, K. K., & Sandahl, P. (2007). *Co-Active Coaching: New Skills for Coaching People Toward Success in Work and Life* (2nd ed.). Davis Black.

11 Important note: The basics of this model have been described in a series of books including *Frogs into Princes* (Bandler & Grinder, 1979), *Neuro-Linguistic Programming Vol. I* (Dilts, Grinder, Bandler, & DeLozier, 1980), *Reframing* (Bandler & Grinder, 1982), *Using Your Brain* (Bandler, 1985), *Turtles All the Way Down* (DeLozier & Grinder, 1995), and *Whispering in the Wind* (Bostic & Grinder, 2001). Following several exchanges with him, John Grinder graciously agreed to have the section written by his colleagues. More than 95% of this section was an original contribution by Bill Phillips and Alessandro de Vita Zublena at AdZ Conseil Coaching for Leaders, based in Lausanne, Switzerland (www.adzconseil.com). Phillips and Zublena are members of The International Trainers Academy of NLP and work in close association with John Grinder and Carmen Bostic St Clair.

  1. Bandler, R., Grinder, J., & Stevens, J. O. (1979). *Frogs into Princes: Neuro Linguistic Programming*, Real People Press.

  2. Dilts, Robert, Grinder, John, Bandler, Richard, & Delozier, Judith (1980). *Neuro Linguistic Programming Volume 1 The Study of the Structure of Subjective Experience*. Meta Publications.

  3. Bandler, R., & Grinder, J. (1982). *Reframing: Neurolinguistic Programming and The Transformation of Meaning by Richard Bandler*. Real People Press.

  4. Bandler R., (1985). *Using Your Brain—For a Change*. Real People Press.

  5. Grinder J., Delosier J., (1995). *Turtles All the Way Down: Prerequisites to Personal Genius* (Updated Edition).

  6. Bostic St. Clair C., & Grinder, J. (2001), *Whispering in the Wind*. J&C Enterprises.

12 Rizzolatti first published his findings in 1996, but later summarized and updated his research in Rizzolatti, G. (2005). The mirror neuron system and its function in humans. *Anatomy and Embryology, 210* (5–6), 419–421.

13 Ramachandran, V. S. (2000, May). Mirror neurons and imitation learning as the driving force behind "the great leap forward" in human evolution. *Edge, 69*, 29. www.e dge.org/3rd_culture/ramachandran/ramachandran_p1.html.

14 Rizzolatti, G., & Craighero, L. (2004). The mirror neuron system. *Annual Rev Neurosci 27*, 169–192.

15 *Calibration*, as the term is used in NLP, is an acute attention to all of a client's conscious and unconscious responses, from changes in voice tone, skin color, blinking, and breathing to choice of words and many more. Because tracking so many details is impossible for the conscious mind, NLP practitioners are trained to allow their peripheral vision and hearing to collect movements and changes, and to respond as if "intuitively" to what others say and do. This is a very specific kind of attention-giving. New Code practitioners are even more highly trained in this, they say, because they work largely content-free, so seeing and hearing is sometimes all they have to guide them. If the coach's calibration is faulty, his or her competence is automatically impaired.

16 Bostic St Clair, C., & Grinder, J. (2001). *Whispering in the Wind*. J&C Enterprises. p. 218. Available at amazon.com (www.amazon.com/Whispering-Wind-Carmen-Bostic -Clair/dp/0971722307)

17 For more on New Code training, go to www.itanlp.com.

18 Salovey, P., & Mayer, J. D. (1990). Emotional intelligence. *Imagination, Cognition and Personality, 9*, 185–211.

19 Goleman, D., (2005) *Emotional Intelligence: 10th Anniversary Edition*; Why It Can Matter More Than IQ. Bantam Trade.
20 Boyatzis, R., & McKee, A. (2005). *Resonant Leadership: Renewing Yourself and Connecting with Others Through Mindfulness, Hope, and Compassion.* Harvard Business Press.
21 Goleman, D., and Boyatzis, Richard. (2002) *Primal Leadership: Realizing the Power of Emotional Intelligence.* Harvard Business School Press
22 Mayer, J.D., Caruso, D.R., & Salovey, P. (2016). The ability model of emotional intelligence: Principles and updates. *Emotion Review*, 8, 290–300. doi:10.1177/1754073916639667.
23 Salovey, P., & Mayer, J. D. (1990). Emotional intelligence. *Imagination, Cognition and Personality*, 9, 185–211. doi:10.2190/DUGG-P24E-52WK-6CDG.
24 Caruso, D.R., & Rees, L.T. (2018). *A Leader's Guide to Solving Challenges with Emotional Intelligence.* New Haven, CT: EI Skills Group.
25 Sheldon, O.J., Dunning, D., & Ames, D.R. (2014). Emotionally unskilled, unaware, and uninterested in learning more: Reactions to feedback about deficits in emotional intelligence. *Journal of Applied Psychology*, 99, 125–137. doi:10.1037/a0034138.
26 Cooperrider, D., & Srivastva, S. (1987). Appreciative inquiry in organizational life. In Woodman, R., & Pasmore, W. (Eds.), *Research in Organizational Change and Development* (Vol. 1). JAI Press.
27 Sloan, B., & Canine, T. (2007, May). Appreciative inquiry in coaching: Exploration and learnings. *AI Practitioner*, http://www.pathfinderplus.com/pdf/May2007AIP.pdf
28 Maturana, H. R., & Varela, F. J. (1980). *Autopoiesis and Cognition: The Realisation of the Living.* Reidel; Maturana, H. R., and Varela, F. J. (1992). *The Tree of Knowledge: The Biological Roots of Human Understanding* (Rev. ed.). Shambala.
29 Heidegger, M. (1962). *Being and Time* (J. Macquarie & E. Robinson, Trans.). Harper.
30 Ontological coaching stems from the work of a number of Chileans: Maturana, Flores, and Echeverria are considered. Echeverria worked with Flores until he and Julio Olalla decided to go their own way and form The Newfield Group.
31 For more on wellness coaching, see the pioneering work of Arloski, M. (2007, 2014). *Wellness Coaching for Lasting Lifestyle Change.* Whole Person Associates. But recent titles includes: Shauna Menard (2019). *Free to Heal: 9 Steps to a Successful, Soul-Satisfying Health*, Coaching practice. Difference Press.
32 Jon Kabat-Zinn has published over the year many books. Here I have decided to site only the most recent published in 2019: *Mindfulness for All: The Wisdom to Transform the World.* Hachette Books.
33 Brock, V. (2008). *Grounded Theory of the Roots and Emergence of Coaching* (Unpublished doctoral dissertation), pp. 2, 6. International University of Professional Studies, Hawaii.
34 Adapted from: Meta-Coach Foundation (MCF). Coaching Models. www.meta-coachfoundation.org/index.php?option=com_content&task=view&id=34&Itemid=57.
35 Whitmore, J. (2009). Will coaching rise to the challenge? *The OCM Coach and Mentor Journal*, 92–93.

Chapter 2

How can an executive coach help leaders and organizations?

Introduction

Introduction

Coaching is not a fad, but it is not something new. We spoke in the previous chapter on the history of modern coaching, but some say it is rooted in a series of philosophies and practices that can be traced to Aristotle, Buddhist thought, Gestalt theory, and others. And within the field of coaching the subspecialty in executive coaching seems to be growing. The taxonomy of executive coaching includes a variety of ancient and modern wisdom woven into a unique tapestry designed to produce real-time, real-world results for executives and leaders who have a lot of responsibility and have little time.

Executive coaching is an individual relationship between the coach and a client, based on the subject's intrapersonal objectives within the organizational context. This is a special case within the business coaching model.

Although both the organization and the manager must commit to coaching so that it can succeed, the idea of hiring a coach can proceed either from the human resources and leadership development programs or from the executives themselves. Previously, it used to almost always proceed from the organizational needs angle, but, given the increasing trajectory of coaching as a tool for the most outstanding employees, more and more executives opt for coaching as an impetus for their professional career paths.

BOX 2.1 COACHING AND LEADING BY VALUES: THE PATHWAY TO POSITIVE CHANGE

By Bonnie Richley, PhD, and Tony Lingham, PhD

In our collective work the pathway to positive change has been singular. Simply stated, understanding the individual, team, and organizational values is crucial to unlocking human potential. To be clear, this does not mean using people solely to produce profit but to help them create lives of meaning which leads to high-quality engagement, building true relationships, and sustainable change.

In our work across the range from undergraduates, masters, and doctoral students, as well as executives and senior executives, it all begins with one thing—*understanding their core values.* This is also true in our work as certified Coaching by Values experts, in our consulting work, and yes, in our personal lives as well. Nothing drives us more in life than connecting what we value to our daily efforts. Understanding how our values drive our behaviors enables deep reflection and heightened self-awareness. Being able to move this further by helping individuals understand the values that drive others leads to interpersonal awareness. We have identified in our work as coaches, using different models of coaching, but especially in Coaching by Values, that values and motivation are intrinsically tied. In our work we focus on the work environment and highlight four fundamental learning motivational needs, which can be identified in real-time engagement at the individual, interpersonal, team, and organizational levels. Our knowledge and practice of Coaching by Values were pivotal in our continued work to foster high-impact engagement in the workplace.

Coaching and Leading by Values is our North Star as we work with everyone to help them uncover what gives meaning to their lives and work. Work and life are not separate values: they are one and the same and are the cornerstone of how we live our lives.

Coaching by Values has also proved to be fundamental when people feel off course in life. Through our coaching we help them to connect with who they are, what they value, and how to begin to engage in the direction of positive change connecting them back to the melding of values, work, and life.

Shared values have been also one of the key ingredients in our work with teams. Over the past 18 years we have developed a unique methodology that we labeled "High-Impact Engagement," where we employ a two-phase approach to create sustainable high-impact engagement, incorporating effective coaching for individuals and teams, which is also critical for the development of leaders in organizations. We have used this approach for numerous organizations worldwide and across diverse industries including for-profit, nonprofit, multinational companies, and educational institutions, and the results have been meaningful and powerful.

Teams live and breathe across organizational sectors (i.e., for-profit, non-profit, educational, and government organizations). Organizations in these sectors are being challenged by new paradigms, new technologies, and multiple generations working together. They need to thrive and adapt to the new landscape of work. This means:

- working effectively at the interpersonal level,
- managing changing goals and expectations,
- designing a team structure poised to succeed, and
- developing a team's quality of engagement.

All of this applies to individuals, teams, and organizations. While not everyone may share the same core values, going through the discovery process of what matters most leads to amazing connections, surprising shared values, and a desire to effect positive change and prosper in this new world.

Lingham T., Richley B., (2018) High-Impact Engagement: A two-phase approach for individual and team development, //www.highimpactengagement.com/

Bonnie Richley and Tony Lingham are cofounders of Interaction Science, LLC, a management consulting company that offers individual and team coaching certification using the Learning Needs Inventory (LNI) and the Team Learning Inventory (TLI), as well as train-the-trainer certification. Both authors are educated in interdisciplinary fields ranging from English literature, engineering, music, and psychology to organization development, and organizational behavior. They have been organization, team, and leadership consultants for more than 15 years, working with managers and leaders in national and multinational companies across the United States, Europe, Africa, and Asia, in both the for-profit and non-profit sectors. Prior to entering academia, they held leadership roles in organizations and as consultants. As academics and researchers, they have taught at some of the leading business schools of the world. Bonnie Richley is the coauthor of *Managing by Values* (2006—Palgrave MacMillan), and Tony Lingham is the coauthor of *Fundamentals of International Organizational Behavior* (2008—Sara Books). They can be reached at: www.highimpactengagement.com/contact/

So, what does it mean to be an executive coach? After examining the academic content of many executive coaching programs, I noticed that different currents of coaching are used (as described in the previous chapter), but the focus is as follows:

- helping executives improve their competence to affect changes in the company (all types of changes—although we focus on cultural change in this chapter or the so-called cultural reengineering);
- helping executives to improve their leadership skills and especially at the time of VUCA in the world we live in today;
- helping executives create and maintain high-performance teams; and
- helping executives overcome all kinds of personal problems (stress, lack of confidence or low self-esteem, fears, conflicts, and others).

All of this requires executives to develop the maximum potential in organizations and to manage people and assets effectively. Unfortunately, many executives are lost, stressed, and looking for help. Increasingly, when I interview high-level executives, I often hear them say: "I live in a VUCA world (Volatile, Uncertain, Complex, and Ambiguous) and it is very difficult to make decisions or act when everything changes." The VUCA world is affecting not only large companies, but also SME executives. And to add more layers of complexity, members of companies are becoming increasingly demanding (the millennia, generation Y, and others), and attracting and retaining talent is becoming more and more difficult.[1]

2.1 Executive coaching and culture reengineering

Changing a company's culture to sustain it in the long run is not an easy task. The executive who likes to do it out of necessity or by conviction needs a coach or a consultant who knows the fundamentals and the stages of cultural reengineering very well. I developed the concept of cultural reengineering along with Salvador Garcia at the end of the last century, when we published our book in Spanish, *Dirección por Valores*, or *DPV* (McGraw Hill, 1997). It was published in English, *Managing by Values*, or *MBV*, in 2006 (Palgrave MacMillan).[2] There, we describe the *MBV* process in four phases:

1. Authentic legitimation of the process by having leadership that is willing to assume the ownership of the process and commit time, resources, and other necessities.
2. Participatory formulation of selecting a short list of final core values and, above all, measuring them and auditing the existing shared values (which is culture).

3. Values in action—Assigning specific project/task teams. Communicating all the desired new values. And from there introducing additional programs via the HR practices for selecting, training, compensating, and assessing performance based on adherence to the new values.
4. Post audit of the coherency of using and conducting behaviors according to the new values.

The nuclear value of *MBV*, which is the "value of values," is trust. If there is no trust among organizational shareholders, the executive coach cannot guide the firm toward culture reengineering. In the next chapters, I will be dealing with Trust: how to measure it and how to build it. But, assuming that there is a minimal base of trust, here are some considerations for undertaking the process of culture reengineering:

• Balance between economic well-being, emotional well-being, and ethical well-being of the company; hence the latter will generate greater internal cohesion and satisfaction, and will lead to greater competitive advantage in the market place.
• Build jointly an exciting idea of where we are going, for what, and with what, in order to enhance commitment to the project;
• Humanize the process in the sense of considering people not merely as "human resources" but as human beings. This will bring you quickly to a cruising altitude in the change process;
• Promote cohesion and credibility of the owners and the management team involved in the change process so that they can project a positive image to other members of the organization and to external clients, suppliers, and society in general

2.1.1 How do we help leaders change culture and do cultural reengineering?

Many managers still act as though they believe that people have the same values they had in the twentieth century. These beliefs are no longer as effective at motivating staff. In the world, a clear change of focus is occurring in management. Managers are required to have a higher level of performance as a result of the company's greater demands on professionalism, responsibility, quality, and customer service. Managers must be able to lead and facilitate the necessary changes and to comply with these expectations. The world has also become a more uncertain and complicated place. Managers must have the skills to cope with increasing and continuous levels of complexity both within and outside the organization.

Thus, in order to survive in the twenty-first century, companies must develop a new way of acting—a new culture. Workers' values must be aligned with the company's vision and mission. In this sense, the leadership by values, management by values, and coaching by values are all integrated, innovative, and systematic concepts for the alignment of individual objectives with the company objectives. In other words, *MBV* is a philosophy that combines personal challenges and priorities with those of the surrounding environment, while core values are the primary element for understanding success in the business of life and in the life of business. Essentially, coaching by values in the context of leadership is a flexible framework (or approach) for the continuous renewal of corporate culture, and it is essential to inspire a collective commitment to the organization and its achievements.

Changing an entrenched culture is the hardest task an executive face. To do this, you must gain the trust of the people you work with and act with wisdom and persuasion. In their book *Blue Ocean Strategy: How to Create Uncontested Market Space and Make the Competition Irrelevant*, Kim and Mauborgne mention four obstacles that an executive-leader has to overcome by trying to instill values in a broad sense for a company. The first is cognitive, as people must have a certain understanding of why a new strategy is needed. The second is limiting resources. Inevitably, changes in the culture of a company require the movement of teams in certain areas. The third difficulty is motivating the workforce. The last step has to do with institutional policies.[3] To overcome these limitations they and many other experts suggest a "tipping point" approach and, from there, manage all other departments:

- First, the change agent (leader-coach) must recognize that they will not be able to introduce all the changes at the same time. They can start with people who are very influential in the company and get their commitment. Once they are involved, the others will receive the message and accept it more easily.
- Second, generate sensitivity to the necessary change (speeches charged with emotions but complemented with data always helps) and look for ways to make people aware of the situation and thus see the necessity of the change.
- Finally, it is necessary to have a clear methodology and simple tools to advance the changes. In this way, it will be easier to build coalitions and design the strategy toward the new direction of the organization. All leaders run the risk of losing contact with what is actually happening in the lower positions, but if they pre-plan benchmarks, are informed by the "Task Force," or by an internal or external consultant, it will help the leader go through the motions, adjust if needed, and focus on the solution.

In a generic manner, the process of changing the company's culture includes the following seven-steps:

1. create a sense of urgency;
2. adapt a philosophy and focus of change (for example shared values);
3. form a Change team;
4. create and communicate a clear vision for the change;

5. eliminate obstacles that may arise;
6. secure some short-term winning points and ensure to broadcast them; and
7. reinforce and build on the change.

BOX 2.2 THE DNA-VALUES METHOD™ TO ALIGN VALUES AT ALL LEVELS IN A COMPANY

Nacho plans

As a strategic consultant who loves team coaching, I was honored when Simon L. Dolan and David Alonso García asked me to teach my DNA-Values Method™, based on Dolan's triaxial model, in the Coaching by Values™ certification and specialization programs. Now there are hundreds (thousands) of consultants and coaches trained in this method in several countries, which is a reason for me to be really grateful to Simon, David, and the whole Coaching by Values™ community.

The method presented here is based on the values alignment at all levels (brand, company, team, and person) with the participation of all the people involved in each level. Let us get into practice!

The "draw-a-circle technique" to identify whose values we are talking about!

"We are not aligned," "Our employees don't feel involved with our business group's values," "I'm afraid our customers are not experiencing the brand values we are aiming for." These are usual expressions in daily business activity. There is *huge confusion* when it comes to talking about values, since most of the time we talk about something we feel, but we don't really know whose values we are talking about! It is frequent to find two people in a Management Committee discussing values with one referring to the Business Group's values, while the other is thinking of Brand values: no one is getting to know why there is such a discrepancy. Or even worse: both people agree on something related to values, but each is referring to different levels, so they will feel repeatedly frustrated when finding action plans do not match their expectations. To solve this problem, I suggest you first *tell the story*, and then *draw a circle around the involved "characters"* (Figure 2.1).

- **Brand values** are those defining the customer experience we want to shape.
- **Company values** are those shared by all members of the company as a large team.

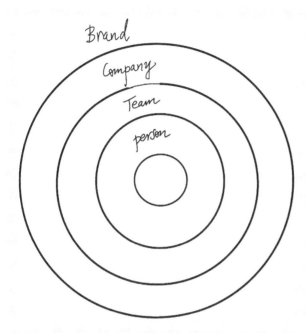

Figure 2.1 The basis of the DNA-values™ method is to define a set of values at all the levels (Brand, Company, Team, and Person) and work on their alignment.

- **Team values** are those shared by a working team to carry out their team mission in an optimal way.
- **Personal values** are those felt by a person as more importantly bringing happiness (or lack of happiness, if these values are missing) to their life.

And we can continue:

- **Business Group values** are those shared by a group of companies comprising a Business Group.
- **Department Values** are those shared by all the people belonging to a Department.
- **Working Center Values** are those shared by all the people working in a working center (for example, our shopping mall, or our warehouse).

And so on. So, whenever we "tell a story":

- *How we would like to develop our employee or customer experience.*
- *How we are going to launch a new product.*
- *How we want to set up a new business.*
- *How we want to change the way we work.*

We need to identify the main "characters," which can be

- An *experience* itself (Brand values for the customer experience, and Employer Branding for the employee's experience), with their own ingredients (environment, behaviors, communication, and so on).
- A specific *system* (the whole group, the whole company in a country, or a small working team).

Once we have a diagram of the whole picture, we can draw circles around these "characters" and determine how we want to work on their values (Figure 2.2). We usually do not have to work on the values of every system, but it is quite advisable *not to miss any of the essential characters in the story*. For example:

- If we have the *group values on the wall*, but if we don't explain our particular way of putting those values into practice, people in our country will look at those values as some sort of external imposition.

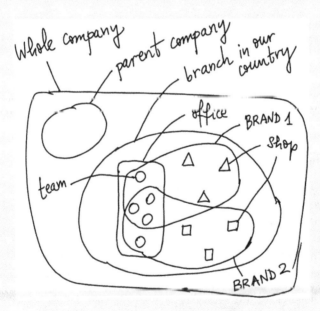

Figure 2.2 A freehand drawing of a more complex example, where there are many levels: brands, teams, offices, shops, the company branch in our country, the parent company, and the company as a whole. Ignoring any of the levels could weaken its development.

- The same applies when we have our *company values on the wall*, but we do not participate in each working center, department, or team, in the transcription of those values into action. Those values become only words! It would be advisable for each team to define their own values and/or strengths, in order to support the company's values.
- **"Fake" company values** are defined. We mean "fake" company values when a set of values is defined to be perceived by the public (in the web, communications to stakeholders, and so on) as if they were the shared values of the people in the company, while they are really a statement of intent from the top management on how the company wants to be perceived as a brand (so, they are actually brand values). Employees would feel those are "fake" values if their daily experience in the company is not aligned with those values.

Ok, we drew the circles, now what do we need at each level?

For each system, we need to know:

1. **Who** we are (to which system that we belong to we are referring to). This allows us to know what system we are working on (person, team, company, brand, and so on).
2. **How** do we do the things we do (based on our system values, criteria, and agreements).
3. Of course, to have a **"why"** and a sense of purpose will definitively push us forward. A clear Vision and Mission for our system, guided (not imposed) by the leaders will push us whether we work at the team, company, or brand level.

These three points will define **our identity, our DNA.**

So at each level, what steps should we follow?

At each level (brand, company, teams, and for each person) we may proceed as follows (Figure 2.3):

1. **Where** do we go? Create an inspirational Vision, communicate it, and, if possible, shape it with participation.
2. **How** do we get there? Create a values map that is participative. If people participate, they feel the values as part of themselves.
3. **Be specific!** Transform the values into criteria (express **what** is our way of doing things here) and (easier for teams and departments) specific **agreements** and **actions** for daily work.

Figure 2.3 (a–d) The DNA-values method™ at the team level: we set where we go, we shape a map comprising our main shared values, we specify precise actions to put our values into practice, and we check them.

4. **Follow up** values, criteria, and agreements; measure to what extent they are put into practice; and correct/adapt whatever is necessary.

In our company, what do we need to feel aligned?

A company is a living system, like a human body. If every cell in our body knows to which organ, system, and human being it belongs to, everything will work fine. Not to mention if we have a clear purpose in life and we know how we want to achieve it!

All the cells in our body share the same DNA, and it is also necessary that they express the particular identity of their organ and system. The same occurs in a company:

KEY IDEA 1: All levels (brands, branches in countries, departments, teams, and every single person) need a clear identity for themselves, as well as a shared DNA with the whole company.

Our identity has to be clear at each level: we know *who* we are, and also *what*, *how*, and *why* we do things (in this company, area, department, brand. And me, as a person, I also know my *who*, *what*, *how*, and *why!*).

What criteria can we follow to have all levels aligned?

- Simon L. Dolan's triaxial model is perfect to check alignment between levels: If you have a brand exhibiting emotional values, and the sales team in charge of its distribution doesn't have a single emotional value in their values map, what can you expect in the final customer experience? Apart from the value-chain, there is also an **emotional value-chain** that we must take into account! And to preserve and enrich this emotional value-chain we need to **align values** throughout all levels!

- In the resulting value-map of different levels (for example, team and brand), the **different zones in Dolan's axis should be in similar proportions** (or at least not too different! Zone 1: economic–pragmatic; Zone 2: social–ethical; and Zone 3: emotional). The proportion amongst zones in the values map tells us **at a glance about the system we are working with.** (If you ask the team "what is the your true DNA?", they wish to share; then the choice will focus on a specific zone, which happens to cover the largest space (or is the dominant zone) relative to the others; there you have information to work with.)

- **Try to ensure that no color is missing.** (It is not critical what value is chosen, but all axes—colors—are important, so I would recommend that they are all represented at least by a single value, as long as this does not conflict with the system's will.)

We extract the following:

KEY IDEA 2: A. There is an emotional value-chain that strongly affects employee and customer experience, and it relies on the alignment of values between all levels in the chain. B. Value alignment is not provided by matching exact values map at all levels, but by a similar proportion in Dolan's axis.

We already have criteria to preserve and work on value alignment between levels throughout the chain. So, we may always come back to a certain level to check our values map and see if we feel it is harmonious with the rest of the levels.

Considering all levels, we can summarize the method as follows:

KEY IDEA 3: Overview of the DNA-values™ method:
1. Elaborate Value-Maps at all levels, guaranteeing *participation*
2. Check value alignment between the levels
3. Write *specific* criteria and agreements to put values into practice
4. Follow up, reward, and review how values are put into practice

What shouldn't be forgotten?

Align all levels and… If you want everybody to be committed… *Guarantee participation* and *ensure specific (documented) outputs* in your DNA definition! Many people claim it is not possible for everybody in the company to participate in defining their shared values. I couldn't disagree more! So, they can ALL work together, long hours, throughout several countries, over the years, but they cannot neglect or disregard the participatory values definition. Once you start and feel the power of value alignment, it becomes a major pillar in your company's strategy, acknowledged by your employees and rewarded by your customers. Good luck!!

The interested reader can check an online video where a team session is carried out using this method (in Spanish): "Pikolinos y Nacho Plans: Alineando Valores de Marca y Equipo," YouTube: https://youtube/qvc3LJoCCto.

About Nacho Plans

Nacho Plans is a strategic consultant who specializes in cultural transformation. During his PhD in Mathematical Engineering, he researched at UCLA and CalTech. Back in Spain, he founded Alicoach, and has worked for companies such as Ericsson, BMW, Bank of Santander, Accenture, and many others. He is a collaborator of Simon Dolan and David Alonso in the Coaching by Values community where he has taught his methodology to hundreds of consultants and coaches. He has written books on Values and Influence and also delivers conferences. He can be contacted at nacho.plans@alicoach.es and LinkedIn. Twitter: @nachoplans.

2.2 Executive coaching and the new leadership competencies[4]

In an increasingly globalized, chaotic, and changing world, the principal role of leaders is to demonstrate that they have the skills to lead. To speak of leadership implies much more than just having knowledge of an area; it has to do with the influence that is exerted on the followers and an awareness of the virtues and the shortcomings that one possesses. Remember leadership is all about followership.

In the course of history, leadership has evolved and been approached from different angles. However, since the beginning of this century it has been common to hear about skills and competencies. Nonetheless, it is difficult to agree on the basic skills and competencies that a good leader needs to possess. Therefore, in this section we will focus on four main groups of competencies: the competency to agglutinate followers around some core values including spiritual values; digital leadership; the critical soft skills of a leader connected with some personality traits; and finally the leader's capacity to overcome situations of stress, conflicts, and other threats.

2.2.1 Leadership, values, and spirituality[5]

One of the main tasks of the leader is therefore to develop a culture of shared values. Values, long ago, were considered "too soft" to be managed effectively. But today, they are accepted as the basis of an organization's identity and as a fundamental principle of its strategy. Although cultural models and values are not new and have been studied since the 1970s, the perspective of the Triaxial Value Model is relatively new and more and more companies are using it as the framework to change or to sustain their organizational culture.

At this point, one may ask: *can we add the spiritual competencies of the leader?* To better understand the connection between effective leadership and spirituality in relationships to happiness at work, it is important to briefly discuss the concept of visionary leadership. Visionary leaders understand that spirituality in the workplace goes beyond themselves and has to do with the meaning of work and its purpose, in addition to the opportunities that the work itself provides. **Visionary leadership is much more than managing followers**. Spirituality comes from inside; leading from within is a way of orienting ourselves toward our inner knowledge and our innate strengths. The key to unleashing the abundant positive energy that springs from within is to resort to our values.

Although spiritual values are not as decisive as the other triaxial axes of values (i.e., they do not directly affect organizational effectiveness), they do provide a platform for aligning instrumental values. In the short term, an organization and a leader can survive without them. However, in the long run, the absence of spiritual values risks that the mission will be turned into something almost impossible. As a result, adding the axis of spirituality is essential for people who exercise leadership in any field.

Talking about spirituality and leadership is risky. Today, business leaders are usually judged for their results and for their ability to generate wealth. Surely, leadership is, in itself, a matter of risk, and a visionary leader does not shun the risk: putting into practice a vision is, in itself, a risky activity.

In 2015, I organized the first World Congress on Spirituality and Creativity in Management at ESADE (Barcelona). I organized it for different reasons. At that time I thought that tomorrow's leaders are not prepared and are not trained in spiritual matters. During the three-day conference, international experts from different corners of the world shared their ideas about the consequences of spirituality at work. Among others they included people like Peter Senge, a reference scholar at the MIT Sloan School of Management, and Naomi Tutu, daughter of African pacifist Desmond Tutu. Leadership experts Richard Boyatzis and Richard Barret explained the latest trends in understanding leadership and their connectivity to spirituality, as well as presenting the Christian approach to spirituality represented by Chris Lowney, a Jesuit who later became a senior executive of JP Morgan, one of the largest consulting management firms. All in all, four themes were discussed (Figure 2.4):

- What is spirituality in management? How is it defined?
- How is spirituality measured? Can it be measured?
- Do spiritual people provide better leadership?
- Are spiritual people also more creative?

Richard Barrett, one of the foremost experts on values, asserted during this congress that people are born with a very high level of creativity, almost to a level of genius. However, we lower our level of natural creativity to conform to pre-established social, family, and cultural structures. This process of socialization diminishes our level of creativity, up to an average of 2% at the approximate age of 25 years. What unlocks this creativity and makes a resurgence of that locked creativity possible, according to Barrett, is the feeling of being able to express who you really are with no fear and in an authentic manner. This happens in the stage of individuation of the psychological development of a person and the basis is very spiritual. At this stage, according to Barrett, you

Figure 2.4 On leadership and spirituality.

leave behind beliefs and fears and leaders begin to discover their true "ME." This is the moment when you start to unlock your creativity, because you find that "ME" is the only place where the passion truly rests (see the Barrett model on Values, in Box 5.2 in chapter 5 in this book).

Some say that a spiritual coach could then help the leaders find a fundamental purpose in their own existence, carrying out an integrated life. Spiritual coaching provides tools and techniques to discover what you really want, and how you can reach it. In this sense, it is very connected with our concept of values where it has to do with the discovery of what is "really important in life."

2.2.2 Executive coaching and digital leadership

Digital leadership is a strategic management approach focused on the quality and functional value of a company's digital assets, including emails, digital documents, audio content, images, movies, and other content stored on digital devices. Digital leadership has to do with digital commitment, collaboration, and accountability.

Digital leaders work in the same way as a CFO, a human resources director, or a COO. Their objective is to ensure that the assets of those responsible have a maximum value. The digital leadership ensures that the system can be understood and used by all others in the firm as they depend on the reliability and speed of the digital/technological system. The CFOs cannot do their job well if they do not have reliable digital information. Human resources management cannot make good hiring decisions if their systems allow false applications for jobs to filter through or candidates are presented without verifying credentials and capabilities. The COOs cannot execute their operations well if they do not obtain reliable data on the raw materials that are delivered.

Currently, in many organizations, new roles are emerging that aim to deal with digital management issues, including the head of data (CDO), the trustee, the data management executive, and the leader of Information Governance. All of these titles are competing to fill a current vacuum in business leadership to ensure the quality and functional value of information.

To exercise digital leadership for the quality and functional value of a company's information, the business has to rely on the people in charge of the digital assets and the information they provide. Validating sources and vetoing the digital information provided by the CIO or another self-proclaimed digital leader, is time-consuming. When digital leadership is properly managed, organizations can move faster and gain a competitive advantage.

Researchers and practitioners seem to agree on the following regarding leaders in the digital age:

1. They need a faster plan, as speed matters in today's world.
2. They need to quickly utilize culture and relationships to further advance the organization (not themselves).

As a result, today, in the digital era, we are witnessing the creation of consultants and executive coaches that help organizations prepare and transform themselves in the digital world. The emergence of new competitors using technology as a base and differential value of their business, including agility and simple processes, is forcing companies that want to survive to redesign. The classic way to demonstrate this is to compare Uber and Cabify to the traditional taxi. Here I provide a short list of soft skills that might allow the leader to lead faster and better.

Digital leader soft skills:

- The skill to quickly gather reliable information, confirm, or adjust the team's composition and/or goals
- The skill to listen to those directly connected to a project and to have the credibility to help solve problems or move strategic projects forward
- The skill to align with all stakeholders to build support, and understand how decisions are made and who has influence over decisions
- The skill to engage the culture to get up to speed on the values and norms that define acceptance behavior, all while working to enhance or change it

In short, executive coaching can help leaders become more successful in the digital age by increasing their ability to adapt quickly to changing technologies and contexts. In particular, leaders must recognize that their behavior and their interpersonal skills are increasingly public and open to the opinions or reactions of a wider range of stakeholders than in the past. They should be aware that simply not participating in online activities does not inoculate them from the effect that digital technologies have on them as well as on their organizations.

SAP is a top worldwide technology firm. Here is what its CEO, Bill McDermott, has to say about the skills of a leader to act fast and with precision:

> The adoption is so fast that the innovation cycle must be much faster for companies. With mobile enabling billions of users to be connected, a new technology augmented reality or digital assistants can reach maturity at a scale in one to two years. The pace of adoption has gone from 10 years to as little as a week. So it's all about speed to innovation and differentiation. Companies that act with urgency will win.[6]

CLBV Reflection ♣ ♠ ♥

Think for a moment about your experiences in which you have considered someone to be a great leader. Individually or in a group, do the following exercise:

On a blank sheet of paper, write the best leader you have had in your professional life. Why was he/she the best? What behavior has he/she displayed? What values have you detected?

Now do the same exercise for a bad leader. I mean, write the name of the worst leader you've ever had. Why was he/she the worst? What conduct has he/she engaged in? What values have you seen in this leader?

If you do this exercise in a team, share with them and enter below some of the conclusions of the conversation. What common themes did you discover in this exercise? Can you identify behaviors that can be taught to others?

2.2.3 Leadership competencies—Toward the future

Such behaviors (or skills) of leaders are called "competencies." Organizations have used executive coaches/consultants to help them identify which competencies are fundamental to their managers. Coaches detect these competencies by interviewing leaders or managers with better performance in the organization. The development of competencies is a multimillion-dollar industry in the current market.

Competencies are socially learned, uninherited, behaviorally specific, and observable skills. The best description of a competency could be: *a skill, a trait, or an underlying personal feature that leads to superior or effective performance.* A skill implies both intent and behavior. The competency assessment usually takes the form of a 360° feedback system (i.e., from supervisors, companions, subordinates, friends, family, and other significant persons). Other methods include interviews about critical incidents or events related to some behavior. These more qualitative methods require the creation of a code-of-competencies book to codify competencies in these interviews. The development of competencies is due to a specific progression: first, after receiving the results of the 360° feedback (or the codes identified in the interviews), people realize that they were not aware of their weaknesses in some competencies (unconscious incompetencies). Then they become aware of their weaknesses in these competencies (conscious incompetence).

In the current working environment, there are numerous competing models for identifying and measuring executives' or leaders' competencies. Some organizations train their managers and leaders in competing models that they themselves develop. Others use the existing models. Given my years of work as Chair of the Future of Work (ESADE) and my current position as president of the "Global Future of Work Foundation," we have developed a futuristic vision on many common tasks of the leaders of the future, and we have developed a list of competencies so that leaders will succeed in the future. In this section, allow me to present for the first time this list of competencies, which incorporates some skills that were developed by others. In addition, we are offering the executive coaches who have confidence in our perspective a commercial online tool that uses a complete 360° Assessment.[7]

How were the leadership skills developed? In my book *Leading, Managing, and Coaching by Values* (in Spanish, 2018) I identified the three main reasons for the failures of leaders, all based on the triaxial model of values, which we will discuss in detail in this book:

1. Leaders lose sight of what really matters. Many leaders are distinguished by their ability to think big and yet when their concentration deviates, they soon begin to think small. Micro-management becomes entangled in the details and the executive begins to be consumed by the trivial and insignificant. A reason for failure, even more subtle, is the obsession of the leader with doing and not becoming, since good leadership work tends to be the result of who is the leader; his/her actions naturally flow from his/her inner vision and his/her character. It is possible for a leader to focus too much on the action as in the process, they lose touch with the most important development of themselves.

2. The leader is involved in an ethical error. The credibility of the leader is the result of two aspects: what he/she does (competencies) and who he/she is (i.e., character and personality). The discrepancy between the two generates a problem of integrity, which is precisely one of the greatest principles of leadership. Numerous studies have shown that a respected leader is one who fulfills his promises, so that when integrity ceases to be the main priority and ethical compromise is rationalized as a means to a greater good, when the achievement of results becomes more important than the means to achieve them, the leader enters a scenario of failure. The same leader tends to see his/her followers as instruments or simple means to achieve an end, confusing manipulation with leadership. In the end, he/she loses empathy and stops perceiving people to devote themselves to indulging them, using popularity as a relief to blame for his/her lapse of integrity.

3. The leader exhibits a loss of contact or passion. Leaders fail when they move away from their first love and dream. Paradoxically, the hard work of leadership should be satisfactory and even enjoyable, but when leaders lose sight of the dream that prompted them to accept responsibility for leadership in the first place, they discover themselves working in causes lacking meaning to them. Therefore, they must cling to what they are passionate about and what motivated them in the beginning, and thus they will be able to maintain the satisfaction of the leadership.

So, at this point, I wish to share the leadership competency model that we have developed. It has a triaxial structure and includes nine competencies classified into three categories (see Figure 2.5):

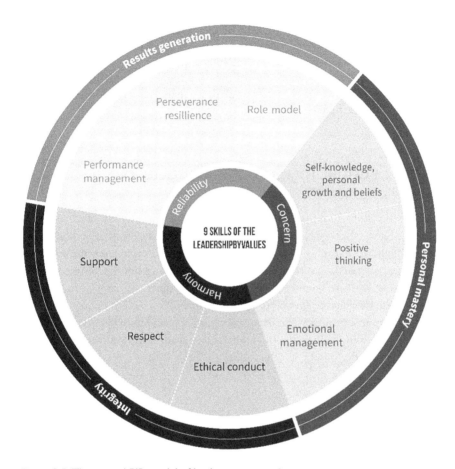

Figure 2.5 The triaxial PIR model of leader competencies.

- The first group of competencies is connected to the leader generating "Results."
- The second group of competencies is connected to the leader's ethical conduct and "Integrity."
- The third group of competencies is connected to the leader's personal traits and attitudes which we labeled "Personal Mastery."

A leader has to generate results

The leader has to manage *the performance*. Obtaining the results desired by the organizations depends on being able to align and integrate the work of the collaborators with the strategy previously defined. In order to do this, performance management processes, which are the foundation of individual and collective compliance in any organization, must be incorporated.

Nonetheless, in order to generate results, the competency of *perseverance* stands out. Perseverance is what the sea uses to dissolve the rocks on the coast; perseverance is what the wind uses to turn the highest mountains into plains; perseverance implies a whole series of qualities such as discipline, constancy or repetition, will, patience, and others.

BOX 2.3 CHURCHILL AND THE CONCEPT OF PERSEVERANCE

There is a story about Winston Churchill when he was already advanced in age. He was supposed to deliver a lecture at a university. He appeared before a large audience, calmly approached the microphone, looked into the room, and after a while he exclaimed, "You should never surrender." Everyone was expecting what he would say next, but he kept quiet. He kept the silence for a long time and again approached the microphone and exclaimed, "You should never surrender." The room burst into applause until again there was silence. He went back to the microphone and again said, "You should never surrender." After this, he left the room.

Another important characteristic of a leader that produces results is his/her being a *role model* to be followed. After all, we have mentioned before that leadership is all about followership. So, followers wish to have a role model to follow; follow a leader who influences our working life in a positive way. Followers want to follow a leader they can point to as an example in almost all the things they do. Good leaders set the pace of their followers for their life-style, behavior, and actions. Followers will become a fanatic of the leader who becomes a mirror through which they see themselves and make adjustments to live a dignified and better life.

A leader has to be integral—integrity includes three competencies: respect, support, and ethical conduct

Respect—respect is mutual. The leader has to respect his followers, but the followers have to develop a respect for their leader. There are many ways to measure the respect of a follower toward a leader, although the greater proof of respect is given when a leader makes a big change in the organization and his respect remains intact. The reasons why people accept the changes of their leaders can be very diverse, but one of those reasons is that they are people who make a difference and want to be part of the vision of the organization.

Another reason may be that the leader has invested a lot of time and energy in his relationships with people and added value to their lives.

Support—imagine that your father or mother is your leader. Can you imagine living without knowing if your parents support you? The same is true of a leader's relationship with his team. I'm not saying that you have to instantly support everything that happens; you have to know that if the rules of the game are being followed, your team can always have the support from you as a leader. Scientific research shows that employees' perceptions of team leaders' support are more positive when the leader gets involved in four types of behaviors: (1) effectively monitor work (giving timely feedback and reacting to problems at work with understanding and help); (2) provide emotional support (to show support for actions or decisions of a team member) and help to alleviate stressful situations for subordinates (3) recognize good work in a private and public way; and (4) consult the subordinates about the work (asking for their ideas and opinions and acting on the ideas or desires of the subordinates).

Ethical behavior—a leader with high ethical standards conveys a commitment to equity, inculcating the confidence that both they and their employees will honor the rules of the game. Similarly, when leaders clearly communicate their expectations, they prevent people from armoring and ensure that everyone is on the same page. In a safe environment, employees can relax, invoking the brain's greater capacity for social commitment, innovation, creativity, and ambition. In the field of neuroscience, this point has been corroborated: when the amygdala registers a threat to our safety, the arteries harden and thicken to handle an increase in demands and even stress. This competition is about behaving in a way that is consistent with their values. If you find yourself making decisions that feel at odds with your principles or justifying actions despite an annoying feeling of discomfort, you probably need to reconnect with your core values.[8]

A leader must apply competencies of personal mastery in his/her conduct

Self-knowledge and personal development—when the leader is willing to grow, the entire team grows because this attitude nurtures growth. All living organisms have an innate need to leave an imprint of their genes. Those at the receiving end feel a sense of gratitude and loyalty. Think of the people you are most thankful for: parents, teachers, friends, mentors. Most likely they have taken care of you, or taught you something important. When leaders show a commitment to our growth, the same primary emotions are exploited.

Positive thinking—having positive thinking helps to give followers a sense of optimism. A show of openness to new ideas encourages learning for all. To encourage employee learning, leaders must first ensure that they are open to learning (and changing course of action) themselves.

Managing emotions—leaders who lack emotional control will not remain in a leadership position for a long time. There has been no shortage of published articles on the subject of emotional intelligence in recent years. After all, being in touch with your emotions as well as being in tune with each other's emotions is an important trait for any leader to possess. Emotional control is a skill that most leaders need to be successful in managing their employees. Workers often look at leaders to see examples of how to behave, especially during times of agitation and change. Therefore, leaders must be prepared to present a serene and rational front. When leaders are highly controlled in expressing emotions, they are seen as more sympathetic, ethical, and working in the interest of the organization.

CLBV Reflection ♣ ♠ ♥

You can do this exercise individually, but results are by far better if you do that in a group.

- **Step 1**: Start by reviewing the theme song or hook from movies and television shows, focusing on those that feature heroes doing incredible things (e.g., *Mission Impossible, Superman, Rocky*) or managing relationship and interpersonal issues (e.g., *The Odd Couple*). Sing the chorus or hook a couple of times to practice.
- **Step 2**: Take five minutes to review something you have accomplished in life that you never thought you'd be able to accomplish. Identify the goal, the obstacles, and challenges, and how it felt to finally overcome them and achieve your goal.
- **Step 3**: Finally, have each participant choose a theme song from the ones you discussed and share it with the group. As the participant takes center stage to tell their story, instruct the group to sing or hum the song the participant chose, as a representation of their struggle and ultimate victory.

Note: This exercise not only feels great, but it also actually helps boost emotional control![9]

2.3 Leadership and trust—The value of values

I have been studying Trust in organizations for over 25 years (with colleagues such as Shay Tazfrir, Yehuda Baruch, Ben Capell, Merce Mach, and Hila Chalutz). We have studied this important construct in different sectors, companies, and contexts. It is not a surprise to see that we have labeled Trust as the mother of all values, the *"value of values."* We build our lives on the basis of trust relationships. The cultures of which we are members, be it organizational, social, political, families, couples, define their qualities based on the trust of their individuals. We trust others to obey basic rules of behavior. We trust that businesses accept our credit cards. Indeed, all aspects of a labor relationship—our organizational cultures—are based on the trust of and toward others.

Much of the conflicts in organizations arise because leaders do not have the capacity to generate and/or sustain trust. How can a leader have followers if they don't trust him/her? Unfortunately, research suggests that in more and more companies (families included if we use it as a metaphor for an organization), it seems that people have lost trust in their leaders and their peers. We note this lack of trust in businesses, government agencies, education, and even in our churches (you only have to listen to the scandals that are published on the corrupt behavior of some priests).

This general distrust in our leaders points to a cultural breakdown. The problem is not a lack of leaders but a lack of a climate of trust where leadership is possible, without which it is impossible.

Unless followers feel confident in fairness and reliability in their leaders, they will not continue following them. Trust can significantly alter individual and organizational effectiveness. It is trust, more than power and hierarchy, that really makes an organization work effectively.

So, if we know that trust is a prerequisite for any attempt by the leader to change the organizational culture, and to sustain the reliability, motivation, and behavior of the followers, why don't we help leaders to improve trust? In my opinion, people use the word *trust* too often in making a generic reference and therefore until we have a clear definition and a simple metric to measure it, we will continue to operate without a compass. The consequence will be simple: the more a leader uses the word trust (without precision), the more the followers and companions will lose interest in listening to him/her and it will naturally lead to disappointment in our leaders.

For this reason, at the beginning of the 2000s, I began to study trust in work settings, in a rigorous and systematic way. In 2004, we published for the first time an article where we identified the three key dimensions of the concept of trust (RCH in English or FIA in Spanish), as we refined the tools to measure it. The three dimensions that emerged from the numerous scientific studies were: **R**eliability, **C**oncern, and **H**armony (Figure 2.6).

The three dimensions of the *RCH* Trust model are:

- **Reliability** is a leader's competence that shows that he is true to his words, makes him/her do what they say, and does it consistently. This dimension is connected to the efficiency of performance and related to the economic–pragmatic axis of the triaxial model of values (our red color in the original "value of values" card game and dark shaded color in this book).
- Concern is equated with the interest that the leader really displays in interacting with his/her subordinates. The leader is involved affectively

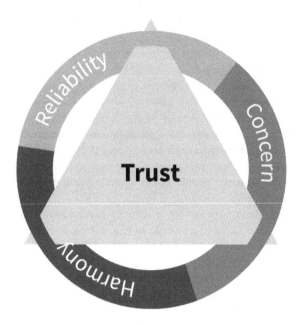

Figure 2.6 Tzafrir and Dolan RCH model of trust. Note: This model was published for the first time in 2004, but was studied in other contexts many times by Tzafrir and Dolan and our collaborators. Within the scientific research of trust in the workplace, there are other definitions and models, but this one has become the most popular and most cited. See: Tzafrir S., Dolan S.L. (2004) Trust me: A scale for measuring manager-employee trust, *Management Research: Journal of the Iberoamerican Academy of Management*, Vol. 2(2):115–132, https://doi.org /10.1108/15365430480000505; Dolan S.L., Tzafrir S., Baruch Y. (2005) Testing the causal relationships between procedural justice, trust, and organizational citizenship behavior, *Revue de gestion de ressources humaines*, Vol. 57:79–89; Mach M., Dolan S.L., Tzafrir S. (2010) The differential effect of team members' trust on team performance: The mediation role of team cohesion, *Journal of Occupational and Organizational Psychology*, Vol. 83(3):771–794 (https://doi.org/10.1348/ 096317909X473903); Chaluz H., Tzafrir S., Dolan S.L. (2015) Actionable trust in service organizations: A multi-dimensional perspective, *Journal of Work and Organizational Psychology*, Vol. 31(1):31–39; Capell B., Tzafrir S., Enosh G., Dolan S.L. (2018) Explaining sexual minorities' disclosure: The role of trust embedded in organizational practices, *Organization Studies*, Vol. 39(7):947–973 https://jo urnals.sagepub.com/doi/full/10.1177/0170840617708000.

and emotionally in the relationship and shares common and complementary goals. It also shows that the leader is concerned and manifests interest in problems that his/her followers and companions might have and shares values such as empathy or sympathy. This dimension is connected to the emotional axis of the triaxial values model (green color in the original "value of the values" card game and medium shaded gray in this book).

• Harmony occurs when there is an ethical–social bond between the leader and his follower. That means that there are elements such as integrity, respect, and other ethical–social facets (blue color in the original "value of the values" card game and light gray in this book).

Today, an executive coach can measure and categorize the three dimensions of trust and translate it into a template such as the triaxial RCH model. With this model we can identify the percentage of trust that the collaborators have in their leader and detect which of the dimensions dominates (it means a good level of trust) and which one has to be improved. To help executive coaches and consultants do a better job in diagnosing low levels of trust and also in designing training or coaching sessions for improving the problematic dimensions, we have developed an online platform that produces a 360° analysis instantaneously (see: www.leadershipbyvalues.com).

2.4 Conclusion

Executive Coaching is a growing profession. However, it seems that many are lost in the quest for a formula of success in the new work landscape. Everything is changing, and changing fast, and leaders need someone to talk to and to reflect on, and perhaps to unlearn and re-learn. Thus, an effective executive coach can become very handy and very helpful. Succeeding in today's organizations requires not only traditional "hard" skills that were sufficient in the past, but also a complete set of new competencies called "soft skills." In this chapter we have identified the main ingredients that open the door to an executive coach to intervene and show his/her added value. Obviously, there are a number of assumptions that need to be repeated. First, the identification of the hard and soft skills that make a good leader (we equate the word leader with executive in this section). Second, that soft skills can be learned. We claim in this chapter that most of these skills can be developed with the help of professional coaches.

These are not competencies that executives learn at universities or other academic institutions. Many of them represent an intimate experience that is learned with a tutor-mentor-coach. We also argue that in order to succeed in the evolution of these competencies, it is necessary to assess what is really important (in life, at work, in the family, etc.) and how to organize and prioritize within it. We think that the executive coaches who are trained (certified) in the concept, methodology, and tools of "Coaching by Values" (as described in this book) can become effective in helping executives become better, healthier, and more productive leaders.

CLBV Reflection ♣ ♠ ♥

Think of the most important information you remember after reading this chapter and then fill in the following phrases:

The main points that I liked about this chapter are ...

1. _____

2. _____

3. _____

The main points that I did not like, or with which I disagree, in this chapter are ...

1. _____

2. _____

3. _____

The next part you can answer only if you are an executive coach

After reading this chapter, I am intrigued by the triaxial model of trust because I see its potential utility for ...

1. _____

2. _____

3. _____

Notes

1 Read: Dolan, S., Makarevich, A., & Kawamura, K. (2015). Are you and your company prepared for the future of work in tomorrowland? *The European Business Review*, 7.
2 Dolan, S. L., Garcia, S., & Richley, B. (2006). *Managing by Values: A Corporate Guide to Living, being Alive and Making a Living in the XXI Century*. Palgrave MacMillan.
3 Kim, W. C., & Mauborgne, R. A. (2015). *La estrategia del océano azul: Crear nuevos espacios de mercado donde la competencia sea irrelevante*. Versión Kindle.
4 This section was inspired by writings in my last book in Spanish: *Liderazgo, dirección y coaching por valores*. New Second Edition. Círculo Rojo, 2018.
5 This theme is very complex and probably merits much more discussion than space affords in this book. We wish to offer the reader some recent articles that we have written, expanding on the connection between leadership, values, and spirituality. You may download the papers from the links provided. See: Dolan, S. L., & Altman, Y. (2012). Managing by values: The leadership spirituality connection. *People*

& *Strategy*, 35(4): 20–25 (http://itemsweb.esade.edu/research/fwc/DolanAltman.pdf); Dolan, S. L. (2015). Values, spirituality and organizational culture: The challenges of leadership in tomorrowland. *Developing Leaders Quarterly*, October 8 (www.iedp.com/articles/values-spirituality-and-organizational-culture/).

6 Source: https://news.sap.com/2018/08/60-new-90-digital-leaders/
7 See: www.leadershipbyvalues.com
8 I recommend that you read a paper that we have published recently on what happens when integrity and ethics symbolize only empty words in the company. It is a sarcastic way to show that talking about values and integrity without practicing them can only lead to deception and demise. Liran, A., & Dolan, S. L. (2016, September). Values, values on the wall, just do business and forget them all: Wells Fargo, Volkswagen and others in the hall. Published in the *Business Times*, and also in the *European Business Review* in 2006. Can be downloaded at: http://itemsweb.esade.edu/research/fwc/news/Liran&Dolan.pdf
9 Source: Emotional Intelligence and Leadership Effectiveness + 69 Exercises (PDF). Offered for free download by the Positive Psychology program at: https://positivepsychologyprogram.com/emotional-intelligence-leadership-effectiveness/

Chapter 3

Coaching, leading, and values, or the "value of values"[1]

3.1 Natural system and human system: The DNA called "values"
3.2 The ABC of values
3.3 Value formation
3.4 Modeling the universe of values: The 3Es triaxial approach
3.5 Values and culture
3.6 Values and education
3.7 Conclusion

3.1 Natural system and human system: The DNA called "values"

The natural system—the universe, the solar system, and the earth—is composed of time, space, and material; it is the most basic world of existence, and it provides living organisms with the fundamentals they need for their existence. If there were no land, water, air, or light, the universe would become an empty space in which no life could exist.[2]

The natural system generates living organisms, letting them grow or become extinct, by physically sustaining its constant state or changing itself, or chemically combining or dissolving its various elements. The stars are moving, exploding, or transforming themselves in the apparently boundless universe by an immeasurable mysterious power. The stars have limitless power and influence over humans as well as all the other living organisms on the earth. These stars have values of sustenance and change, values of combination and dissolution, values of conservation and generation, and values of inaction and movement. Weight, energy, objects, and light realize various values.

Tong-Keun Min, formerly of Chung Nam University, Korea (see the second footnote in this chapter), has classified values using qualities such as individual and social, natural and artificial, and personal and impersonal. The following is a partial list of the classes of values he's identified:

- individual values and social values
- natural values and artificial values

- physical values and mental values
- instrumental values and intrinsic values
- temporary values and permanent values
- exclusive values and universal values
- lower values and higher values
- unproductive values and productive values
- active values and inactive values
- personal values and impersonal values
- theoretical values and practical values
- relative values and absolute values

Values are indeed manifold and countless, and values in an individual's life are interconnected. For example, artistic values and social values depend on physical values because we cannot engage in artistic or social activities without our lives or bodies. Science, education, and political activities depend on economic values because we need some degree of economic support for these. Intellectual and political values influence our economy just as remarkable talent or an excellent policy can make a home or a nation prosperous.

Values are strategic lessons learned and maintained. They remain relatively stable over time. These lessons teach us that one way of behaving is better than its opposite if we are to achieve our desired outcome(s)—that is, our values and value systems guide our behavior toward that which we think will turn out well for us. Thus, to the extent that they constitute deliberate or preferentially strategic choices, in the medium to the long term, for certain ways of behaving and against others, toward the survival or *good life* of a system, values form the nucleus, the DNA, of human liberty.

Today humans face a multitude of potentially catastrophic problems: environmental pollution, human alienation and unemployment, the depletion of natural resources, crimes, drug addiction, megacities, exploding populations, the disintegration of the family, mistreatment of the elderly, the threat of weapons of mass destruction, unequal distribution of wealth, food, educational opportunities, and resources, and many more. These challenges cause chaos and disturb the established sense of values across cultures. In this chaos, we are losing our reference point.[3]

Solving these problems will require both individual and group efforts: the efforts and cooperation of social organizations, government agencies, business leaders, the academic community, and international organizations. At the core of these efforts must be healthy, sustainable values. Educating and enlightening citizens so that they are guided by conscience rather than compulsion will be an important step in activating these values.

3.2 The ABC of values[4]

In many of my previous writings I've stressed the importance of understanding personal values and becoming clear about what is most important to us in our life in general (including family and friends) and in our work. But in over 40 years of research on values, I have not yet come across a credible source that tackles this critical concept with enough depth. Most of the studies on value research take you through a process of eliciting your current values and leaves it at that.

In the past 15 years, I've developed a concept, a methodology, and tools for engaging in culture reengineering, primarily in corporations. Extensive global experience (visiting several continents, many countries, and multiple cultures) has led me to the conclusion that changing a company's culture always starts with a micro-change in a corporate leader's values. Only when a leader starts to understand his or her own values, modify or adjust them if necessary, and connect them in a holistic way with the organization and/or its stakeholders can the candid journey to change and value alignment really begin. Until then, all attempts at culture change remain superficial; even in the best possible scenario, any attempt at culture change—if not ignited by a shift in the leader's values—will stall far short of the height of excellence it was designed to achieve.

Leaders in today's world often ask themselves, "Who am I?" and "What am I to do?" In past decades, leadership depended on institutional and bureaucratic power, but now leadership depends on the capacity to articulate and inspire an organization's mutually selected values.[5] Values, once considered "too soft" to be considered in any serious approach to management, have become a central part of organizational strategy. But there is still a long way to go.

In this chapter, I will extrapolate from my experiences with leaders in organizations and delve much deeper into this rich subject. I will examine the concepts of "values" and "value," looking at their genesis and the relationship between values, beliefs, attitudes, and norms. I will then introduce you to the triaxial model, a framework for intelligently identifying our values and understanding their significance in our lives. This model will give us the means to detect and classify not only our personal values but also those of systems, such as the family, our work environment, society, and so on. We can also use it to determine whether our values are likely to lead us to our goals and whether our current goals are in fact those that will truly fulfill us.

Achieving relative happiness and fulfillment requires aligning our values with our goals and then seeing how the systems in which we live, and work, are congruent (or not) with these. In the following chapters, I will discuss this in depth. I will also offer methodologies and tools to achieve value alignment—using the triaxial model as a fundamental stepping-stone in the process of Coaching by Values, or *CBV*.

Values: But what are they?

If you go into any bookstore that specializes in management and enquire about books on values, chances are you will be sent first to the section on stock markets or to the section on business ethics and ethical investment. You will find books about share values (the worth of a share in a corporation) and books dealing with the relationship between values and business results. In these books, you will come across several interpretations of the word *value*.

Values are not only words. Values guide and direct our behavior and affect our daily experiences. But the words we use to identify our values and the definitions that we assign to them are particularly powerful; they give meaning to and direct the channeling of human efforts, both on the personal and organizational levels.

The term *axiology* refers to the study of values and originates from the Greek word *axios*, meaning "valuable, estimable, or worthy of being honored." Significantly, it is also the root of the English word *axis*, the point around which the essential elements turn.

Milton Rockeach of the University of Minnesota is a world authority on the study of values. His definitions[6] of "value" and the "value system" have become classics:

> A value is an enduring belief that a specific mode of conduct or end-state of existence is personally or socially preferable to an opposite or converse mode of conduct or end-state of existence. A value system is an enduring organization of beliefs concerning preferable modes of conduct or end-states of existence along a continuum of relative importance.
>
> (*The Nature of Human Values*, p. 5)

In many Latin languages, the words *value* and *valor* (from the Latin *valēre*, meaning "to be worthy; to be strong") represent three different, but complementary, meanings that can be categorized in the following dimensions:

- **Axiological dimension:** In Greek, the word *axios* means "worthy" or "worthy of dignity"; it also signifies a focal point or center around which other elements turn.
- **Economic dimension:** In this sense, value is a criterion used to evaluate things in terms of costs, benefits, and relative worth, as in today's expression, the "added value" of a person to a firm.
- **Psychological dimension:** Equated with ethics, this dimension also includes the courage that moves companies and people forward in confronting new frontiers without fear.

Similarly, one can understand the definition of values through three perspectives that, as we will see later, are the foundation of the triaxial model of values: the economic–pragmatic, the ethical–social, and the emotional–developmental.

The economic–pragmatic dimension: Worth

From an economic perspective, "value" is the measure of the significance or importance of something. In this sense, values are criteria used to evaluate things with respect to their relative merit, adequacy, scarcity, price, or interest. By "things", I mean people, objects, ideas, actions, feelings, and facts. For example, one may speak of the value of mutual confidence, of the value of creativity at work, or of the value a process adds to the products the customer buys. One can also talk of the value of money, the value of a machine, or the value of an expert working for a firm.

"Value analysis" refers to the process by which one determines if a product or service is generating optimal customer or user satisfaction at minimum cost. It is important to note that it is human values like creativity, confidence in the company, and commitment that activate and sustain the behaviors and actions that add value to a product. In fact, "continuous improvement," which became so popular in the management jargon of the 1990s, is based on a set of values.

Another economic concept is the "chain of value," which is the linked set of a company's activities, logistics, operations, and marketing that add or subtract value to a product, leading to the total or final value of the product. According to Michael Porter from Harvard, the chain of value of a company reflects its history and strategy and is a critical and differentiating element for achieving a competitive advantage.[7]

But even more important, the chain of value of a company reflects the shared values of the people that constitute the company. Lack of shared values damages a company's value chain, like in the old (but appropriate) adage, "A chain is only as strong as its weakest link." Ask yourself: What are the weak links in my company's value chain? How does this impact the *value* of my organization? This same logic can apply to your personal or family life: What constitutes the weak links in your relationships or your family's value chain? How does this impact the *value* of your relationships or your family?

The ethical–social dimension: Preferential choices

This concept means that an individual might choose quality in work or life in preference to its opposite—the botched, improvised, or rushed job. Similarly, genuine concern for people in the company or family might be preferable to feelings of contempt or indifference. Other examples of these values are the creation of wealth rather than ruin or destruction; autonomy (healthy independence) instead of unhealthy dependence; honesty as opposed to fraudulence; and team spirit and cooperation versus individualism. Our true, or core, values are revealed through our actions rather than our words, or what we merely state as being a value.

Values that are demonstrated through behavior are "lived values." "Espoused values" are those that are expressed, either verbally or in writing, but are not consistently embodied or realized in action. An example of a person expressing espoused values is the individual who adamantly states that health is his or her number one value but goes on to smoke cigarettes, take harmful drugs, or never exercises. Similarly, an organization might have a company values statement that lists honesty as its highest value while it engages in questionable bookkeeping practices or withholds critical information from employees or other stakeholders. In both cases, the values are espoused values: They look good on paper or sound good in conversation, but they fail the test of consistent and enduring lived behavior. Espoused values represent a mismatch between what we say and what we do.

A respected sociologist, Floyd Henry Allport, said that when there are no clearly formulated value options in a society, the society is said to be "anomic."[8] Organizational anomia exists when an organization has no articulated and shared values, when values do not *mean* (in both senses of the word—semantically and in terms of their worth) the same thing throughout the organization. Anomia helps explain the lack of vitality, collective coherence, morale, and unwillingness to make an effort that can be observed in many companies today. Understanding the various types and definitions of values can help individuals and organizations develop a common language regarding an often fuzzy, complex, and critical aspect of personal and professional lives. Thus, values can either be a strong link between people and their organization or the weak link that breaks this all-important bond.

The emotional–developmental dimension: Personal fulfillment

The notion of what constitutes individual happiness and fulfillment varies from person to person, from culture to culture. The emotional–developmental values are those related to freedom and happiness, or more broadly, to personal fulfillment. They represent the type of passion that motivates and sustains people who are trying to realize a dream. Walt Disney believed "all our dreams can come true if we have the courage to pursue them." And Martin Luther King famously declared, "I have a dream that one day on the red hills of Georgia the sons of former slaves and the sons of former slave owners will be able to sit down together at the table of brotherhood."

When one is confident about his or her emotional–developmental values, dreams that once seemed too risky or too far beyond one's capabilities now appear not only reasonable but compelling. This security allows one to live up to one's potential and accomplish dreams that in earlier stages of one's life may have been too frightening to embrace.

Passion and creativity are becoming the most characteristic descriptors for the increasingly educated segment of Western society, say sociologist Paul H. Ray and psychologist Sherry Ruth Anderson, who coined the term *Culture Creatives* to describe the 50 million adult Americans—and an estimated 80 to 90 million Europeans—who since the 1960s have moved beyond the dueling paradigms "progressive" and "conservative."[9] Values connected with personal fulfillment might be some of the best indicators of behavior, they say, adding that Cultural Creatives attach great significance to the following:

- authenticity (actions must be consistent with words and beliefs)
- engaged action and whole process learning (seeing the world as interwoven and connected)
- idealism and activism (including helping others and valuing their unique gifts)
- concern that business and society overemphasize making money and consuming
- support for the common good
- global issues and ecology
- elevating the importance of women

Not everyone, however, agrees that education and values connected to personal fulfillment are markers of concern for the environment, compassion for the disenfranchised, and disregard for the act of consuming as an end. While Ray and Anderson have found more and more people who are actively supporting such values and beliefs, the disparity between the classes in the United States has become a yawning chasm. Economists like Nobel laureate Joseph Stiglitz argue that this growing inequality is stifling innovation and constricting opportunities, as the wealthy (and those who emulate them) lose empathy for others, lack interest in the common good, and value profits over planet and people.[10]

Values, beliefs, norms, attitudes, and behavior

There are three important concepts taken from the general literature in psychology that are closely related to values; these must be understood both as concepts and in their relation to each other—that is, the sequence in which they are formed (see Figure 3.1)—to implement the Coaching by Values method. These are beliefs, norms, and attitudes.

What are beliefs?

I have already said that values may be generally understood as the strategic choices we make regarding what is required to achieve our goals. It is important to recognize that these choices, in turn, are derived from basic suppositions or beliefs about human nature and the world around us. In short, each person chooses to think and act in specific ways according to what he or she believes about people, things, events, ideas, and the world.

One very common assumption is that beliefs are the same as supposed "truths." However, beliefs are deeply rooted structures of thought that we develop over years of learning and experience to explain and make sense of our reality. These structures precede the formulation of our values. For example, being convinced that never having enough time is a sign that someone is successful may encourage one to hold the value that hard work is worthwhile. Believing that what counts are immediate results could support one's valuing immediate benefits, speed in production or work, and even, perhaps, a quick botch job over a quality outcome that takes longer to achieve. Believing that poor quality results in a higher cost in the long run will likely lead to one's embracing good quality as a value.

The relationship between beliefs and values is extremely close. For this reason, in this chapter, I speak of "changes in beliefs and values" much more often than changes in values alone. And throughout the process of Coaching by Values, it is important to keep in mind that beliefs precede values, so a shift in values requires a shift in beliefs. As illustrated in Figure 3.1, the unlearning of some beliefs is essential if one is to replace or renew values, change behaviors, and be a positive influence.

Norms and values

Values play a special role in the formation of norms or the so-called rules of the game. Our values inform us about what we believe is ethical, good, valid, competitive, appropriate, beautiful, and desirable; they are continually being generated and reinforced throughout our lives. Values are held at the level of the individual; norms tend to emerge from group interactions. Norms are rules of conduct adopted by consensus, whereas values are criteria for evaluating, accepting, or rejecting norms. Further, noncompliance with norms usually incurs external sanctions (e.g., ostracism, fines, or imprisonment), whereas noncompliance with values results in feelings of guilt or "internal" sanctions.

Attitudes and values

Often the concept "change of attitude" is used wrongly to refer to the change of something else, namely, a change in values, conduct, beliefs, or behaviors. Consider these examples: a change of values, such as commitment; a change of

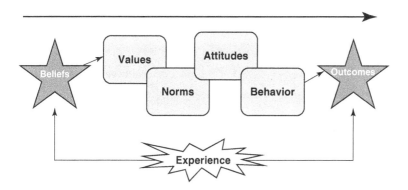

Figure 3.1 Sequence from beliefs to outcomes.

conduct, such as lack of punctuality; a change of beliefs, such as "it is dangerous to detect errors in others and then publicize them." This is partly the result of the popularization of the concept of "attitudes" and of trendy uses of "change in attitude" (for example, in social surveys). Usually the confusion originates from researchers in the field of management or psychology who find it easier to measure attitudes than values.

An attitude is a consequence of the values and norms that precede it. It is an evaluating factor or tendency, either positive or negative, toward other people, deeds, events, things, and so on. Our attitudes reflect how we feel toward someone or something and predict our tendency to act in a certain way. For example, if we have a positive attitude toward a particular job or project and dedicate ourselves to it enthusiastically, this conduct (e.g., pursuing the assignment, embracing the hard work involved) stems from the possibility that this project will let us put into practice a certain value (e.g., creativity), which in turn stems from certain beliefs (e.g., we must be creative in order to thrive in our market; creativity is personally fulfilling) (Figure 3.2).

Attitudes and behavior

Attitude is a feeling, or an opinion, of approval or disapproval toward something. Behavior is an action or the reaction that occurs in response to an event or internal stimuli (e.g., thought). People hold complex relationships between attitudes and behavior that are further complicated by the social factors influencing both. Behaviors usually, but not always, reflect established beliefs, values, and attitudes. But behavior can be influenced by several factors beyond attitude: preconceptions about self and others, monetary factors, social influences or norms (what peers and community members are saying and doing), and convenience, among others. For example, in a society in which premarital abstinence is embedded as a value, a man who believes strongly in abstinence before marriage may choose to remain a virgin until his wedding night. But if

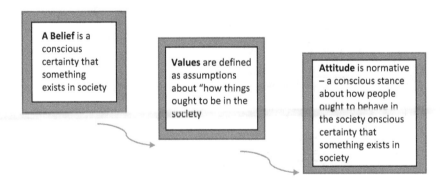

Figure 3.2 Beliefs, values, and attitudes.

that society is rife with messages tying masculinity to sexual activity, that same man may engage in premarital sex, succumbing to these social messages despite both his convictions and the avowed values of his society.

Ideally, positive attitudes manifest well-adjusted behaviors. But, in some cases, healthy attitudes may result in harmful behavior. For example, someone may remain in an abusive and potentially deadly domestic situation because he or she holds negative attitudes toward divorce.

Studies have clearly demonstrated that in some cases pointing out inconsistencies between attitudes and behavior can redirect the behavior. And some coaches focus on changing attitudes in order to change behavior. This is the essence of cognitive-behavior therapy, which combines two types of techniques: those designed to change irrational ways of thinking (e.g., attitudes and/or beliefs)[11] and those aimed directly at correcting the resulting inappropriate behavior.[12] Actually, this approach works well in many cases, but I've found that rather than attempting to change attitudes to modify behavior, it is more effective to modify the values and beliefs that underlie the conduct. This produces a deep and lasting change. The process, however, is more complex.

The stress connection

In an ideal world, everyone would be able to create environments in which his or her beliefs, values, norms, attitudes, and behaviors were perfectly aligned. But rarely is reality so neat. Demands on our lives and work are increasing more rapidly than ever. Factors such as globalization, new technologies, heightened competitiveness, mounting pressure on companies to do more with less, the growing premium on multitasking, and organizations that increasingly require everyone to accomplish tasks once divided among several people have created a world in which people are perpetually "on call." Rarely are any of us unplugged from the perpetual motion swirling around us. The convergence of these dynamics activates—and by activating, brings into strong relief—a basic relationship between beliefs, values, and behavior: stress.

Today stress is usually referred to as "the entire process by which people perceive and interpret their environment in relation to their capability to cope with it."[13] Under this definition, stress is present when the environment poses (or is perceived to pose) a threat to an individual in the form of either excessive demands or insufficient resources. Although most of us can respond adequately to stressful situations most of the time, our bodies and minds have a limited capacity to respond to stressors. When we are exposed to too many stressors over a long period, our ability to cope with them diminishes; constant activation of the stress response (and the corresponding secretion of such hormones as adrenaline and noradrenaline) takes a toll on us, physically and mentally.

Specific beliefs and values are activated (or inhibited) when we react to stress. Values associated with high performance—including, among others, friendliness, creativity, achievement, and commitment—tend to be inhibited when we are either under- or overstimulated. Understimulation leads to boredom; overstimulation can lead to hyperactivity, which can result in exhaustion and, finally, in what is commonly referred to as a "burnout." Both scenarios depress values that play a crucial role in a healthy, fulfilled life.

Although there is a plethora of research on stress, the knowledge gained from all this studying has not sufficiently migrated into our lives or work. The need to develop work and life environments in which stress is manageable is becoming increasingly important—as stress levels are rapidly rising. But this requires a major shift that will only occur when we all recognize the conditions that activate stress and understand the serious toll it can take on our lives. Those in positions of influence, such as leaders, parents, and coaches, must be aware that negative levels of stress can impair individuals—and that when this happens, not only people but also (business and other) outcomes will suffer tremendously.

In more-developed countries, an interesting phenomenon has occurred over the past several years. In cultures in which performance has become highly valued and financially rewarded, people shift their behavior trying to become "super-achievers." Although they may have other values, such as family happiness or harmony, these values recede into the background as people focus on those dominant cultural values associated with high achievement. This super-achiever behavior is widely known as Type A behavior. Research shows that Type A individuals tend to create stress for themselves and make already stressful situations worse than they otherwise might be. Furthermore, particular aspects of the Type A personality (specifically anger, hostility, and aggression) may lead to heart attacks. Interestingly, Type A behavior was first described and is continuing to be on the rise in the same countries in which Ray and Anderson are discovering a growing population of Cultural Creatives.

It should be noted that values in and of themselves are neither good nor bad. It is the extent to which an individual expresses a value through behavior that gives the value its negative or positive association in that situation. For example, an individual who values power may demonstrate this value by dominating or controlling others or by relentlessly pursuing financial acquisition, while someone else who values power uses it judiciously to achieve shared organizational goals or to promote a fair and just workplace.

Table 3.1 provides some examples of how typical beliefs and values can lead to harmful behaviors and outcomes (column A) and how we can alter our beliefs and values to produce positive behaviors and outcomes (column B).

3.3 Value formation

Individual values are formed in infancy, childhood, and adolescence based on the models of parents, teachers, friends, and the like. Values are learned, oftentimes unconsciously imbibed, and transmitted to others. Values are caught and taught. I've been affected, influenced, and changed by the values and virtues

Table 3.1 Beliefs, Values, and Stress

	Column A Negative	Column B Positive
Beliefs	• *Without exception*, we must complete all work within the minimal timeframe; • Work is our first and only priority; • Behavior is either "right" or "wrong"; • If you are not aggressive, people will not respect you (you either step over people or they will step on you); • Showing symptoms of stress is a sign of weakness; • Self-esteem is based on success and rewards from work.	• We need to evaluate the situation and achieve the best results within reasonable parameters; • Individuals should seek a balance between energy deployed at work, at home, and for personal needs; • We need to develop flexibility in how we evaluate people and situations; • We need to differentiate assertiveness from aggression and understand how our behavior can create negative or positive outcomes; • Creating healthy boundaries helps us to be physically and psychologically healthy; • Self-esteem is based on a holistic notion of a happy life to include work, relationships, and many other aspects that bring us joy.
Values	• Efficiency; • Achievement; • Performance; • Power; • Personal fortitude; • Recognition.	• Adaptability; • Life balance; • Fairness; • Emotional self-control; • Well-being; • Harmony.
Behaviors	Behaviors that predispose stress and may lead to illness: • frustration; • perfectionism; • isolation; • anger/rage.	Behaviors that favor emotional control and promote wellness: • pragmatism; • learning; • affiliations; • happiness/satisfaction.
Outcomes	• Poor physical or mental health; • Failing or limited personal relationships; • Decreased performance over time.	• Sound mental and physical health; • Fulfilling relationships; • Improved performance over time.

Source: Dolan, S. L., Garcia, S., & Richely, B. (2006) *Managing by Values: Corporate Guide to Living, Being Alive and Making a Living in the 21st Century*. London: Palgrave Macmillan. p. 42. Used with author's permission.

of people with whom I've been in contact over the years (see the discussion of my evolution in the Introduction). Similarly, my values and virtues have touched other people's lives. Often, I receive warm and affectionate messages from former graduate students thanking me for my mentoring, which I take to mean teaching them not only the necessary hard skills, such as doing research, but also the soft skills, such as instilling values and enjoying the process of conducting that research—skills that I believe are equally necessary.

In this context we can appreciate yet another definition of values: "the ideals that give significance to our lives, that are reflected in the priorities that we choose, and that we act on consistently and repeatedly." As ideals, values are both tools and goals for social transformation, for the renewal of public life and for the renewal of the community and society.

Values and needs

In the book *Values Shift: A Guide to Personal and Organizational Transformation*,[14] Brian Hall identifies eight stages of value formation. Many of these stages are influenced by popular theories of human motivation and need as those espoused by Maslow.[15] The stages are (a) safety, (b) security, (c) family, (d) institution, (e) vocation, (f) new order, (g) wisdom, and (h) world order in that sequence. Each stage includes core values that serve as both its goals and the means to achieve it. The values in each stage are associated with specific behaviors and can explain subsequent developments of people in and out of organizational life.

Even though it is outdated, Maslow's hierarchy of needs is still being used by therapists and coaches today. Maslow claimed that values reflect a person's judgment and help him or her sort out what is important in life. In other words, needs are already embedded in our values. In his later work, Maslow described what he considered the important values that define an individual's *being*; he called these "Being Values," or "B Values." According to Maslow, people who are self-actualized tend to have incorporated more B Values than those who are at lower levels on the need's hierarchy. The B Values include the following:

- wholeness/unity/oneness
- perfection/just-so-ness
- completion/finality/ending
- justice/fairness
- aliveness/full-functioning
- richness/intricacy
- simplicity/honesty
- beauty/form/richness
- goodness
- uniqueness/idiosyncrasy/novelty

- effortlessness/ease/perfection
- playfulness/joy/humor
- truth/reality/beauty/purity
- self-sufficiency/independence

Value formation, the evolution or purposeful development of values, manifests itself in personal renewal (for the individual) and social transformation (for the collective). Renewal and transformation require going beyond the survival phase of life, which is focused simply on securing one's safety. Because all phases of life have corresponding values, which act as both goals and means, moving from one stage to another requires modifying values.

The value shift from personal survival to living with a sense of belonging to a family or an institution includes accepting their goals-values and means-values. Further transformation or renewal would mean entering a still higher phase of life, preparing for, and dedicating oneself to one's life work (calling, vocation, or profession) in view of constructing or renewing the social order. This again requires discovering new goals and purposes in life and, in conjunction, forming new values. For the next level of renewal and transformation, one must learn and embrace the value of interdependence, which makes possible productive and fulfilling relationships between people on a global scale. In this stage, values of prophetic wisdom and world order are acquired and developed.

Some people believe that understanding needs is more important than understanding values, because, they claim that needs are more likely to explain behavior than values. No doubt we all have needs. Also, there is no doubt that basic needs have to be satisfied regardless of our values. We need to breathe fresh air, and unless we continue to breathe, we will die. No matter how much we value a healthy ecosystem and fresh air, if our immediate survival needs are so profound that satisfying them requires all our energy, those survival needs will explain our behavior more than our values will. In a couple of popular films, people survived an airplane crash by eating the flesh of their dead buddies. As terrible as this may sound, their actions fulfilled survival needs. I am convinced, however, that in all situations where survival is not at stake, values are by far more important than needs.

This is because our values help us make choices about what to commit to. If you commit time and energy to something that violates one of your core values, you will eventually feel resentful or frustrated. This may start with a niggling in the back of your mind, telling you that something is not right. If you persist in choosing activities and relationships that don't honor your values, you will develop a full-blown and persistent sense that something is terribly wrong. Your values are the qualities that define you; they are at the core of who you are. Without them, you would not be you.

Think of a time when life was rich, fulfilling, exhilarating, and flowing. Maybe there were some challenges, but you were on a roll. It may have been minutes, hours, or weeks; the length of time doesn't matter. What was important was the experience itself, but what about that experience which made it so powerful? What values were you honoring?

Now, think about things that drive you nuts, make you angry, or leave you frustrated. Examine each of these, and I'm certain you'll discover that a value dear to you is being violated. What value is being neglected or stepped on in these situations?

After these two quick self-reflections, consider what it is that you can't live with and still be true to yourself? What is so much a part of you that you haven't thought of putting on the list yet?

Value formation in an organization

Some specific factors influence the formation of values in an organization. Of the many variables that we can identify, the following seem to be the most important:

The beliefs and values of the founders: Every company starts its life as an impulse from an idea, and within this burgeoning enterprise, some principles are implicit. To implement their idea, the founders assemble the necessary financial, human, and material resources. These founders, in general, determine how the company is defined, how it resolves its problems, and how it adapts externally and integrates internally. The founders not only possess a high degree of determination and self-confidence but also usually have very firm ideas about how the world works, the roles that different people can play, how to arrive at "the truth," and how to exert control over time and space. The ideas and principles of the founding group tend to be dissipated over time as the company grows, unless special efforts are made to encourage their continuation. Many companies that exhibit an especially strong cultural identity have managed to maintain a coherence and strength of values inherited from their founders.

The beliefs and values of the current management and the system of rewards: At any given time, the management of a company can decide to perpetuate, revitalize, or even radically modify the beliefs and values of the founders. One of their tasks is to manage the perennial conflict between the traditional and the modern in all aspects of an enterprise's operations. This is also one of the basic problems underlying generational succession in companies.

One of the strongest formative influences on beliefs and values in employees is the existing mechanism of compensation. For example, it is pointless for the management to make speeches about the importance of innovation if they do not stimulate and compensate creative efforts.

Training and the influence of coaches: An essential mechanism for modifying beliefs and values is training. Earlier I had mentioned that changing values and behaviors required "unlearning" beliefs, and in keeping with this, true learning consists of unlearning irrelevant beliefs and replacing them with new ones. Such training may take the form of attending courses, reading suitable publications (such as this book, I hope!), or interacting with coaches. In addition to inculcating new values, it is often important for a company to focus on values that have previously been learned and partially forgotten. Senior managers with professional training can be very effective in reactivating these, helping to ensure continuity throughout the life span of an organization. Clearly it would be unrealistic to think of promoting values like honesty and initiative through attendance at seminars. Competent, professional business coaches can also play a major role here.

Legislation: Legislation covering employment, the environment, taxation, and the like in each country significantly influences the beliefs and values in companies.

The "rules of the game" in particular markets: The degree of free competition in any market, as well as accepted conventions or customs, imposes certain rules of the game that condition the beliefs and values of companies. Among the beliefs most strengthened by competitive pressure is that it is important to beat your rivals and gain short-term advantage or benefit, using any means necessary to achieve this regardless of the long-term effect on the viability of the business or society.

The prevailing social values of the period: At the beginning of the twentieth century, the predominant social values in the developed countries were different from those now, which in turn will be different in the future. For example, transparency is a relatively emergent value; previously confidentiality was of utmost importance. And employees are now referred to as "organizational members," whereas in earlier times they were considered merely cogs in the metaphorical organizational machine.

The cultural tradition of each society: In every society, the social values and business values influence each other mutually. A large part of the economic success of Japan was due to its urge to show the Western world its collective strength, which was achieved by the incorporation of its traditional social values—such as the drive for continuous improvement, harmony, loyalty, and pride in belonging to a family or a group—into its industrial arena.

The history of success and failure of the company: Lastly, it must be stated that the systems of beliefs and values of the company are self-sustaining if its results are considered good. If a company does well profit-wise and explicitly includes values such as dealing honestly with its customers in its systems, then it will tend to perpetuate that value as essential for its business. This is the "winning formula" factor. In contrast, if this company builds up losses, it is likely or at least possible that it will reconsider its system of values.

Hierarchy of values: The value of values

At the root of my thinking about values—derived from my own experience and validated in my work over decades and across continents—is that the hierarchy of your values will determine what you do and how you live your life. It is almost impossible to align all your values at the same time with all your goals. And the attempt to do so can be so overwhelming that you may want to give up. But you can make significant progress to a healthier and more fulfilling life by identifying your core values, putting them in order, and choosing a strategy for aligning those at the top of the list with your goals. This synchronization of your values and goals will be effective as long as your values hierarchy does not change, but, in reality, the hierarchy is dynamic and may change.

Claims, in Best-selling books such as *The Secret*,[16] that by using positive energy and focusing on aligning several values one can attain all life goals simultaneously are utopian. Not only are such messages chimerical, but they also mislead readers with claims that positive thinking can effect real-world outcomes, which can actually be very dangerous. *The Secret* offers false hope to those in true need of more conventional coaching.

So, how do we organize our values? What are the criteria for the hierarchy? The truth is that there are no rules, and each person's hierarchy is unique. Philosophers, theologians, and other thinkers have, however, wrestled with this for millennia, with some arguing that certain values are absolute or that there are criteria for prioritizing values or determining the value of specific values that hold true across time and place. In "A Study on the Hierarchy of Values," Tong-Keun Min, a Korean scholar steeped in combined Asian and European philosophies, offers some principles identified by M. Scheler (1874–1928) that are useful in ranking values[17]:

- **Timelessness:** The longer the value lasts, the higher it is. For example, while the value of pleasure lasts for the duration of the feeling of pleasure, the mental value remains after the disappearance of the circumstances.
- **Indivisibility:** The harder it is to reduce the quality of the value as its carrier divides or the harder it is to increase the quality of the value as its carrier enlarges, the higher the value is. For example, while the value of material goods reduces as the goods divide, the value of mental goods is indivisible and not related to the number of people concerned.
- **Independence:** The higher value becomes the base for the lower value. The fewer other values the value has as its base, the higher it is.
- **Depth of satisfaction:** There is an intrinsic relationship between the rank of the value and the depth of satisfaction from its realization. In other words, the deeper the satisfaction connected to the value, the higher the value is. For example, physical satisfaction is strong but shallow. On the

contrary, the satisfaction derived from artistic meditation is a deep experience. The depth of satisfaction is not related to its strength.

- **Absoluteness:** The less the sense of the value is related to the existence of its carrier, the higher the value is. For example, the value of pleasure has significance in relation to the sense of sensuality. The value of life exists for those with the sense of life, but the moral value exists absolutely and independently from those who feel it.

The more we explore values and try to deal with them in our lives and work, the more complex the subject becomes. Although many associate the word *value* with economics (and we saw earlier in this chapter that there is an economic dimension to value), value is not the same as price. In fact, the value of a thing or service is often not truly reflected in its price. The price of a thing is its exchange value, which varies from time to time, from place to place, from people to people; it is always changeable and changing. Not attributing a price to something, or making it available at a low price, does not necessarily mean that it has no value or limited value. For example, we do not put a price on air, but it is very valuable to us. Tap water is cheap, but water is essential to human life and has almost boundless value. Land, the sun, and light also have boundless and essential value for humans, animals, and plants. A nurturing and caring spouse or mother is another example. We cannot measure nurturing and caring as values, but we know how essential they are to present and future happiness. Air pollution, water pollution, the destruction of the ecosystem, and loss of nurturing and caring are, conversely, grave anti-values that threaten the existence of humans and other living organisms.

Most of us will agree that we hold a set of principles to be important, that we value integrity, and accountability, freedom, and respect for others. Most organizations will describe their values as including care for the customer, safety of their employees, innovation, and performance. But it is idealistic to believe that every action can fulfill all of these, and the test of "walking the talk" has become a cliché. Most employees in most organizations will say that what is written on the wall (or published on the company's website) is far from reality. It is not that companies do not believe in these principles; it is simply impossible to achieve them all. A company, like a person, must choose, and in these choices the company's true values hierarchy is revealed. A hierarchy of values is seen most clearly when there are limited resources, and choices must be made regarding how they will be applied. These choices become symbols of what is really valued.

Creating a hierarchy of values is not a simple task. In the next section, I will present a method and a logic to help you develop your hierarchy of values. I will introduce you to the triaxial model, which allows you to classify all your important values on three axes (dimensions) and then explore the relative dominance (meaning) of each axis. This method is very flexible: You generate the axes from your individual values, but as you continue to work with it, you refine and rethink those. By the end of the process, you may not have the same values in the model as you had when you began. The anchor is the axis; the relevant importance of specific values and the hierarchy will come later in the process. Let us begin by understanding the logic for the triaxial model.

3.4 Modeling the universe of values: The 3Es triaxial approach

What are your core values? What are the core values of your corporation? What are the core values of your family? Your community? Your country? Which values of yours would you select and place in a hierarchy that will become a guide for your actions, a guide for your behavior? Why—or under what circumstances—would you be prepared to adjust your values, and your hierarchy, to create a better fit with your mate, family, work, and the like? Which values are you not prepared to modify? What is the best way to discover whether your core values are being supported or undermined by your work or family?

While grappling with these questions, my colleagues and I developed a model that can describe any universe of values. We call it the *3Es triaxial model of values*.[18] Figure 3.3 encapsulates the primary elements of this model, and Figure 3.4 is an example of a triaxial structure in use. The triaxial framework is flexible; one can use it to detect or uncover values, to categorize values, to clarify and prioritize values, and to help align values. The beauty of this model is not necessarily its completeness but rather its simplicity (parsimony) and applicability to various individuals, corporations, and communities. In this section, I will familiarize you with the basic structure of the model.

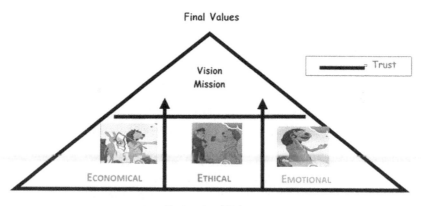

Figure 3.3 The 3Es triaxial model of values.

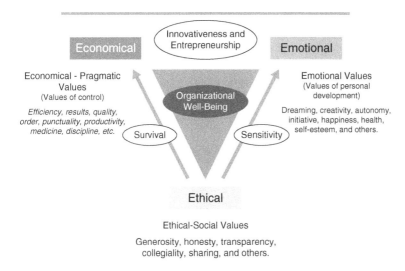

Economical

Innovativeness and Entrepreneurship

Emotional

Economical - Pragmatic Values
(Values of control)

Efficiency, results, quality, order, punctuality, productivity, medicine, discipline, etc.

Organizational Well-Being

Survival

Sensitivity

Emotional Values
(Values of personal development)

Dreaming, creativity, autonomy, initiative, happiness, health, self-esteem, and others.

Ethical

Ethical-Social Values

Generosity, honesty, transparency, collegiality, sharing, and others.

Figure 3.4 An organizational triaxial model and possible outcomes of value alignment.

The underlying assumption of the 3Es triaxial model is that values can be detected in all fields (personal, family, organization, and community) regardless of their nature, mission, or vision and once identified, they can be classified according to three core dimensions or axes: *economic–pragmatic axis, ethical–social axis*, and *emotional–developmental axis (the 3Es)*. Also foundational to this model is the assumption that all personal and organizational values are situated in one of these dimensions. (We refer to the 3Es triaxial model, for short, as either the "3Es model" or the "triaxial model.")

These axes were identified, and the model developed through both classical research and primary empirical research; I tested it and refined it in hundreds of workshops and seminars across the globe (different countries, cultures, sectors, and categories of employees). The reaction of the participants was overwhelming.[19]

The model borrows some ideas developed in the 1970s by Milton Rockeach, who divided individual values into *terminal/final values*, which are desirable end-states of existence (e.g., happiness and wisdom), and *instrumental values*, which are desirable modes of behavior (e.g., acting honestly and earning lots of money). A functional relationship exists between these two: Instrumental values describe behaviors that facilitate the attainment of terminal values (and instrumental values can be detected and categorized using the 3Es model). The former has received more attention in the literature than the latter and is more widely used by researchers and practitioners to describe an organization's culture.

Let us start by observing the simplest and most fundamental organization that we all know, the family. Think about your family or others with whom you are familiar. Most of us know intuitively that if a family is to be successful as a unit, a balance must exist between the axes that are shared by the couple. Most of us also know that the family (and marriage, more specifically) in the twenty-first century is in crisis: Rates of divorce and separation are alarming, violence within the family is growing, and a general sense of uneasiness and marital dissatisfaction is on the rise. Why is this happening?

A family, like any other organization, has objectives (final values). If these are not shared by the couple, and if the couple's instrumental values—which can be plotted along the three axes—are not aligned with their final values, the family is doomed to fail. Thus, agreement on the final values alone will not ensure success. The family will likely fail even if one of the following exists:

• There is discordance between the couple's economic–pragmatic values.
• The couple's ethical–social values are not in sync.
• One or both parties lose passion for the relationship (the most critical emotional–developmental value binding the couple).

If we think about families and close-knit groups of friends as living organizations that struggle to survive and be happy in a complex world, we can see that challenges confronted by larger organizations such as corporations and governmental bodies are far greater. The same shared values necessary for positive, sustainable relationships in the family and among friends are critical in the workplace. It follows then that assessing an organizational culture by identifying core values, the level of which they are shared, and the extent to which they are congruent with organizational members' personal values is very important. The CBV methodology, which I'll present in depth in the following chapters, enables us to plot these values around these three axes.

Figure 3.4 shows a 3Es model and certain values associated with each axis. It also shows the following relationships or linkages between the axes and the outcomes of these congruencies:

• Congruency between the emotional axis and the economic–pragmatic axis leads to greater innovation and entrepreneurship.
• Congruency between the economic–pragmatic axis and the ethical–social axis leads to enhancement of survival.
• Congruency between the ethical–social axis and the emotional–developmental axis increases sensitivity and makes the organization more socially responsible.

The following examples illustrate these linkages:

• **Survival** (economic–pragmatic values and ethical–social values): A company that is involved in unethical behavior (e.g., manipulation of accounts or participating in fraud) will certainly not survive. Likewise, a husband cheating on his wife, or vice versa, endangers the survival of the couple as a unit.

- **Innovativeness and entrepreneurship** (emotional values and economic–pragmatic values): The best innovations are born of people's positive passion. There are hundreds of examples to illustrate this. Take the invention of Post-it Notes. Art Fry, a 3M new-product-development researcher, created the sticky yellow notes as a substitute for scrap paper bookmarks that kept falling out of his church choir hymnal. Frustrated with his bookmarks, he remembered a strange weak adhesive a 3M scientist had developed while searching for its opposite, a super strong glue. Fry put the accidental adhesive to use. His persistent curiosity, coupled with personal desire, led him to invent a product that revolutionized office work and research.

- **Sensitivity** (ethical–social and emotional–developmental values). You don't need to wait for legislation requiring you to separate your garbage for recycling. If you are concerned about the environment, you can take the time and make an effort to separate your household (and workplace) trash and recycle it regardless of the need for legal compliance. You will do it because of your sensitivity. In the same vein, you will not smoke in places where you think it may bother others, even when smoking is permitted.

Pages and pages of examples exist. Why don't you try this simple exercise: Identify the crossing of values that enhance your survival, sensitivity, and moments of innovation by identifying the interface of relevant values.

CLBV Reflection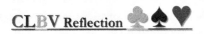

Values intersection exercise

Think of a family context, a work context, or a community context. Complete the following sentences:

I am more *sensitive* to my Family/Team/Community (circle only one) because of the interaction of my following core values:

I am more *innovative* within the context of my Family/Team/Community (circle only one) because of the interaction of my following core values:

I know that I am adding to the *survival of* my Family/Team/Community (circle only one) because of the interaction of my following core values:

Here I need to add a very important note that will be critical later. Although Figure 3.3 presents a perfectly symmetrical triangle, most triangles developed using the triaxial model are not symmetrical and need not be symmetrical. Moreover, although the symmetry of Figure 3.3 may imply that all three axes have equal importance in one's hierarchy of values, this is certainly not the case in many such hierarchies. For the purpose of this introduction, I used an equilateral triangle almost metaphorically to emphasize that the aggregate of the three axes is the universe of values that represents the world being examined. In Chapter 5, I will show you how to draw an actual triangle based on your values and the axes into which they fall.

3.5 Values and culture

Every culture has a set of moral and social values. These derive from its prehistory and are modified with each generation. Some cultures or societies change faster than others, but there is stability found in a common set of values. These values, true enough, are often held as ideals rather than implemented as realities. Still, the accepted set of values, ideals, goals, and standards are part of the character of a culture. One of the basic goals of every community, tribe, and nation is to maintain its own identity as a group. The specific values found in a culture relate to this maintenance. There are numerous disciplines that define the common aspects of values found in all human societies. These have been developed by sociologists and anthropologists in detail. In this section, I will try to provide a brief overview of some of the common characteristics and the roles of values in the following levels of culture: organizational culture, family culture, community, and national culture. These are the principal levels of interventions for coaches, and so I thought that some additional information might be useful.

Best-selling author Riane Eisler has developed two extraordinary models—domination and partnership—that can be used to view any culture. She claims that every system falls somewhere along the continuum between the two models; no culture is purely one or the other. Eisler also identifies values connected to each model and shows how these affect every relationship in our lives: parents and children, women and men, government and citizens, humans and nature. She focuses on seven key relationships and has developed key practices for strengthening them: (a) our relationship with ourselves: body, mind, and spirit; (b) our intimate relations: the heart of the matter; (c) our work and community relationships: the widening circle of caring; (d) our relationship with our national community: why politics matter; (e) our relationship with the international community: the world around us; (f) our relationship with nature: from mother earth to biotechnology; and (g) our spiritual relations: putting love into action. Partnership living begins with you.

Values and organizational culture

Basically, organizational culture is the personality of the organization, but it is not often easy to put your finger on it.[20] Culture is composed of the assumptions, values, norms, and tangible signs (artifacts) of the principal stake-holders of an organization and their behaviors. It is difficult to express or describe, but everyone recognizes a culture when they experience it. Members of an organization, for instance, soon come to sense the organization's unique culture even if they cannot articulate it, which is often the case. Certain broad types of cultures are quite distinct: The culture of a large for-profit corporation is different from that of a hospital which is different from that of a university. You can tell the culture of an organization by the arrangement of furniture, what employees brag about, what members wear, and the like; in the same way, you can get a feeling about someone's personality by being attentive to his or her language, tone of voice, and appearance. But cultural recognition is one thing, and understanding it on a deep level is another.

Corporate culture can be looked at as a system. Inputs include feedback from, say, society, professions, laws, stories, heroes, values placed on traits such as competition or service, and so on. The process is based on assumptions, values, and norms, such as values on money, time, facilities, space, and peo-ple. Outputs include organizational behaviors, technologies, strategies, image, products, services, and appearance, among others.

The concept of culture is particularly important when attempting to man-age an organization-wide change. Coaches and organizational consultants are coming to realize that despite the best-laid plans, if an organizational change initiative does not focus on modifying corporate culture as well as changing structures and processes, it will not succeed.

A great deal of literature has been generated over the past decade about the concept of organizational culture, particularly about how to change it. An overwhelming majority of organizational change efforts fail. Usually, this failure is credited to a lack of understanding about the strong role of culture and the role it plays in organizations. Because of this, many strategic planners now place as much emphasis on identifying strategic values as they do on an enterprise's espoused mission and vision.

An organization in which staff respond to stimulus because of their align-ment with the organizational values is considered to have a "strong" culture. Conversely, if there is little alignment between staff and organizational values and if the management must rely on extensive procedures and bureaucracy to maintain control, the culture is considered "weak." When the culture is strong, people do things because they believe that is the right thing to do. This type of culture develops, for example, when there is a strong reliance on a central charismatic figure in the organization or an evangelical belief in the organization's values. It can also arise when a friendly climate is at the base of the company.

Edgar Schein, an MIT Sloan School of Management professor who has written extensively about organizational culture,[21] defines organizational cul-ture as "the residue of success" within an organization and claims that it is more resistant to change than any other element of the organization—products, services, founders' beliefs, and leadership. His organizational model, described from the standpoint of the observer, contains three cognitive levels of organizational culture:

- The first and most cursory level refers to the organizational attributes that can be seen, felt, and heard by the uninitiated observer, and it includes the facilities, offices, furnishings, visible awards, and recognitions, the way that its members dress, and how each person visibly interacts with each other and with organizational outsiders.
- The next level deals with the professed culture of an organization's members. At this level, company slogans, mission statements, and other operational creeds are often expressed, and local and personal values are widely expressed within the organization. Organizational behavior at this level can usually be studied by interviewing the organization's members and using questionnaires to gather attitudes about organizational membership.
- At the third and deepest level, the organization's tacit assumptions are found. These are the elements of culture that are unseen and not cognitively identified in everyday interactions between organizational members. Additionally, these are the elements of culture which are often taboo to discuss inside the organization. Many of these "unspoken rules" exist without the conscious knowledge of the members. Those with enough experience to understand this deepest level of organizational culture usually become acclimatized to its attributes over time, thus reinforcing the invisibility of their existence. Surveys and casual interviews with organizational members cannot draw out these attributes—rather, much more in-depth means is required to first identify and then understand organizational culture at this level. Notably, culture at this level is the underlying and driving element often missed by organizational behaviorists.

Schein's model not only gives us a way to begin to understand paradoxical behaviors in organizations—behaviors that seem to be out of sync with the organization's espoused mission and vision statement—it also constitutes an argument for formulating new methods of attempting to effect change in organizations based on a more profound understanding of culture than those often crafted by traditional organizational change agents (we will discuss this more in Chapter 4). Furthermore, his model may begin to give us a way to look at the importance of the relationships between people in the organization, including the way in which they are "managed."

Studies confirm that the way people are managed and developed delivers a higher return on investment than new technology, R&D, competitive strategy, or quality initiatives. In addition, a culture that emphasizes employee effectiveness is linked to shareholder returns. It is no wonder that many CEOs use the now-clichéd phrase: "The most important asset of our organization is our people." The broader implications of this are obvious for corporate contenders striving to enhance value through quality and customer-centricity in an increasingly complex, professionally demanding, and continuously changing global market.

The system of beliefs and values that shaped the Western management and organizational model at the beginning of the twentieth century is impotent in the new business paradigm. Rigid management models based on hierarchical control of employees under conditions of relative stability externally and internally are a shaky foundation for companies in today's global turmoil and rapid technological change. Traditional command-and-control management practices stifle the sparks of creativity critical to innovation in and adaptation to a diverse environment and essential to the ability to successfully compete in that environment. The changes of the twenty-first century have fueled the drive for a fundamental rethinking of organizational structure and operating philosophy toward a renewal of corporate culture. Values are now understood to be the essence, the DNA, of corporate culture, and shared values are vital to the robust versatility required for success in today's global market.

Stability must be created from within an organization and be embedded in a culture that preserves the best of its past and simultaneously fosters new ways of thinking and doing. While just about everyone agrees with this in theory, putting it into practice is another matter. Determining which values and beliefs to change, how and when to initiate the change process, how far to take it, and, most important, how to lead and steer cultural reengineering without complete collapse presents, at the very least, major stumbling blocks. The Coaching by Values process addresses these issues and provides specific tools for keeping a change process on course and on target.

Since my colleagues and I first articulated our ideas about the significance of values to corporate leaders and organizational change agents in our 1997 book *Managing by Values*,[22] we have seen wonderful successes that have helped us refine the Coaching by Values process. In a 2010 *Harvard Business Review* blog, Rosabeth Moss Kanter summarized the logic behind such a values-based change process and suggested specific ways leaders can strengthen their companies by keeping values front and center[23]:

1. Values should be a priority for leaders; they should be invoked in their messages and on the agenda for management discussions.
2. The entire workforce should enter the conversation; employees should be invited to discuss or interpret values and principles in conjunction with their peers, who help ensure alignment.
3. Principles should be codified, made explicit, transmitted in writing in many media platforms, and reviewed regularly to make sure people understand and remember them.
4. Statements about values and principles invoke a higher purpose, a purpose beyond current tasks that indicates service to society. This purpose

should become part of the company's brand and a source of competitive differentiation.

5. The words should become a basis for ongoing dialogue that guides debate when there is controversy or initial disagreement. Decisions should be supported by reference to particular values or principles.

6. Values should guide choices, in terms of business opportunities to pursue or reject, or in terms of investments with a longer time horizon that might seem uneconomic today.

7. As they become internalized by employees, values and principles should substitute for more impersonal or coercive rules. They should serve as a control system against violations, excesses, or veering off course.

8. Actions reflecting values and principles—especially difficult choices— become the basis for iconic stories that are easy to remember and retell, reinforcing to employees and the world what the company stands for, the company branding.

9. Values are aspirational; they signal long-term intentions that guide thinking about the future.

10. Principles, purpose, and values should also be discussed with other stakeholders, such as suppliers, distributors, and other business partners, to promote consistently high standards everywhere.

BOX 3.1 MY PERSONAL EXPERIENCE WITH VALUE-DRIVEN LEADERSHIP

Michele Hunt

I have been a student and a teacher of values-driven leadership all my life. My life has been a journey of discovering, witnessing (and being a part of) the extraordinary things values-driven leaders have accomplished in their organizations, communities, and personal lives.

Values powerfully and beautifully shaped my life

My life was conceived and nurtured by the two greatest people I have ever met. My parents gave me the gift of witnessing the "value of values." My parents came from very challenging beginnings. My father was the second oldest of 12 children. They lived in extreme poverty in the inner city of Detroit, Michigan. His passion was the arts; he was gifted with a beautiful, classical baritone voice. He also played every wind instrument. In spite of his many talents, his mother told him that his dreams of singing and performing around the world were unrealistic. My mother lost her mother at the young age of seven, and her father deserted her and her siblings. They were moved four times to different homes by the time she was ten. Life was hard; my mother even suffered abuse, but she escaped through books. She journeyed around the world through the stories she read, imagining she was in exotic places. Her most cherished dream was to have a family and give them the love and support she had missed as a child.

Despite their beginnings, when my parents married, they consciously and deliberately envisioned the family and the life they wanted to create together, and they committed to a set of nonnegotiable values with which to guide their decisions and actions. My parents succeeded in making their hopes and dreams come true. Dad sang and performed all over the world. He produced elaborate USO shows with audiences of more than 10,000 people. My mom's vision of a family bonded by love also came true. She was at the heart of the creation of love, beauty, and joy in our home. Her family is the center of her life, and to this day we are extraordinarily close. Her vision of traveling to exotic places was also fulfilled; we lived in Alaska, Arizona, Kentucky, and the country of Panama. I experienced in a very personal way "the value of values":

Values were the magic of Herman Miller

I served on the executive leadership team as vice president for people at Herman Miller. Under the leadership of Max De Pree, I saw how the power of shared values transformed this Fortune 500 company from near failure into *Fortune*'s Most Admired Company in the World. We learned the hard way that nothing fails like success.

After decades of success, we had started becoming irrelevant. We had become complacent and insulated and had developed a touch of arrogance. Most damaging, we had failed to pass on the company values—the secret sauce of our 60 years of success. When we were small, we could share the values through stories and relationships, but we had become large, complex, and impersonal. The consequences would have been dire had we not changed. Max called for a company-wide renewal. We renewed our mission and created a shared vision. We accomplished this in a unique manner. We created a disciplined process that authentically engaged every work team and every individual in the company. All the employees wanted the same thing—to reclaim our leadership, "to be a reference point for quality and excellence."

Max insightfully understood that a vision without values is empty and potentially dangerous, so he asked a very important question, "What values do we need to embrace and build into the organization to become a reference point for quality and excellence?"

Once again, we went to the people. After hearing their input, we settled on seven core values that would guide everyone's decisions and behaviors:

1. **Customer-focused vision:** Put the customer at the center of our vision.
2. **Participation and teamwork:** Recognize the value and collective genius of people. People have the right and responsibility to contribute their gifts.
3. **Ownership:** Treat employees like owners. Allow everyone to be responsible and accountable for the decisions that affect their work.
4. **Uniqueness:** Encourage people to bring their whole self to work and to contribute their uniqueness to help achieve the company's goals.
5. **Family, social, and environmental responsibility:** Work, family, community, and the environment are inextricably connected, and our actions had to respect that connection.
6. **Become a learning organization:** Continual learning was a shared commitment.
7. **Financial soundness:** This is essential, but it is not the single aim of our work. It is the result of our commitment to our vision, values, and goals.

The results were amazing! Within 18 months, Herman Miller became:

- *Fortune's* Most Admired Company
- Best Products by *Business Week*
- One of the 10 Best Companies to Work For
- Best Company for Women
- Best Company for Working Mothers
- Winner of numerous environmental awards
- Recipient of the White House Presidential Citation for environmental responsibility
- The Best Managed Company in the World (from the Bertelsmann Foundation)

In addition, sales increased by 20%, and we returned to double-digit growth.

Values-based coaching

For the past 16 years, my method of coaching has been to help leaders mobilize their people around a compelling shared vision born out of their deeply held shared values, engaging their people in transforming their vision, values, and goals into reality. The results have consistently been outstanding. Two of the companies were invited into *Fortune*'s 100 Best Companies to Work For after engaging in this process. This is the same methodology we used at Herman Miller; it transcends time, cultures, and sectors. The secret to success is a commitment to the organization's shared values. When leaders connect the hearts of people through values to accomplish shared goals, amazing things happen.

Michele Hunt is a transformation catalyst and a "thinking partner" on cultural transformation and leadership development for leaders around the world. She is a speaker and the author of *DreamMakers: Putting Vision & Values to Work* and *DreamMakers: Agents of Transformation*. She contributed chapters to Peter Senge's *Fifth Discipline FieldBook* and Robert Rosen's *Healthy Companies*. Michele served in President Bill Clinton's administration as director of the Federal Quality Institute, as a part of the Reinventing Government Initiative. She served on the senior leadership team of Herman Miller as corporate vice president for people.

Values and culture: The family

In this section, I will try to illustrate the relationships between values and family functioning. To begin with, the meaning of "family values" is vague, but most often associated with social and religious contexts. Its meaning varies as a function of time and national culture. In the United States, for example, from the middle to the end of the twentieth century, the term *family values* (at least as it was bandied about in political debates and the media) referred to fundamentalist Christian values that included several specific rigid principles requiring followers to hew to certain behaviors within narrow bounds. But twenty-first-century surveys show a shift in the definition toward the broader principles of "loving, taking care of, and supporting family members." Surveys in the United States also noted that 93% of women thought society should value all types of families.

The more conservative formulation of family values includes valuing "traditional marriage" and a traditional role for women while opposing sex outside conventional marriage. Social and religious conservatives often use the term to promote a conservative ideology that supports traditional morality or "Christian" values. American Christians often see their religion as the source of morality and consider the nuclear family to be an essential element in society.

Liberals, on the other hand, have used the phrase to support family planning, affordable child care, and maternity leave as well as equal roles for men and women in raising children and undertaking work outside the home (paid jobs) or within the family (unpaid jobs). According to Riane Eisler, the essence of the family relationship is changing in the developed Western world as the domination of the male is gradually decreasing and more women are establishing collaborative agreements with their male spouses regarding partnership and care.[24]

Confucianism exerts a strong influence on the family culture and values in China and other Asian societies. In Confucian thought, family values, familial relationships, ancestor worship, and filial piety are the primary basis of the philosophical system and are considered virtues to be cultivated. Filial piety is the highest virtue in Chinese culture. The term *filial*—meaning "of a child"—denotes the respect and obedience that a child, originally a son, should show his parents, especially his father. This relationship has been extended by analogy to a series of five cardinal relationships: ruler and subject, father and son, husband and wife, elder and younger brother, and friend and friend. These values are manifest in many aspects of Chinese culture even to this day. Examples are extensive filial responsibilities children have to parents and elders and the profound and enduring concern of parents for their children.

Some communities separated by great distances manifest similar views of the family and stress the strength of one's commitment to it throughout life. Hispanics and many Arabs, for instance, value the family above all else; they prize family relationships more than any other communities I have encountered in my extensive travels. When they are growing up, young Hispanics and many young Arabs do not envision their future as a life outside the family unit, and in fact they remain intimately connected to their birth family for the rest of their lives. Children grow up hanging out with their brothers, sisters, and cousins. Parents care for their children, provide for them, and protect them. This acceptance and love, in turn, engenders more of the same. Individuals who grow up in such families develop and exhibit the same love and acceptance for their parents and for other children in the family. This bonding continues through adulthood and into old age. Some sociologists cite it, together with mutual assistance, as the reason there was not a revolution in Spain when unemployment soared to record heights in 2010 and 2015 (over 20% for adults and over 37% for people under 25). Most economists say that when unemployment hits these numbers, a social revolution follows, which did not happen in Spain.

Table 3.2 summarizes the hierarchy of values I've seen in some societies based on general value characteristics in these communities. I don't mean to suggest that every member of these communities holds these values or prioritizes them in this way—in fact, they certainly don't. Nor do I mean to stereotype these cultures or present the value systems with any judgment.

Table 3.2 Comparative Hierarchies of Values in Families

English-speaking families	Hispanic (and many Arab) families	Asian families
Freedom	Family security	Belonging
Independence	Harmony	Respect
Self-reliance	Parental guidance	Harmony
Equality	Age respect	Age respect
Individualism	Authority	Group
Competition	Compromise	Collaboration
Efficiency	Devotion	Quality

BOX 3.2 A PRACTICAL GUIDE FOR USING THE *VALUE OF VALUES*: TOOLS AND METHODOLOGY WITH CHILDREN AND FAMILIES

Anat Garti

In this short vignette, we wish to briefly explain a model that we have developed which extends the 3Es triaxial model with other psychological models used in family therapy to help educators, parents, and family coaches use it in their practice. The last decade brought many challenges to parents and the confrontations often ended up harming their feelings and placed in them doubts about their parental capability. So, at the risk of being too simplistic, we are proposing three main factors that challenge parental capability today:

1. In the past, the parent had the knowledge and the experience, and the child aspired to learn from him/her. Today, parents feel that their children know more than they do and that their experience as adults is irrelevant in the new reality. As an outcome, many parents feel confused as to their added value to their children.
2. In the past decade we have witnessed a significantly increased influence of the virtual world (i.e. internet, the social networks, instant mass communication, marketing systems, and influential figures in the media: the so-called cultural heroes). All these and other factors, such as natural disasters, wars, new diseases, and epidemics, to mention a few, find their way instantly to our children in different stages of forming their personality. And again, this creates a major challenge to the parental influence and the parents' attempt to educate and instill values and to constitute an authoritative figure.

3. The economic situation and the emerging social norms which encourage self-fulfillment brings many parents to spend many hours at work away from home. This situation creates the "remote control parenting." In a period and a complex society like the one we are having today, "remote control parenting" is a very challenging mission.

All in all, these realities bring many parents to a state of despair—a feeling of inadequate parenting. So, we suggest handling this complexity as an opportunity for parental work, which will allow high parental capability despite the complexity. The parental work that we are talking about is "The Parent as a Value Anchor." The latter includes all the following aspects, but thereafter we will touch only some of the points:

*   understanding the anchor that enables a behavioral space;
*   understanding the three groups of values that constitute the universe of value anchors;
*   defining the set of value anchors;
*   understanding and dealing with the psychological needs of a person;
*   implementing and translating values into everyday behavior;
*   improving decision making via value assessment;
*   creating an environment that supports behaving by values.

Understanding the anchor that enables a behavioral space—Using "value anchor" and not just "value" emphasizes that the value is not a dichotomy (having it or not) but a phenomenon that runs on a different continuum characterized by behavioral space. Behaving by values means behaving in boundaries that the rope of the anchor enables—not too firm and not too flexible. An honest person is not a person who has never lied but a person that in his essence is honest and the times he has been dishonest are very low in importance and frequency. Each person decides for himself the correct length of his rope. When one's rope is too long and his behavioral space is too wide, or when a person behaves most of his time in spaces far away from his anchor, then we will say that this person is dishonest. As the anchor is designated to confine a sea craft to a certain place in the ocean, without it the vessel can be carried away by the wind, the waves, and the flow of the ocean or any additional factors. Similarly, the value anchor is designated to confine the person to a correct behavioral space, without him/her being carried away by inner (psychological needs) or outer (social pressure) determinants.

The model offers parents to teach their kids that there are margins. Otherwise the kids will torment themselves for every blunder or will give up their values system altogether as their concept will be that it is impossible to handle. In both possibilities, whether they torment themselves or give up, they will feel that it is not possible for them to act by the conscience order that their parents gave them. If we educate them to a value anchor, instead of a dichotomy, when they exaggerate and stray from the anchor, the rope of the anchor will bring them back. The rope of the anchor in the first stages of the child's development is the parental voice. During the course of the child's development, this voice will be internalized and will become an inner voice. Each parent has to decide what the values are and what the length of the rope would be that is tied to each anchor. Each value will have a different length of rope. The parent may think that the value of respect should have a short rope, while the value of persistence should be long.

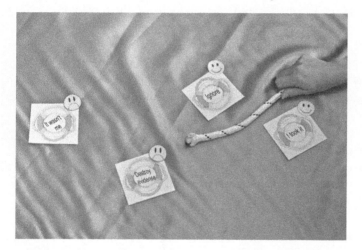

Understanding the three value groups that constitute the value anchors—
The anchors should be selected from the three groups that are proposed by Dolan's 3E triaxial model: economic, ethical, and emotional. When a child is missing one of the groups, the quality of his/her life is significantly limited. Imagine a child that does not manage himself in a pragmatic way. A child that has difficulty in getting organized in the morning, completing school chores and homework, defining goals for himself/herself and to effectively act in order to achieve them. A child bearing these characteristics, even if he/she has excellent relationships, and is involved in things that are of interest to him/her, may not experience a high level of quality of life, hence he/she cannot achieve the things that are important to him/her and to his/her relationships. For example, he/she will be late for school, at school he/she

will not be able to meet the demands of his/her friends, and the results will be that the parents will be upset with him/her, because of not carrying out his/her obligations. Finally, he/she may experience a sense of failure that will harm his/her personal image and probably harm his/her relationships as well.

Similarly, if a child is missing correct management in the social group and if he/she does not acquire the respective social skills required to manage himself/herself in society, he/she may be socially hurt time after time, and he/she may feel unwanted and unappreciated in society. Furthermore, this may bring about behaviors in society that will not enable him/her to achieve his/her goals.

Likewise, if we look at the third group, the emotional–developmental group, we can imagine a child that manages himself/herself effectively, and he/she is surrounded with friends, but he/she does not have joy in life. This is a child whose parents do not understand why he/she is sad most of the time and is like a successful manager who is surrounded by friends but is still depressed.

Therefore, in order to make sure that the children's quality of life is good, the model suggests that parents make sure that children acquire important skills in each one of the groups of values—that they know how to manage themselves in an effective way in order to achieve their goals, how to conduct themselves in society, and what makes them feel good and direct themselves in that direction. In other words, they are productive, ethical, and satisfied kids, adolescents, and grown-ups.

Defining the set of value anchors—The first step that parents have to do is to define the set of value anchors from each group that the parents think are important to be internalized by their children and choosing the length of the rope for each anchor. An effective way for this important process is using "the value of values" game.[25] This game enables the process of identifying personal, couple, and parental values which then leads into family dialogue examining the respective values and understanding the 3E triaxial model of each member of the family. A discussion of the important values to the family can be followed which involves the choice of a balanced set of values—a set of values that is composed of the three groups of values. The parents should discuss between themselves and with their children the significance of the values, how they are translated into our everyday conduct, and what is the meaning of the rope that is tied to each value anchor.

And remember, values are abstract concepts. For us to be able to conduct our everyday life according to our values, we must turn these abstract concepts into behaviors. Moreover, young children cannot understand abstract concepts and so in order to educate them to conduct themselves by values, we have to translate the abstract concepts into concrete concepts. If you are a parent and you follow these guidelines, you will see how the quality of your parenting will improve.

In sum, the model which we have developed proposes to parents a strategy based on values and behavior that includes the following components:

- Create a set of value anchors that will light up the way.
- These value anchors are composed of values taken from the three groups of the 3Es triaxial model: economic–pragmatic, ethic–social, and emotional–developmental.
- Part of these values are family values. Part of these values are from other entities of the child's life, such as belonging groups, and some are his private values, which also provide the child some freedom for being unique and adhering to specific different values.
- Have the values translated into objectives, and in our everyday behavior transfer messages that include the value, the objective and the recommended behavior
- Define the length of the rope for each value and the objective that directs the flexibility of the behavior concerning this value and this objective.
- Translate the values and the way they are manifested into objectives, ensuring that they are congruent with the psychological needs of the family members.
- Assist by performing an analysis of the value decision scale in order to examine what the correct choice of our set of values is in order to enable a value conversation with the child concerning the decisions he made.
- Internalize effectively a set of value anchors by using a combination of conscience, the desire to belong to certain groups, and profitable reasons.

Good luck!

***

Anat Garti is a Coaching by Values trainer who specializes in family therapy. She is one of the most celebrated coaches in Israel. She teaches part time in several academic institutions and is currently completing her doctoral studies at the University of Haifa.

Values, community, and national culture: A brief description

Although there are numerous ways of looking at the national and community levels of culture, given the limited scope of this book, let us consider the ideas of one seminal figure in the field of national culture whose pioneering work has greatly influenced the current conversation. Geert Hofstede, a Dutch organizational sociologist, has studied the interactions between national cultures and organizational cultures. He argues that there are national and regional cultural groupings that affect the behavior of organizations and that these are persistent across time. By and large, Hofstede and his colleagues have shown that these cultures affect the behavior of individuals.[26] As editor-in-chief of *Cross-Cultural Management—An International Journal*, I invited Hofstede and a colleague to reflect on the evolution of their pioneer work.[27]

They identified five characteristics that define a culture and influence organizational and personal behavior:

- **Power distance** is the degree to which a society expects power differences to be there among people. A high score reflects the belief that some individuals should wield more power than others. A low score reflects the view that all people should have equal rights.
- **Uncertainty avoidance** is the extent to which a society accepts uncertainty and risk.
- **Individualism vs. collectivism** is the extent to which people are expected to stand up for themselves or to act as a member of a group or organization.
- **Masculinity vs. femininity** is the importance a society places on traditionally male and female values. Male values, for example, include competitiveness, assertiveness, ambition, and the accumulation of wealth and material possessions.
- **Long-term vs. short-term orientation** describes a society's "time horizon" or the importance attached to the future as opposed to the past and present. In long-term-oriented societies, thrift and perseverance are valued highly; in short-term-oriented societies, respect for tradition and reciprocation of gifts and favors are valued more. A high score indicates a long-term orientation. Eastern nations tend to score especially high here, with Western nations scoring low and the less-developed nations very low; China scored highest and Pakistan lowest.

Hofstede's doctrine has generated controversies; it has been both undervalued and overused. His conceptualization of culture as static and essential has attracted criticism especially. Some culture experts claim to have found inconsistencies in both its theory and methodology.[28] Many think that he identifies cultures with nations based on the supposition that within each nation there is a uniform national culture—a suggestion Hofstede explicitly denies when he insists on the resilience to change despite all this diversity.

3.6 Values and education

The different views about education in values are related to questions such as: What are values? What is valuation? What is the relationship between education in values and the educational project? Is it the role of home/school/ university to train for values? How will the school/college/university measure the training and development of values? These questions raise concerns and worries for parents and educators alike.

Many of these concerns accompany the present world in a more general way. We talk about crises of identity, faith, and epistemology of identity by pointing out the absence of a clear sense of belonging and by a lack of common unifying projects. Many claim that it is characterized by the inability to believe in something, for the impossibility of change, and the lack of trust in the future.

Some say that we live in a society without values; others say that a new breed of values has appeared which is associated with the new socio-economic and cultural paradigm. There are also those who say that the problem lies in the lack of existence of a coherent model of values and that causes confusion and disorientation in the performance and valuation of teachers and students alike. While all this is happening, perhaps it would be worthwhile to address the matter, taking into account that in all societies and at different times man has had to face his own development challenges, and why could it not be done before the accelerated scientific-technological development and globalization of the planet?

Educating in values, then means extending the scope of education so that it does not limit itself to the teaching and learning of subjects, skills, and topics but focusing on morality and civics, with the goal of forming responsible citizens. Through education, there are some values we try to strengthen and by doing so we are strengthening the culture and a way of being and behaving based on respect for others, the environment, and the ideas of solidarity. If teachers, parents, politicians, or even educators will not do that, the young ones will take matters into their own hands to affect changes. As I write this book, there is a case of Greta Thunberg, a 15-year-old young Swedish climate activist, who gave a sensationalistic speech at the COP24 UN Conference in Katowice that became widely popular. She blames the politicians and the corporate world that by neglecting the value of a friendly environment, they are stealing the future from the next generation. People will rise to the climate challenge whether we like it or not, and if the schools, family, and politicians will not educate them on these core values, your children will.[29]

Although education by values is a broad and complex concept, which ideally requires the involvement of both teachers and the educational community and, especially, parents and society, in general, in recent years we have developed concepts, methodologies, and tools to facilitate the tasks of parents and teachers. That is the essence of our concept of "Educating by Values." In Box 3.3 that follows this section, Ani Paez is sharing an amazing original angle to teach values. Ani is a teacher who lives in Madrid and has been trained in Coaching by Values and from there has developed her own methodology in which she combines the game *Value of Values* and the tale *The Magic Carpet and the Islands of Values*.

BOX 3.3 ANOTHER EDUCATION IS POSSIBLE

By Ani Paez

The digitization and robotization of our present-future are making educators think of new ways of teaching and training the new generation "Z." How do we prepare these students? What needs and skills should they have and develop in order to become successful people?

During the Industrial Revolution, a similar situation arose. From there, we developed the education system that we know today. This education system has worked well, but our current technological advancements have created the need for new change.

According to the theories elaborated by big businessmen and students of the future of work, among them Simon Dolan, the new generations must be prepared to demonstrate their personal worth. They must develop social and emotional tools and skills in order to be able to compete with the intelligent machines that lack these skills.

The global transformation will depend on what is done in the classrooms. We will have to start by leaving aside a training based on hard skills, the logical ones, and move forward to develop soft skills that are based on the development of emotional intelligence, creativity, and critical thinking.

Taking this approach as a starting point, anticipating what is to come, and understanding my students from their foundation as human beings is essential. Values have always been present and have been the beginning of the understanding of people. Values, seen as the DNA of behavior, will be the ones that help to focus on the change toward an education where the development of creativity for the resolution of conflicts, learning to learn or reflective thinking, teamwork, and proactivity become the goal.

To do this, developing a new methodology is crucial. That is why this new approach to Coaching and Values in the classroom is so essential. It is a new educational method that provides the keys to educate and develop future leaders while strengthening their strengths and working on their weaknesses.

To do this, we must begin to provide tools that will help students develop their soft skills, without neglecting the learning of the content in the annual educational program.

If values are the engine of our behavior, when incorporating them in the daily routine of the classroom, they will become part of the content, activities, and performance of the students. An activity as simple as guiding students to elaborate and manage their work according to a new value every 15 days costs very little and yet opens many doors.

Using the Model of the Three Anchors of Values (Anat Garti 2016) in the classroom with the card game of the *Value of Values*, together with the tale of *The Magic Carpet and the Islands of Values* (Dolan) has helped me to detect incongruities and needs that my students have when meeting their goals. According to the triaxial model, proposed by Simon Dolan, there are three axes of clearly identified values. Children should learn to understand the importance of having these values and using the values of the three groups: pragmatic, social–ethical, and emotional.

The tale of "The Magic Carpet and the Islands of Values" is a great tool to introduce the abstract value of words for the proper development of the sessions. These words can be patience, respect, determination, silence, and listening. Emotional values such as fun, creativity, affection, and empathy will complement the cooperative work in the classroom.

The activities, both with the tale and the card game, have served for different moments during my sessions. Using the characters of the tale as examples for understanding, reflection, and elaboration of strategies based on values facilitates the internalization of the different values. Students understand the difficult vocabulary of values by role-playing the characters of the tale, who live in the same situations as them. Values become magic words that help them to be better people. In short, they learn to use values with a meaning.

The power to combine questions that facilitate reflection and identify their difficulties is a new way of giving students tools to solve their own conflicts, inside and outside the classroom, in the school environment, as well as in their family. Using values in the playground to solve their conflicts is a starting point to reduce all sorts of aggression and leads students to consider dialogues to analyze the root of the problem. If students have a clear understanding of the essential values of their group, as soon as there is a disagreement, the conflict is taken to the field of values and from there the resolution is fast and direct.

Values are worked at each moment and in each subject. A good example could be to use the values of respect, empathy, and privacy with the learning of any subject related to the human body. When working on mathematics, for example, the values of effort, perseverance, order, and planning can be reinforced. Everything is a matter of focusing from the same angle. Even learning a new language becomes easier and faster when what you have to share matters so much and is so personal. Students make a double effort to communicate their experiences, emotions, what moves them, and their values.

Knowing the individual values that each student chooses helps to facilitate their learning and to avoid labeling them for example, the case of a student with difficulties to complete his tasks, fulfill his duties, and interact with his classmates and teachers. When working with the card game of the *Value of Values*, he only chose emotional values, leaving clear evidence that pragmatic and ethical–social values were not present in his life. I immediately understood what the problem was, and we dedicated to work on them together with his family and the rest of the teachers and classmates. After five months, this student was able to finish his classwork, hand in his homework, and began to relate better with his classmates, teachers, and family. This is a clear proof that values are the engine of our behavior.

At the school level, we can also use values in order to internalize and live them. For example, a way of doing this is working with the pragmatic values during the first term. During the second term, we work on the social–ethical values and during the third term, we introduce the emotional values combined with the previous values.

Note: Photo used with the mother's permission.

I have also been able to develop new tools to help me control the discipline in the classroom. For example, the "Contract of the Magic Words" that consists of establishing the values that will be used for the good performance of a specific task. The rules are clear and if they are not met, I just refer to the document created because when there is a commitment, the students fulfill their tasks better.

I would like to say that inclusion and diversity are completely met when using this methodology while learning a second language. Students talk about what they feel and believe, and this is a non-stop tool to motivate them to learn new vocabulary.

Ani Paez is passionate and committed to education, with more than 30 years of experience in teaching English as a second language to children and adults. She is a civil servant and a qualified English teacher. Ani works with several publishers in the educational field—collaborating on webinars, training workshops on specific methodologies of teaching English, and adapting science textbooks to the English language. In addition, she is an author of two *Teacher's Didactic Guides for Social and Natural Sciences in English* for the first grade of primary school. Ani is a teacher trainer in the CLIL methodology, and she tutors teachers for the state exam in the English language for the community in Madrid. She is an expert in Coaching by Values and certified in Education by Values, methodologies endorsed by Simon Dolan. Ani is the creator of her own methodology in Education by Values, combining her experience with current educational and pedagogical methodologies to create a unique teaching method. She is a pioneer in teaching English through values and shares her passion in two practical manuals, "The Parent as a Value Anchor," "Valores: La Brújula para Personas y Organizaciones de Futuro," and on her blog:

http://cuentosporvalores.blogspot.com.es/

She can be reached via e-mail at: anipm00@gmail.com

3.7 Conclusion

Values are critical determinants of our behavior; they represent our highest priorities and our most deep-seated driving forces. Values are priorities that tell us how to allocate our limited resources (e.g., our time and energy), right here and right now. And these priorities matter. It is critical to our satisfaction, health, fulfillment, and happiness that we understand them and their consequences. This is why:

1. Time is our most limited resource; time does not renew itself. Once we spend a day, it's gone forever. If we waste that day by investing our time

in actions that don't produce the results we want, that loss is permanent. We can earn more money, improve our physical bodies, and repair broken relationships, but we cannot redo yesterday. If we had infinite time, then values and priorities would be irrelevant. But our life spans are limited, and if we value our mortal lives, then it makes sense that we'd want to invest them as best we can.

2. We as human beings tend to be inconsistent in how we invest our time and energy. Most of us are easily distracted. It's easy to fall into the trap of living by different priorities every day. One day we exercise; the next day we slack off. One day we work productively; the next day we are stricken with a bout of laziness. If we don't consciously use our priorities to stick to a clear and consistent course, we will naturally drift off course and shift all over the place. And this kind of living yields poor results. Imagine an airplane that went wherever the wind took it: Who knows where it would eventually land? And the flight itself would likely be stressful and uncertain.

Our limited time and typically low index of distraction make it extremely important that we know what our values are and consciously live by them.

Our values are informed by everything that has happened in our lives and everyone we've known—our parents and family, our religious affiliation, our friends and peers, our education, our reading, and more. Effective people recognize these environmental influences and identify and develop a clear, concise, and meaningful set of beliefs, values, and priorities. They also recognize that some values may be more important than others in a given moment or context. Our personal hierarchy of values must be versatile; it needs to be refined, tuned, and synchronized with our surroundings (family, friends, workplace, and community).

When we join an organization, community, or family, we bring our deeply held values and beliefs with us. There they co-mingle with those of the other members to create an organization or family or community culture. But the subject is a little more complicated than this. As we've seen, existing organizations already have a deeply embedded set of values, as do nations, communities, and families. These determine their behaviors and may or may not agree with their espoused values, which are much easier to identify. In addition, the structures of these systems often give some people more power than others to establish or shift entrenched values. What do we do if we begin to feel uncomfortable in our surroundings or start to sense a disconnect from the cultures in which we live and work?

Sometimes we need help understanding our values. We also may need help understanding the culture and values of the places in which we live and work—especially in today's increasingly culturally diverse environments. Coaches can play a major role in helping people understand their values and the values of their surroundings. Coaches can also help people make choices and adapt, creating a positive fit between people and their surroundings. Sometimes the choice may be to find a situation more in sync with your values. Or it may mean working hard on yourself or in concert with your partner, team, or organization. Whatever we need to do to attain it, a positive fit makes for a happier person, and a happier person will be more successful. We will learn more about how to create this fit in the remaining chapters.

CLBV Reflection

Think of the key message(s) that you retained after reading this chapter. Then complete the following sentences:

The principal point(s) I liked in this chapter include:

1. _____

2. _____

3. _____

The principal point(s) that I did not like or disagreed with in this chapter include:

1. _____

2. _____

3. _____

Complete this section only if you are already a professional coach:

After reading this chapter, I am intrigued by the 3Es triaxial model of values because I can see its potential utility for:

1. _____

2. _____

3. _____

Notes

1 The "Value of Values" is a registered trademark of Gestion MDS Inc. of Montreal (Canada) and Simon L. Dolan in Spain (© 2010). Nowadays it is available as a brand in many countries around the world as it is used jointly with the community of "CoachingxValores" in more than 19 languages. Used with permission.

2 This section was greatly inspired by the writings of Tong-Keun Min of Chung Nam National University, Korea, in particular *A Study on the Hierarchy of Values* (www. bu.edu/wcp/Papers/Valu/ValuMin.htm); the excellent presentation he gave at the Twentieth World Congress of Philosophy in Boston (August 10–15, 1998). I made

numerous attempts to contact the author and obtain permission to begin this chapter with his beautiful description of values and the natural system but was unable to reach him. A Korean doctoral student at ESADE who has been graciously assisting me in this effort discovered that Tong-Keun retired from the university in 1995. At the time we prepared this edition, we were unable to locate Professor Tong-Keun Min.

3 For more on these issues, read Raich, M., & Dolan, S. L. (2008). *Beyond: Business and Society in Transformation.* Palgrave Macmillan; Raich, M., Eisler, R., & Dolan, S. L. (2014). *Cyberness: The Future Reinvented.* Disponible in Amazon.com. www.amazon .es/Cyberness-Future-Reinvented-Mario-Raich/dp/1500673382

4 This section has been greatly inspired by my previous writings, specifically Dolan, S. L., Garcia, S., & Richley, B. (2006). *Managing by Values* (chapter 2). Palgrave Macmillan; Dolan, S. L., & Lingham, T. (2008). *Fundamentals of International Organizational Behavior* (chapter 10). Sara Books; Dolan, S. L., & Kawamura, K. M. (2015). *Cross Cultural Competence.* Emerald. And, Dolan, S. L. (2018 in Spanish). *Liderazgo, dirección y coaching por valores.* Círculo Rojo.

5 See, for example, Dolan, S. L., & Richley, B. (2006). Management by Values (MBV): A new philosophy for a new economic order. *Handbook of Business Strategy,* 7(1), 235–238; Raich, M., & Dolan, S. L. (2009). Managing in the new landscape. *Effective Executive, 12*(10), 48–56; Ulrich, D., & Ulrich, W. (2010). *The Why of Work.* McGraw-Hill.

6 Rockeach, M. (1973). *The Nature of Human Values.* Free Press.

7 Porter, M. L. (1985). *Competitive Advantage: Creating and Sustaining Superior Performance.* Free Press.

8 Allport, F. H. (1924). *Social Psychology.* Houghton Mifflin.

9 Ray, P. H., & Anderson, S. R. (2000). *The Cultural Creatives: How 50 Million People Are Changing the World.* Harmony Books.

10 Stiglitz, J. E. (2011, May). Of the 1%, by the 1%, for the 1%. *Vanity Fair,* pp.126–129. www.vanityfair.com/society/features/2011/05/top-one-percent-201105.

11 See, for example, Blau, S., & Ellis, A., (2000). *The Albert Ellis Reader: A Guide to Well-Being Using Rational Emotive Behavior Therapy.* Citadel.

12 B. F. Skinner, the father of modern behaviorism, has written extensively on the subject since the early 1940s. For a typical example of his message, see Skinner, D. F. (1971). *About Behaviorism.* Knopf.

13 For more details, read my book on stress: Dolan, S. L. (2007). *Stress, Self-Esteem, Health and Work.* Palgrave Macmillan.

14 Hall, B. (1994). *Values Shift: A Guide to Personal and Organizational Transformation.* Twin Lights.

15 Maslow, A. (1943). A theory of human motivation. *Psychological Review, 50,* 370–396.

16 Byrne, R. (2006). *The Secret.* Atria Books.

17 Min, Tong-Keun. (August 10–15, 1998). *A Study on the Hierarchy of Values.* Paper presented at the Twentieth World Congress of Philosophy (www.bu.edu/wcp/Pape rs/Valu/ValuMin.htm).

18 See Dolan, S. L., Garcia, S., & Richley, B. (2006). *Managing by Values: Corporate Guide to Living, Being Alive and Making a Living in the 21st Century.* Palgrave Macmillan.

19 My colleagues and I have been conducting a 30-country validation study on the meaning of values. The project was called VAC (Values Across Cultures), and we have focused on public sector employees in each of the 30 countries. The participating countries are spread across the globe. The results confirmed the efficiency of the triaxial model of values. See: Dolan, S. (ed.) (2013) Values across cultures (VAC): Mapping differences and strengths in the public sector. *Cross Cultural Management,* 20(4), the entire special issue, op cit.

20 For more, see my discussion of culture reengineering in Chapter 6.

21 Schein, E. H. (2005). *Organizational Culture and Leadership* (3rd ed.). Jossey-Bass. First edition was published in 1985.

22 Garcia, S., & Dolan, S. L. (1997). *Dirección por Valores*. Madrid: McGraw-Hill; Dolan, S. L., Garcia, S., & Richley, B. (2006). *Managing by Values: Corporate Guide to Living, Being Alive and Making a Living in the 21ˢᵗ Century*. London: Palgrave Macmillan.

23 Kanter, R. M. (2010, June 14). Ten essentials for getting value from values, *Harvard Business Review* blog. http://blogs.hbr.org/kanter/2010/06/ten-essentials-for-getting-val.html.

24 In *The Chalice and the Blade* (1988, HarperOne); Eisler traces the powerful effects of everyday exposure to a dominator and shows the difference between those and the effects of the partnership model in every area of life.

25 The game "the value of values" was developed by Professor Simon Dolan and Avishai Landau. The web page of the game: www.learningaboutvalues.com or https://tienda-coachingporvalores.com/

26 See Hofstede, G. (2001). *Culture's Consequences: Comparing Values, Behaviors, Institutions, and Organizations Across Nations* (2nd ed.). Sage; Hofstede, G., & Hofstede, G. J. (2005). *Cultures and Organizations: Software of the Mind* (Revised and expanded 2nd ed.). McGraw-Hill.

27 Minkov, M. (with Hofstede, G.). (2011). The evolution of Hofstede's Doctrine. *Cross Cultural Management—An International Journal, 18*(1), 10–20.

28 See, for example, Taras, V., Kirkman, B. L., & Steel, P. (2010). Examining the impact of *Culture's Consequences*: A three-decade, multilevel, meta-analytic review of Hofstede's cultural value dimensions. *Journal of Applied Psychology, 95*(3), 405–439.

29 I recommend you to watch Greta's speech at the UN climate change conference COP24: www.bing.com/videos/search?q=greta+speech+in+the+UN&view=detail&mid=AEBC9B38742904387F7BAEBC9B38742904387F7B&FORM=VIRE

Chapter 4

The secret of coaching and leading by values

Alignment and realignment

DOLAN 3Es

Triaxial Model of Values

4.1 If the shoe fits, wear it; if it doesn't, change it

I will start with a metaphor. Try and walk for a while in shoes that don't fit. What will happen? If the shoes are too small, you will start to feel the pain after a few steps. The pain will grow gradually to the point that you cannot take it any longer, and you will change the shoes. The same thing will happen (though it will take a little longer) if you walk in shoes that are too big. First, you will slide a bit inside; your socks will tear, but there won't be any physical damage. But if you keep walking, for longer distances and repeatedly, you will feel the impact of the oversized shoes. Now, what would you think if people said to you, "You really need to adjust your feet to fit the shoes." Wouldn't it be more reasonable to just adjust—or change—the shoes? And if you can't find the proper shoes in Store 1, you will shop around until you find them. This could take a while, and the new shoes may not fit forever, but they will provide the comfort you need at the time—and your life will be better for it.

The same thing happens with values. If your values (whatever they are) do not fit the values of your spouse, team, organization, community, or even country, you will feel miserable; you will feel that you're a misfit, and the growing psychological pain will end in physical pain. It is normal for people to look for the right culture—one in which they sense a better (if not perfect) fit between their values and the values of their environment.

Do organizations offer us new shoes, or do they expect us to readjust to the shoes offered? Almost always, they expect us to adjust. The reasons organizations developed, and in some cases continue to maintain, cultures characterized by rules, regulations, and control is that they are easier to manage, they worked well for centuries, and they derive from the paradigm of efficiency (producing more with fewer resources). Organizations today have to struggle with the tension of exercising control on the one hand and developing their employees on the other.

A great majority of companies today are strategically designed according to traditional organizational models oriented toward hierarchical control. An over-reliance on control and rational processes, while relatively comfortable and predictable, contributes to an environment in which employees are indifferent, uninspired, and excessively dependent on leadership. I am not suggesting that control is bad, but I strongly believe that a more integrated,[1] flexible, and learning-oriented design will contribute to a robust culture and, therefore, a successful business.

Resolving the dilemma between security and risk (between control and development) is essential to the survival and growth of an organization. Both options imply certain distinct, but related, systems of values. My consulting experience has taught me that a company that clings to values of concentration, preferring rigid departmental boundaries and a parochial view to an open-minded and forward-thinking vision, is very likely to stagnate, because it will not be receptive to changes in the environment (e.g., market demands, new technologies, or resources). Excessive order and control cause loss of vitality and drive. Companies have been known to die of boredom, not just figuratively but literally; their best people have gotten fed up and left. Take the "Control vs. Development Values Quiz" in this chapter to see where your organization (or family or team; see the note below the quiz) lies along the control–development values continuum. The second part of the quiz will let you begin to see how well your values are aligned with those of your organization.

##

Control vs. development values quiz

(**Note:** This quiz was created for organizational settings, but it works for families and small groups; just slightly adjust the questions.)

A. Rate the following elements of your organization from 0 through 5 according to the given characteristics.

		0	1	2	3	4	5
1.	Structure	Fluid					Rigid
2.	Innovation	High					Low
3.	Risk orientation	Risk taking					Risk averting
4.	Vision	Wide/global					Narrow/local
5.	General orientation	Process					Results
6.	Conformity	Low pressure					High pressure
7.	Learning climate	Relearning					Retention
8.	Changes	Embraced					Resisted
9.	Tolerance to diversity	High					Low
10.	Task orientation	Multitasking					Specialized tasking

Add your answers to get your organization's total score: ☐

Interpret your score:

0–15 Your organization seems to be development oriented.

35–50 Your organization seems to be control oriented.

B. Assess your own values and preferences. Think about your values and general preferences and think about the kind of organization in which you like to work.

Fill out the quick-scoring quiz below. On the righthand side, put any number from 0 through 5.

I prefer to work in (or be associated with) a culture where there is

1. Fluid structure (0) ....Rigid structure (5)   ___
2. High innovation (0)..............Low innovation (5)   ___
3. Risk taking (0) ....Risk averting (5)   ___
4. Wide/global vision (0)...........Narrow/local vision (5)   ___
5. Process orientation (0)...........Results orientation (5)   ___
6. Low pressure to conform (0) ....High pressure to conform (5)   ___
7. Learning climate (0)..............Retention climate (5)   ___
8. Openness to change (0).........Resistance to change (5)   ___
9. High diversity tolerance (0)......Low diversity tolerance (5)   ___
10. Multitasking orientation (0).....Specialized task orientation (5)   ___

Total score   ☐

Interpret your score:

0–15 You seem to have a preference for development-oriented cultures.

35–50 You seem to have a preference for control-oriented cultures.

Now calculate the gap between the two scores. It is the size of the gap that causes discomfort. Remember the metaphor of the shoe. Oversized shoes and undersized shoes can cause similar discomfort. The smaller the gap, the more the congruence (or fit) and the less difficult it will be to be involved in the change process. The larger the gap, the more challenging achieving congruence will be from a coaching perspective.

4.1.1 The meaning of values: Control-oriented organizations vs. learning, or development-oriented, organizations

Values, as we saw in the previous chapter, are concepts that we identify and define using words. We name our values. But the names (the words) we give them may be used in very different ways to mean very different things according to the context. Most cultures (organizations, nations, families, and others) think of "good" as a value to be prized. But for some, being good means being resigned and patient, whereas for others, it means being enterprising and original, having the courage to say what one thinks or believes. The word is the same, but it represents two very different ways of being. Similarly, values such as support, respect, integrity, and efficiency can take on a variety of meanings depending on whether they are formulated in a culture oriented toward control or in a culture focused on learning and development. In this and the next few sections, I will focus on the meaning of values in organizations, but the thinking can be applied to values in any culture, system, or environment.

A culture of learning and development is rooted in values that support and encourage both organizational and human potential. Often these distinctions are thought of as twentieth-century versus twenty-first-century organizational cultures or simply old versus new, or traditional versus innovative, cultures. Table 4.1 compares the entirely different meanings certain values have in both cultural types.

4.2 The importance of reshaping and realigning values

Organizational leaders spend too much time drafting and redrafting vision statements, mission statements, values statements, purpose statements, aspiration statements, and so on. They spend nowhere near enough time trying to understand the nature of alignment of their organizations with the values and visions already in place.

Researching, and sometimes working closely with some of the world's most visionary organizations, has made it clear to me that they concentrate primarily on the process of alignment rather than on diagnosing and understanding what kind of alignment is really needed. To do that, we need to, again and again,

Table 4.1 Meanings of Specific Values: Culture of Control and Culture of Development

Values	Twentieth century: Culture of control	Twenty-first century: Culture of learning and development
Control	Supervision focused on control geared toward correcting deviations from anticipated results; results are determined by top management; hierarchical structure	Managers encourage autonomy and employee responsibility; control is interwoven in policies and procedures to ensure quality assurance, safety, etc.; results are derived through participatory processes that are inclusive and aimed at getting appropriate and accurate information; flatter organizational structure
Support	Saying what you believe others want to hear; approving and praising; helping to hide errors	Helping others to check the effectiveness of their work; learning from errors
Integrity	Staying put in one's own principles, values, and beliefs; not giving in	Open disposition toward situations and people with different belief systems
Respect	Not questioning the rationale of other people and more specifically those in positions of authority	Showing consideration for others regardless of organizational "rank" and being open to their opinion, ideas, perspectives, etc.
Self-confidence	Demonstrating self-confidence through persuasion and "winning"; an admission of errors is akin to "losing face and status"; posturing is a way of life	Demonstrating self-confidence as well as accepting others' opinions; ability to admit mistakes and to learn from others regardless of position

come back to the basics and ask fundamental questions like: What are our core values? What is our primary reason for existing? What do we aspire to achieve and become? These are very important questions that get at the true vision of an organization.[2]

Vision is one of the least understood, and most overused, words. Vision is simply a combination of three basic elements of an organization: (1) its fundamental reason for existing beyond just making money (often called its "mission" or "purpose"); (2) its timeless, unchanging core values; and (3) huge and audacious—but ultimately achievable—aspirations for its future. Of these, the most important elements of great, enduring organizations are their core values.

There is a big difference between being an organization with a vision statement and a truly visionary organization. The difference lies in creating alignment—alignment to preserve an organization's core values, to reinforce its purpose, and to stimulate continued progress toward its aspirations. When you have superb alignment, a visitor could drop into your organization from another planet and infer the vision without having to read it on paper.

Creating alignment is a two-part process. The first is identifying and correcting misalignments. The second is creating new alignments, or what I call "reengineering the culture with mechanisms of real reinforcement."

4.2.1 Correcting misalignments

Identifying misalignments means looking around the organization, talking to people, getting input, conducting organization culture audits, and asking: If these are our core values and this is fundamentally why we exist, what are the obstacles that get in our way? For instance, many organizations say they respect and trust their people to do the right thing, but they undermine that statement by doing X, Y, and Z. The misalignments exist not because the statements are false; these companies believe what they say. The misalignments occur because years of ad hoc policies and practices have become institutionalized and have obscured the firm's underlying values. The first task for leaders, then, is to create an environment and a process that enable people to safely identify and eliminate these misalignments.

The task of a business coach is to show senior executives the misalignments, to discuss the consequences, and to help the leader develop a policy for encouraging open debate and dialogue around the core values.

Figure 4.1 presents an example of a corporate alignment strategy. Note that both arrows in the graphic are of the same color shade. Information is flowing throughout all levels of the organization. There is a balance between the left and right sides of the triangle. How often is such a strategy really followed? In

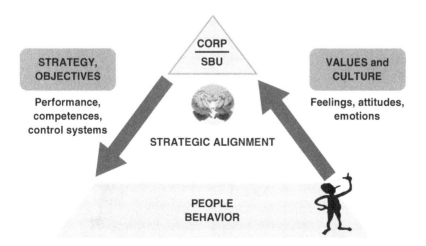

Figure 4.1 Corporate alignment strategy.

most cases, when senior members of an organization craft strategies to align people's behavior with the corporation's goals, they do not recognize that complete alignment requires both sides of the triangle—the left side (strategy and control) and the right side (values and culture)—and input from all members.

Most companies rely on a unit called SBU (Strategic Business Unit) to develop their goals and objectives and to formulate strategies to align people's behavior with these goals. For years, companies tried to force alignment by focusing on the left side of the diagram in Figure 4.2: crafting performance standards, ensuring technical competencies, and employing a variety of control systems (e.g., titles, perks, salaries, promotions, or withholding promotions). This is like using only the left hemisphere of the brain (rational thinking and linear reasoning). And for a long time, it worked; it produced good results. However, today's workforce is by far more educated and less susceptible to manipulation. At the same time, the environment is far more complex (nonlinear) and is becoming even more so. In this kind of business environment, organizations that fail to also use the right side of the brain (artistic, poetic, and sensitive) and listen to the people in the organization will not be able to create an alignment.

In Figure 4.2 we see why corporate "alignment" strategies so often fail. They are in fact "misalignment" strategies and look more like the diagram in Figure 4.2 than in 4.1. When people's feelings, attitudes, and emotions are not aligned with the organization, the brain will not be aligned, and the entire system will not work. To create a better alignment, we need to work simultaneously with the two sides of the brain.

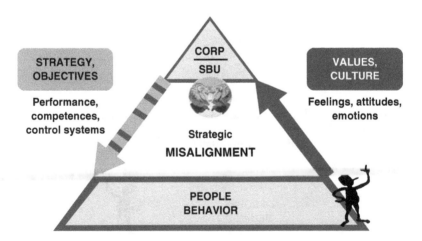

Figure 4.2 Why so many companies fail to achieve strategic alignment.

There are ample books, writings, and consulting firms claiming that they can help any organization enhance performance by setting objectives, developing incentives and control measures, crafting policies, and initiating practices connected with the rational paradigm (left side). But the right side has not been given nearly as much attention. To help remedy this, let us look at the values and culture side of the equation.

4.2.2 Creating new alignments

Creating something that doesn't yet exist but ought to is not easy. True alignment means being creatively compulsive. It means going over the top. It requires a combination of factors and conditions. The most important ones are openness and the will to change. Overcoming resistance to change and sponsoring a process of culture reengineering requires a courageous leader. One who is not afraid to take the risk; one who understands that it is not possible to *set* organizational values; it is only possible to *discover* them. Nor can you "instill" new core values into people. Core values are not something people buy in to; they must be predisposed to holding them. Thus, the task for the leader is either (a) finding people who are already predisposed to sharing their core values or (b) changing and adapting to the core values of the rest of the members of the organization.

The process of culture reengineering involves identifying the core values, identifying gaps between the core values and the mission and vision, attracting and retaining people who share the core values, and letting people who aren't predisposed to sharing these values go elsewhere. This last action may sound harsh, but you can do this by showing people that this might be good for *them*, because it opens up opportunities for them to find situations in which they will be happier and more likely to succeed. Leaving an organization, a country, a community, or a family is not necessarily a bad thing.

Every institution, team, group, family, or enterprise must wrestle with this vexing question: What should change and what should never change? It's a matter of distinguishing timeless core values from operating practices and cultural norms. Timeless core values should never change; operating practices and cultural norms should never stop changing. Timeless core values in a family are respect for each other and trust in each other. This should never change. At a university, a core value should be freedom of intellectual inquiry. The moment this core value begins to wither, the institution risks losing the vision necessary for it to advance and create new knowledge. But going back to the critical question above, it's important not to conflate core values with other things. At times, institutions cling doggedly to practices that are in truth nothing more than familiar habits. As a result, they fail to change things that ought to change. And by defending outmoded practices under the banner of core values, they might be betraying their true core values.

Many organizations exist with value misalignment. Many leaders forget about the importance of values. Few institutions take responsibility for value alignment. An inflexible hierarchy, overdependence on competition, and constraints on behavior guarantee frustration in any environment. Value alignment is critical to successful organizational endeavors. In the next sections, I will provide a quick overview of the research showing the concrete positive consequences of value alignment (value congruence) and the negative consequences of value misalignment (value incongruence).

Before moving to the next section, take a moment to list the possible consequences of congruence and incongruence in any environment in which you work or live by doing the Consequences of Value Incongruence and Value Congruence exercise.

CLBV Reflection ♣ ♠ ♥

Consequences of value incongruence and value congruence

Jot down the possible key consequences of incongruence (left column) and congruence (right column) between your values and the values of your environment (e.g., your company, team, family/partner, or workgroup).

If you are discussing this in a team, see if the team can identify the ten most important consequences of value incongruence (anything positive or negative such as performance, motivation, and health, just to mention a few), and the ten most obvious possible consequences of value congruence.

Possible significant consequences of value incongruence	Possible significant consequences of perfect (or near-perfect) value congruence

BOX 4.1 THE VALUE OF VALUES IN THE COACHING EXPERIENCE

Dave Ulrich

A few years ago, I was honored to be invited to coach a high potential leader in a large company. He had many of the technical skills that predicted success, but the executives felt that his softer skills could use improvement. So, he agreed to coaching. When I asked him why he was interested in being coached, he said because he was told it would be good for him. When I asked why I was considered as his possible coach, he said because I was known in some coaching circles and he could tell others he was being coached by me. It was my shortest coaching experience ever. When I left after cutting short my interview, I told the HR leader that this high potential individual was not prepared to be coached or to learn. He saw coaching not as a commitment to change but as another "check" on his rise to executive ranks and his name-dropping of his coach as a point of personal pride.

I have often reflected on this experience. What did I learn? I realized the "value of values" in coaching and being coached.

Value focuses outside; values come from within. Value emphasizes what others get from our efforts; values emphasize who we are. Value can be created and developed through innovation and hard work; values are generally inherited and may be honed through self-awareness and experience. Values can be measured by impact; values are measured by the strength of our character. Value derives from the worth of our work to stakeholders; values reflect the worth of our work to us.

As a coach, my value is created when I help those I coach understand their values and learn how to use their values to create value for others. When my values as a coach do not align with the values of those I coach, the experience will fail for both of us.

As a coachee, the value of coaching comes not only from learning about oneself but also from learning how one's personal values (and style, behaviors, and predispositions) do or do not create value for others. Being coached requires being willing to look into a value mirror to determine how one can make personal changes that help others.

To understand the value of values, we believe we have to start with the "why" question. Psychologist Wendy Ulrich and I spent the last few years trying to figure out why people work and how their reasons for work both reflect their values and affect the value they create for others. We discovered that people find more value in, derive more value from, and add more value to their work when they know why they do it.

In the book *The Why of Work*, we identify seven factors—and corresponding questions—leaders can explore to become meaning-makers who help employees recognize the values that drive them at work and thus deliver more value from the work they do. Exploring these factors and asking these questions (slightly revised for coaches) can provide coaches and coachees personal insights about how their personal values can help them deliver more value through coaching:

1. **Identity:** What do I want to be known for as a coach? How does my approach to coaching reflect my strengths so that they will strengthen others? How can I help my clients (coachees) better recognize their strengths and use them to serve others?

2. **Purpose:** What do I want to accomplish as a coach? What do I want my clients to be able to know more and/or do more after my coaching experience? How do I help my clients recognize and clarify their personal aspirations and definitions of success?

3. **Relationships:** How can I form personal relationships with those I coach in a professional setting? How can I overlook the foibles of those I coach and care for them? How can I help those I coach learn to surround themselves with personal relationships that are supportive?

4. **Work environment:** How do I coach individuals so that they can understand and adapt to the work environment in which they work? How can I build a positive work environment in the microcosm of the coaching experience? How can I help my clients be sensitive to the work environment they create by their actions and decisions?

5. **Work itself:** What is it about coaching that is energizing and exciting to me as a coach? What do I like about the work that I do? How do I help my clients discover the work that energizes them?

6. **Learning and growth:** What am I learning as a coach? How am I different because of each coaching experience? How can I help my clients desire and recognize their learning agility?

7. **Fun:** How can I have fun even in the midst of demanding coaching assignments? How can I help my clients recognize the playful side of their lives even as they accept increased responsibilities and accountabilities?

In the *Why of Work*, we argue that leaders who resolve these seven domains become meaning-makers who build abundant organizations that make cents (money) and sense (purpose). I suggest that coaches and coachees who reflect on these questions will discover that coaching is a way to create the value of values.

If the individual I had met and did not coach worked through these questions or if I had been more explicit about them, both he and I would have had a better experience.

Dave Ulrich is a professor of business administration at Ross School of Business, University of Michigan, and co-founder of the RBL Group. He serves on the board of directors of Herman Miller and the board of trustees of Southern Virginia University and is a Fellow of the National Academy of Human Resources. He has written 23 books that cover topics in HR, leadership, and organizations. For more on Ulrich, his work, and his publications, visit www.daveulrich.com.

4.3 Value alignment and positive outcomes

4.3.1 Value alignment and positive organizational outcomes

The term *value alignment*, or as it is often called in the coaching field, *value congruence* or *value fit*, has received much attention lately from both scientists and business leaders. The concept of value congruence is intuitive; when there is a match between the employee's and the organization's value systems, positive outcomes will result. In this section, I will explain the benefits of value congruence—and the negative consequences of values incongruence—as I see them.

In previous chapters, we saw that both individuals and organizations have value systems that dictate their attitudes and behaviors and the ways in which they allocate resources. Research has shown that value congruence can lead to several valuable outcomes for both the organization and the individual[3]:

- **Job satisfaction**: Job satisfaction is a positive emotional experience associated with one's job. Satisfied employees are more productive and experience less stress than dissatisfied employees.
- **Organizational identification and commitment**: Organizational identification derives from an employee's sense of belonging to the organization. Employees who feel like they belong are likely to be more committed to the organization, more productive, and more likely to engage in extra-role behaviors—helping behaviors that go beyond the duties of one's position.
- **Intent to stay**: Intent to stay is an employee's intent to remain with the organization over some period of time. Intent to stay is contingent on job satisfaction and organizational identification.
- **Performance**: When a person has the knowledge and skills to perform well, value congruence can lead to even better performance by positively affecting job satisfaction, organizational identification, and commitment.

- **Reduced conflicts**: Value congruence decreases conflicts. Group value consensus has been found to be a key factor in reducing conflicts.

Although the link between value congruence and positive organizational outcomes has been firmly established, until recently, it was not clear how value congruence leads to such outcomes. Some research studies indicate that value congruence directly affects positive organizational outcomes, while other research proposes that value congruence results in positive outcomes indirectly by enhancing communication and trust between the organization and the employee. Figure 4.3 shows the proposed sequence from value congruence to positive outcomes.

Recently new positive outcomes of value congruence have surfaced in the work and organizational behavior literature: OCB (organizational citizenship behavior) and enhanced work engagement. Early evidence suggests that when value congruence occurs between an employee and his or her organization, organizational citizenship behaviors result. These are behaviors that go beyond an employee's written job description and are not a part of his or her formal job requirements. They contribute to overall organizational functioning. The ability of managers to direct the values of employees toward organizational goals greatly affects the degree to which the employees engage in OCBs throughout their careers.

Work engagement is a positive, fulfilling, work-related state of mind that is characterized by vigor, dedication, and absorption. The findings of scholars studying work engagement suggest that engaged workers have high energy, high self-efficacy, and a positive attitude about work and life. Despite the lack of systematic research connecting the two, my experience has shown that there is a strong link between value congruence and work engagement. In its highest form, it can become what positive psychologists call "flow." Flow is

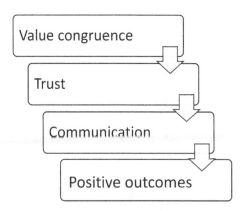

Figure 4.3 Proposed chain from value congruence to positive outcomes.

the mental state of operation in which a person in an activity is fully immersed in a feeling of energized focus and complete involvement in the process of the activity and is able to achieve goals and objectives successfully. Flow is completely focused motivation. It is single-minded immersion and represents perhaps the ultimate in harnessing emotions in the service of performing and learning. When one is in flow, his or her emotions are not just contained and channeled but positive, energized, and aligned with the task at hand. The hallmark of flow is a feeling of spontaneous joy, even rapture, while performing a task.[4]

In sum, individuals are more comfortable in organizations that are consistent with their own values. The congruence of personal and organizational values enables employees to feel a connection to the company and its mission. To gain a competitive advantage within the industry, organizations need employees who will go well beyond their expected work responsibilities. Aligning values and enhancing congruence seem to lead to multiple direct and indirect positive outcomes.

4.3.2 Does value congruence enhance mental and physical health?

With the emergence of positive psychology,[5] we are learning more and more about the positive aspects of health and well-being. Value congruence leads to work engagement, which has been found to enhance mental health as well as psychosomatic health. Value congruence also leads to relative happiness, which in turn has been correlated with both mental and physical health.

Positive psychology focuses on positive emotions, strengths, and good mental health, all of which are related to value congruence. Happiness and life satisfaction are linked to value congruence. My colleagues and I have seen that value congruence coupled with support and optimism leads to faster recovery following surgery. Although some people take it even further and suggest that there is a link between positive psychology and cancer survival, this has yet to be proven.

While wellness is experienced at the individual level as happiness, joy, health, and longevity, many of its causal factors extend well beyond the individual. Similarly, while wellness promotion strives to increase the joy, health, and longevity of individuals, its strategies go well beyond the individual and include environmental, social, and other collective interventions because the etiology of wellness and well-being depends on, among other factors, value congruence (the social environment) and the physical environment.

Research stemming from positive psychology on subjective well-being, positive affect, and life satisfaction; the development of the Values in Action Classification of Strengths; and the study of how those strengths can be applied by individuals to improve their social interactions are all very important additions to the evolving explanation of the enhancement of well-being.[6]

4.4 The negative consequences of value incongruence

One thing is certain: a prolonged state of value incongruence leads to stress, and stress is a condition that debilitates the body and the soul. I have written many articles and books on the sources and consequences of stress (at work), and as I mentioned in the last chapter, I am convinced that the latter negatively affects our physical and mental health.[7]

There has been ample research on stress in the past 30 years or so, even if—as I suggested in the previous chapter—the knowledge it has generated has not permeated our lives and work. Interestingly, though, the medical and biological literature has started to borrow concepts from psychology and sociology, such as stress, to explain the mutation of cells (or diseases). Traditional medical textbooks classify diseases by the affected organ or system, and frequently by the agent involved, for example, viral and bacterial diseases. But increasingly, mental and physical diseases are appearing that cannot be explained sufficiently in this manner—among them some illnesses that we now know are related to

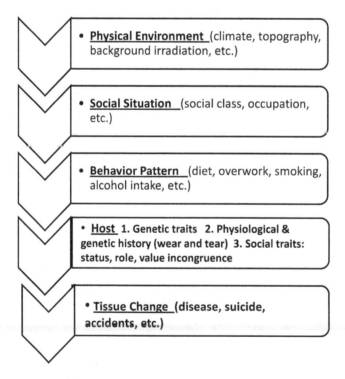

- **Physical Environment** (climate, topography, background irradiation, etc.)
- **Social Situation** (social class, occupation, etc.)
- **Behavior Pattern** (diet, overwork, smoking, alcohol intake, etc.)
- **Host** 1. Genetic traits 2. Physiological & genetic history (wear and tear) 3. Social traits: status, role, value incongruence
- **Tissue Change** (disease, suicide, accidents, etc.)

Figure 4.4 The etiological chain. Source: Modified from Saxon, G. (1974, November) The sociological approach to epidemiology. *American Journal of Public Health*, 64(11), 1046–1049.

stress. The models of diseases have changed, and the new paradigm includes the social phenomenon involved in the etiology of a disease. One of the social factors that has been identified in this context is value incongruence (see, for example, Figure 4.4, which shows the proposed etiological chain of disease published in a 1974 medical journal).

When an individual experiences chronic value incongruence, the likelihood of health-related problems increases dramatically. In our own research, my colleagues and I found out that nurses who felt trapped in their jobs (they wanted out because of value incongruence), but were forced to stay in their positions because of economic needs, experience a higher level of job burnout and also have an incidence of metabolic syndrome higher than expected given their age.[8] Metabolic syndrome is a key predictor of heart disease and type 2 diabetes. Burnout—an unpleasant and dysfunctional condition that both individuals and organizations would like to avoid—has been established as a stress phenomenon. It presents a pattern of health correlates one would expect to find with the following conditions: headaches, gastrointestinal disorders, muscle tension, hypertension, cold/flu episodes, and sleep disturbances, among others. Stress phenomenon is also a form of mental distress characterized by (a) a predominance of dysphoric symptoms such as emotional exhaustion, (b) a predominance of mental and behavioral symptoms, and (c) decreased work performance resulting from negative attitudes and behaviors.

The scientific evidence for the negative outcomes of chronic value incongruence for both organizations (e.g., productivity loss, or incapacity to retain talent) and individuals (e.g., likelihood of mental and physical diseases) is overwhelming.[9] I am not talking about a form of temporary or transitory incongruence; I am talking about a permanent feeling or a permanent perception. Just think about yourself. What do you think will happen to you if you feel completely and continually incongruent with your partner? With your family and friends? With your organization or your community? The likelihood that it will affect your mental and physical health is very high.

Despite the obvious connections, the relationships between values, cognition, stress, and illnesses are complex and not fully understood. But science is advancing our understanding of psychological experiences. We now know that these experiences in some ways both arise from (or are manifestations of) and affect brain chemistry and biology. It appears that cognitions leading to stress influence biology. A basic example of this is that when we are stressed, we experience muscle tension and increased heart rate. The strength of the relationship between thoughts and pathologies such as cancer cannot yet be determined, and because of this, I'd view any absolute statements about this with healthy skepticism. Nonetheless, coaching advice and interventions to improve psychological health by reducing incongruence among values will likely be beneficial not only for enhancing mental health and quality of life but also potentially for increasing physical health. This is not to suggest that coaches are therapists, but it is important to recognize that reducing incongruence will have multiple positive effects on overall health.

Several theories from different research fields in management, psychology, and medicine claim that human beings are generally inclined to reduce cognitive or motivational discrepancies and that such incongruences are associated with negative outcomes such as psychological distress or dissatisfaction. So, by and large, high levels of incongruence are hypothesized to be an essential cause of the formation and maintenance of a variety of psychopathological symptoms.[10]

CLBV Reflection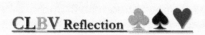

Discovering congruence: Write your obituary

Here is an interesting way to self-diagnose congruence and incongruence in your life. To do this, you need to be (a) totally honest and (b) creative.

As a celebration of life, help write your obituary. Think of what others in your life will say:

1.   About the differences between what you say and what you do
2.   Which key values they would have liked you to exhibit to be congruent with their expectation?

What would your life partner say about you?	
What would your children say about you?	
What would your friends say about you?	
What would your coworkers (or business partners) say about you?	
What would your parents say about you?	
What would your neighbors say about you?	

When you have completed it, post this form on your refrigerator for members of your family and e-mail it to friends, neighbors, and colleagues. Let each of them respond and correct. Then ask yourself, "Do I need to make any adjustments?" After reflection and discussion with your coach (or friends and family), make a shorter list of adjustments you need to make.

My coherent behavior and legacy:

I want to be remembered for ...

Discuss this short legacy with your coach (or family and friends) and use the analysis to plan future changes in your behavior; it is another exercise in value alignment.

4.5 Conclusion

The name of the game is value realignment. Throughout this chapter, I have tried to show why we need to pause, assess our values, compare them with those of our cultures or environments (partner, family, colleagues, organization, or the entire community) and see if there are discrepancies, or incongruences, that require realignment. I showed that poor alignment will likely negatively affect our health and the people around us. Also, our productivity will suffer. Alternatively, while it is not certain that enhancing congruence will lead directly to enhanced well-being, the likelihood that it will is high, and certainly it will enhance wellness and general happiness. There is strong evidence that in work contexts, congruence between a person's values and those of his or her job, work, or organization leads to more meaningful work, higher levels of engagement, and improved performance.

In the next chapter, I will show how you can put value congruence to work in your organization, in your family, or even in your community using techniques for value realignment. Value realignment is not entirely a new concept. But the methodology I present in this book, based on the triaxial model, is unique. I will describe this methodology in detail in the next chapter.

CLBV Reflection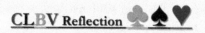

Think of the key message(s) you retained after reading this chapter. Then complete the following sentences:

The principal points I liked in this chapter include:

1. _____

2. _____

3. _____

The principal points that I did not like or disagreed with in this chapter include:

1. _____

2. _____

3. _____

Notes

1 By a more integrated design, I mean one in which relevant aspects of control and development are woven together throughout the organization.
2 For a more thorough discussion of vision and mission, see Dolan, S. L., Garcia, S., & Richley, B. (2006). *Managing by Values: Corporate Guide to Living, Being Alive and Making a Living in the 21st Century.* Palgrave Macmillan.
3 This summary is based on two excellent pieces of research: Edwards, J. R., & Cable, D. M. (2009). The value of value congruence. *Journal of Applied Psychology, 94*(3), 654–677; Bao, Y., Vedina, R., Moodie, S., & Dolan, S. (2013, March). The effect of value congruence on individual and organizational well-being outcomes: An exploratory study among Catalan nurses. *Journal of Advanced Nursing, 69*(3): 473–497; Dolan, S. L. (2016, July). Reflections on leadership, coaching and values: A framework for understanding the consequences of value congruence and incongruenece in organizations and a call to enhance value alignment. *The Study of Organizations and Human Resource Management Quarterly, 2*(1): 56–74.
4 To read more about the concept of flow, see Csikszentmihalyi, M. (1988). The flow experience and its significance for human psychology. In Csikszentmihalyi, M., & Csikszentmihalyi, I.S. (eds.) *Optimal Experience: Psychological Studies of Flow in Consciousness.* Cambridge University Press, pp. 15–35.
5 Positive psychology defines itself as a "science of positive subjective experience, positive individual traits, and positive institutions" that seeks to "understand and build the factors that allow individuals, communities, and societies to flourish."
6 Seligman, M. E. P., & Csikszentmihalyi, M. (2000). Positive psychology: An introduction. *American Psychologist, 55,* 5–14.

7 Dolan, S. L. (2007). *Stress, Self-Esteem, Health and Work*. Palgrave Macmillan; Dolan, S. L., & Arsenault, A. (2009). *Stress, Estime de soi, Santé et Travail*. Presse de l'Université du Québec; Moodie, S., Dolan, S. L., & Arsenault, A. (2011). Exploring the multiple linkages between metabolic syndrome and stress: An empirical analysis of the relationships between stress, health, and metabolic syndrome among Catalan nurses, Document presented at the *International Conference on Prehypertension and Cardio-metabolic Syndrome*, Vienna, 24–27 of February; Moodie S., Dolan, S. L., & Burke, R., (2014). Exploring the causes, symptoms and health consequences of joint and inverse states of work engagement and burnout. *Management Research: The Journal of the Iberoamerican Academy of Management, 12*(1), 4–2.

8 Moodie, S., Dolan, S. L., and Arsenault, A. (2011). Exploring the multiple linkages between the metabolic syndrome and stress: An empirical analysis of the relationships between stress, health, and metabolic syndrome among Catalan nurses, *First International Conference on Prehypertension and Cardio Metabolic Syndrome (PreHT)*. Vienna.

9 For a very good synthesis of this theme, see Bao, Y., Dolan, S. L., & Tzafrir, S. (2012). Value congruence in organizations: Literature review, theoretical perspectives, and future directions. *ESADE Working paper # 239* (http://proxymy.esade.edu/gd/facult ybio/publicos/1351517718381Value_congruence_in_organizations_Literature_rev iew_theoretical_perspectives_and_future_directions.pdf).

10 Dolan, S. L. (2016, July). Reflections on leadership, coaching and values: A framework for understanding the consequences of value congruence and incongruence in organizations and a call to enhance value alignment. *The Study of Organizations and Human Resource Management Quarterly, 2*(1): 56–74; Moodie, S., Dolan, S. L., & Burke, R. (2014). Exploring the causes, symptoms and health consequences of joint and inverse states of work engagement and burnout. *Management Research: The Journal of the Iberoamerican Academy of Management, 12*(1), 4–2.

Chapter 5

Methodologies and tools for everyone

5.1 Values and success in the life of business and the business of life
5.2 CLBV methods for reengineering the business of life
5.3 The Gift of Values: A coaching enrichment module
5.4 The history, validation studies, and co-evolution of the 3E triaxial model of values
5.5 CBV processes, methods, and tools for reengineering the life of business
5.6 Values and ethics in organizations
5.7 Conclusion

5.1 Values and success in the life of business and the business of life

Throughout this book, I have emphasized that values act as our compass. This compass keeps us on course every single day and brings us back on track when we've drifted away. If we follow our compass, each day we will move in a direction that takes us closer to what we envision as the "best" life possible. This best, of course, is highly individual. Your best may not be—and likely isn't—my best. And even though neither of us may ever reach our ideal, as we proceed along the path toward it, we will enjoy increasingly positive states of well-being.

Much of life exists on a continuum. There are some discrete markers like marriage or having children: One is either married or not married (though even this may have shades of gray, and marriage means different things to different people in different cultures); one either has children or doesn't. But most things are achieved gradually: Health, financial status, relationship intimacy, and happiness come in degrees; they are changeable; they get better and worse. Rarely can anyone instantly achieve the state of "best" in any of these areas. But one hopes that, cumulatively, the "betters" increase throughout one's life. I think it is safe to say that, for most of us, more is better than less, whether it is health, happiness, wealth, intimacy, inner peace, or love.

Moreover, because everyone has a different definition of the best life, some things mean more to one person than to another. For some people, good health is an absolute must. For others, being compassionate is most important.

And for each of these values, every person is at a different point along his or her own continuum. Let's go back to the metaphor of the airplane in chapter 3. Imagine that there are now several airplanes in the air, each having taken off from a different location and each heading towards a different destination airport—a different best. It's impossible to plot one course that would bring every plane to its destined airport. Each plane requires its own individual course.

Continuing this conceit, let's say that the planes and their routes represent not different people but the trajectory of different values in an individual's life. Each person is in a different state of health right now, and each person is aiming for a different best possible state of health. So the course each person takes from his or her unique starting point to attain her own best state of health will be different. Because we cannot do everything at once and because we have limited time, we have to prioritize. We may not be able to land all the planes within the span of our lives because we most likely do not know how long our lives will be, nor can we be certain how long it will take us to land each of these planes. But the closer we bring each plane to its destination airport, the better that area of life will be.

The journey to your values: A generic methodology, a dyad method, and corporate action plans

In this chapter, I hope to give you a deep understanding of the processes of alignment and realignment, or reengineering. I will set the stage by laying out an overall methodology, which can be transferred to various settings, cultures, and environments by adjusting the procedures involved. This step-by-step process will show you how to create a personal values hierarchy and align it with your goals. You can use it to get a sense of whether your life, in general, is going in the direction you want to take, and you can use it to analyze specific areas of life (e.g., work, marriage, friendships, and other relationships); with this basic method, you will be able to create a values hierarchy for any context or culture and to determine whether it is congruent with yours. This is the generic Coaching and Leading by Values (*CLBV*) method.[1]

You can work through the *CLBV* process with or without a coach; I will point out steps for which a coach's intervention may be helpful. If you are working through it yourself but at the end fail to achieve congruence, you may then want to seek out a coach. Professional coaches may find this process useful both in their practices and in their lives.

I will also present an encapsulated step-by-step dyad model for coaching in pairs—the coach and the coachee. This model follows the basic outline of the generic model and can be successfully transferred to couples, friends, teams, and larger groups, as I will show you.

After describing the in-depth generic Coaching by Values model and the brief *CLBV* dyad model, I will provide examples of concrete action plans I use in corporate enterprises as part of Managing by Values (*MBV*). This section of the chapter applies to coaches, managers, and leaders. When engaging in culture reengineering in the corporate (for-profit or large nonprofit organizations) world, even a professional coach may want to collaborate with a business consultant or a leader or a manager in the organization who has been trained in transformational change.

Before we delve deep into the *CLBV* methodology, I should let you know that going through this process will take a while as it requires concentrated attention. If this is not a good time for you to do this, come back to this chapter later. Even if you think you don't have time now, read just the first step; in fact, you might discover that you are so engaged you can't stop reading! It will help you begin to answer the question "What is important in my life?."

5.2 CLBV methods for reengineering the business of life

The generic CBV methodology

The generic Coaching by Values methodology is graphically displayed in Figure 5.1, which shows the progression of the process.

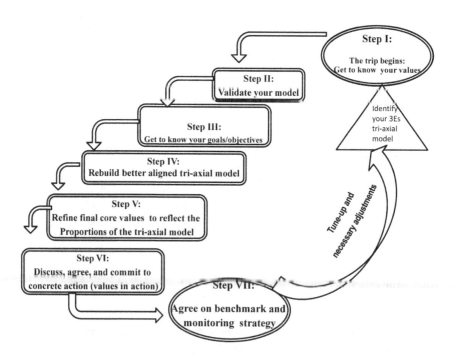

Figure 5.1 Coaching and Leading by Values: The generic process.

Step I: Get to know your preferred values: The journey begins with or without a coach. The idea is to be involved in the process through which you will get to know your preferred values. To do this, you need to do some brainstorming to identify your preferred values. Then you need to answer the question, what is truly important to me in my life? This is a question that you will be asking throughout this generic process.

Step Ia. *List your values*: To make this task easier for you, my colleagues and I have put together an extensive list of values, which you'll find in Appendix 1. We suggest that you select 10 from the list of 51 possible values. Do not worry about the order of your list at this stage. Just put everything down in writing. Remember we are talking about preferred, or *core*, values. If you are in a rush, the same exercise can be done by selecting only five values. Otherwise, the step-by-step methodology will become too complicated to manage.

You might end up with a list that looks something like this:

- health
- wealth
- playfulness
- happiness
- economic success
- care
- generosity
- adventure
- security
- empathy

There is no hard and fast rule for how long your list should be, but if it includes more than 5 to 10 values, consider shortening it. Are there some marginal values that barely made your list? Consider cutting those, or combine nearly identical values like achievement/accomplishment.

Step Ib. *Attribute meaning; build an initial triaxial model of your values*: In the previous chapters, we saw that there are different ways to analyze values. Here, I'm going to show you how to do this using my 3Es triaxial model discussed in chapter 4. Begin by placing the values in your list in the three dimensions, or axes, of the model (for the sake of this discussion, we'll use the values in the list below):

economic–pragmatic: wealth, economic success, security
social–ethical: care, generosity
emotional–developmental: health, playfulness, happiness, adventure, empathy

Next calculate each axis's percentage of the whole, according to the number of values we've placed in it. We see that the economic–pragmatic axis, with four values, comprises 30% of the total values; the social–ethical, with two values, comprises 20%; and the emotional–developmental, with five values, comprises 50%. Using the triaxial structure (i.e. a template is provided in Appendix 2), we connect these points (3, 2, 5) on each axis to form a triangle (note that the point at which the axes intersect is not given a number and the first number on each axis is 0). This becomes the initial triaxial model that will play an important role in your life. It is graphically displayed in Figure 5.2. You can use the template provided in Appendix 2 for repeated calculations.

Step II: Validation of the triaxial model: Again, this step can be done with or without a coach. Look at your 3Es model and ask yourself, "What are my dominating values? Are they economic, ethical, or emotional?" If you are not satisfied with your answer, either change some values by swapping them for others or assign new meaning to some of your originally selected values by reclassifying them—that is, by putting them in another family or dimension (axis). Now recalculate your triaxial model. This analysis is very personal. You need not consult other people during the classification phase.

In this step, we see one of the beauties of the 3Es triaxial structure. It gives you a visual way to begin to understand the "big picture." The number of values that fall in each axis (the percentage of your total values that each axis represents) shows you something that is essential to your life philosophy. What shape is the triangle? (Remember from chapter 2 that it will almost never be equilateral.) Which axis or axes dominate? Does one dominate in a way that seems disproportionate to you? Does this tell you something about yourself? Or does it not really reflect who you are? For example, you find that the values

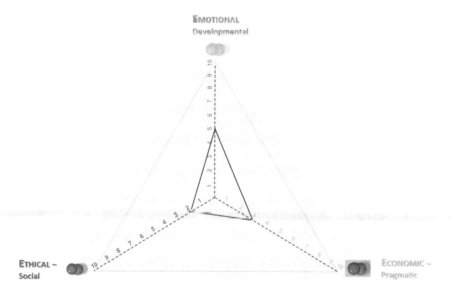

Figure 5.2 Sample-selected values represented proportionally Dolan 3Es triaxial model.

you chose in Step I fall mainly in the economic–pragmatic dimension, but you think of yourself as primarily an emotional, socially conscious person. Perhaps you'll want to choose new values more in sync with those dimensions. Or perhaps you will decide to reevaluate your sense of what is most important to you. As this process continues, you will revisit this again and again.

Step III: Define (and refine) your goals and objectives: This phase may require a professional coach (e.g., a life coach), but it can be done independently. Your life goals should be things you would really like to accomplish—maybe some things that you would love to attain and that you would be proud of.

Step IIIa. Define your goals: No two people have identical life goals/objectives, so I can only suggest a few ideas. Basically, you should look inside and see what your goals really are. Perhaps your life goals would look like this:

work: to have a job that I am very good at, that matches my talents, and that I love
career: to own my own company in the field in which I am most capable
money: to become a millionaire
romantic: to develop a deep relationship with someone that is really fulfilling
creative: to create something outstanding that is of great value to other people
social: to contribute to and help other people as much as possible
spiritual: to develop spiritually and to become a fully spiritually awake person

Step IIIb. Refine your goals: If you are not happy with your first list, change it. Refine it until you feel most comfortable, or satisfied, with it. This is a great opportunity to do some deep thinking about your goals. Go for it, keeping this in mind: Life goals can give you direction and success; they represent the experiences that you feel are part of the best life you could live—not just a good life or even a great life, the *best* life. The idea is to develop an optimum level of goals without setting unrealistic ones. Very often, people set unrealistic goals and dedicate their entire lives to achieving the unachievable. These people usually end up paying with their health. They suffer from burnout and stress—and the life-threatening (and sometimes life-ending) conditions these can lead to.[2] One of the tasks of a life coach is to engage the coachee in discussions about what is real, what is achievable, and what goal(s) should be abandoned.

Step IV: Rebuild a better aligned 3Es triaxial model: Having gotten a broad understanding of the big picture through your work on Steps I, II, and III, you are now ready to move on to a more refined analysis and to align your values with your objectives and goals.

Step IVa. Match your goals with your values: The books and scholars that dominate the field of coaching suggest that you derive your goals from your values. I recommend a more flexible approach—deriving both your values from your goals and your goals from your values. This is a more dynamic process. At a certain point, I realized that when I tried to use only the first approach, I ended up being more frustrated. I always felt I was missing something, because my static values list never seemed to allow me to achieve certain goals. Eventually, I figured out that goals can be adjusted, and values can also be adapted to fit those goals; when a goal is reached, then a whole new values hierarchy can be created. In this step, rethink your values by considering the goals you identified above. Select the values that you believe will most likely help you achieve those goals.

As a university professor, I always wanted to achieve the goals of first getting tenure and then becoming a full professor which is the top in the rank. When I had achieved both goals, becoming one of the youngest full professors at the university where I taught, I realized the process of getting tenure was not congruent with my values of playfulness, creativity, and being an agent for social change. After receiving tenure, I decided to never again engage in projects that don't generate creativity, playfulness, and opportunities for social change, and I placed the economic–pragmatic values on the back burner, as their relative proportion in my 3Es model had been significantly diminished. This does not mean that I wouldn't have done all the hard work necessary to get tenure and become a full professor over again if I had the choice. This work allowed me to concentrate more effectively and enjoy more deeply the emotional–developmental and ethical–social values I'd put aside during that time. Now, I could re-embrace those values and bring them to the top of my hierarchy.

Step IVb. Recalculate your triaxial model to match your goals: Select the final 3Es model that will make you happy. For the sake of this discussion, let us say its proportions are 60% emotional–developmental (EMO), 20% economic–pragmatic (ECO), and 20% ethical–social (ETH), which are different from those in Step I. Now do you see the problem with having a static list of values throughout your entire life. How is a single list of values going to allow you to be aligned with all your goals? The values that will make you a millionaire probably are not the same ones that will get you married. At some point in your life, however, you will need to focus intently on one of these goals while letting the others slide.

Although there will always be challenges and you may have some doubts, you need to get to the point in your evaluation that you are comfortable with the match between your 3Es model of values and your refined goal(s). The task of a coach is to help you achieve this.

Step V: Refining your core values: The next step is to prioritize your individual list of core values and create your hierarchy of values. This is a time-consuming and difficult step because it requires some intense thinking. A coach can be instrumental in helping you reflect on the choices you will be making here. The core values you decide to use here should be limited to five, six, or seven. You may select them from your original list or choose values that were not included in that list. What is important is that you select these values in proportion to your corrected triaxial model from the previous step.

Next, begin to construct a hierarchy of your values by asking yourself these questions: Which of these values is truly the most important to me in my life? If

I could only satisfy one of these values, which one would it be? The answers to these questions are your number one value. Once you have identified the top value, move on to the second-highest value, and so on, until you have sorted your values into a hierarchy from the top to the bottom.

Sometimes the highest priority value will be obvious to you. At other times you will have it narrowed down to a few choices but will have a hard time figuring out which one is really the most important among those. If that happens, try to be creative by inventing a scenario for each value, and then comparing those scenarios. An experienced coach can develop these scenarios for you if you need help.

For example, if you are trying to decide which is more important to you, health or wealth, ask yourself, which would I rather do—spend my time exercising and traveling to health food or whole food stores to get healthy food, or spend my time thinking about how to generate more money? This example assumes that exercising and trying to get healthy food would satisfy your value of health and that making an effort to engage in business opportunities would satisfy your value of accumulating more wealth, each to roughly the same degree. Creating scenarios such as these can help in listing the tough-to-prioritize values, and the best ordering becomes evident.

So, let us say we have sorted our list, and respecting the proportions of the final triaxial model in Step IV (60% EMO, 20% ECO, and 20% ETH), we have come up with the following priority list:

1. health (EMO)
2. playfulness (EMO)
3. happiness (EMO)
4. wealth (ECO)
5. care (ETH)

Getting to this point can tell you a lot about yourself. When you understand your values hierarchy, you should have a fair chance of predicting your behavior. The questions are as follows: Do you really live (truly and honestly) your values? Do you, for example, make a constant daily effort to improve or maintain your health (first priority on your list)? Do you engage in situations permitting you to have fun (playfulness; second priority on your list)? Are you happy (your third priority)? Do you take the necessary initiative and accomplish what you can to enhance your wealth (your fourth priority)? Can you list ways in which you show care for others (your fifth priority)?

If you have answered yes to these questions, you are experiencing value congruence: Your values are well aligned with your life. But if your core values, those that you've decided are the most important and meaningful to you, are not aligned with your daily life (are not realized in your behaviors), then you are living in a situation of misalignment, or incongruence. This, as we've seen, can take a heavy toll on your happiness and well-being. And to reverse this, so you can lead a more satisfying and healthier life, you will need a considered and thorough process of realignment.

Step VI: Values in action: If you get to this step and congruence is apparent, you have reached the end of the process. Your values seem to be aligned with your goals and objectives. You can always, and will probably want to, repeat this process in the future, to ensure continuous alignment. But if your values are not aligned with your life, it is time to think about taking concrete behavioral measures (actions) to bring about congruence so that you are "walking the talk" and your behavior is consistent with your values.

When you decide to commit to change, it will help to (a) form concrete plans (actions), (b) define a time frame for accomplishing actions, and (c) identify major challenges you will need to overcome. This can be done alone, but an experienced coach may make the process much easier by providing a variety of techniques, tools, and incentives for change and by helping you establish your timetable. Most coaches work with a preferred methodology, ranging from the simple GROW model to the very nuanced and complex NPL, from Emotional Intelligence to Appreciative Inquiry. Some coaches are eclectic and employ a variety of techniques and approaches depending on the situation and the client. In chapter 1, I provided an overview of a few of these, to give you an idea of what is available. In the next section, I will show you some concrete action plans I use in the context of organizational change. Once you agree on specific actions, you need only start the change process. But to make sure you stay on course; you will want to put in place a monitoring plan.

Step VII: Define the criteria for success and design monitoring follow-up: The final step is (a) establishing a time frame for assessing your progress and fine-tuning your action plan if necessary, (b) choosing benchmarks to meet along the way, and (c) deciding on general criteria for success. A coach will clearly be helpful during this period.

The CBV dyad process: A method for reengineering the business of life

The generic model described in the last section can be used by a single person without a coach. However, the process can be made easier and smoother with a coach's help. The following is an example of a coaching process that follows the general outline of the generic *CBV* model. In this example, the objective is to increase congruence between a coachee's values and her goals in her couple's relationship. It can, naturally, be applied to any context—such as family, life, business, community—as I will describe later.

We will use the following symbols to represent the coach and the coachee:

☺   Coach
♀♂   Coachee

☺   **Step 1:** The coach provides a list of values.
♀♂   **Step 2:** The coachee selects five or ten values from the list (see Appendix 1).
☺♀♂   **Step 3**: The coachee, with the help of the coach, builds an initial triaxial model.

☺♀♂   **Step 4:** The coach and the coachee begin a dialogue to ensure that the model is valid. They correct the triaxial model.

☺♀♂   **Step 5:** The coach and the coachee discuss the meaning of success in a specific area of life or work (in this example, in her partner relationship). The coachee, with the help of the coach, defines her meaning of success in this relationship. This becomes the goal for the remainder of the coaching.
♀♂   **Step 6**: After a dialogue with the coach, the coachee selects five values reflecting her perception of her partner's primary values regarding the relationship. A triaxial model is constructed based on these values. This is the partner's value model.

☺♀♂   **Step 7:** The coach and the coachee compare the two triaxial models. They identify and discuss congruence and incongruence. They craft action plans to reduce such incongruence.

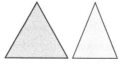

☺♀♂   **Step 8:** The Coach and the coachee (after some time has passed) discuss the experience and the actions the coachee has taken. They address problems she's encountered, agree on steps to realignment, and fine-tune her action plans.

Applying the CBV dyad process to larger groups

With some slight modifications, we can apply the same methodology to larger coaching contexts, such as couples coaching, family coaching, and coaching a team or even a larger unit. First, the coach works with both partners or with all members of the team together, facilitating group discussions and the building of triaxial models. After they define and establish overall goals, the coach works with members individually in dyad relationships.

Here are some suggestions for arriving at a diagnosis and crafting a strategy of alignment ("team" in the following can be a couple, family, group, or another system):

- The coach conducts a value audit of each member of the team.
- Each member of the team builds his or her own triaxial model based on his or her own preferred values.
- The team discusses current state and identifies values manifested in current team culture.
- Based on values detected in the previous step, the team develops an aggregate team culture triaxial model. This triaxial model represents the current *real* culture in the team.
- Members of the team begin a dialogue based on the triaxial model above. They identify gaps between their own models and the group model. They discuss the direction they'd like the group to go in and define success in the team. They agree on a final desired culture. This culture embeds the definition of success. The team selects five, six, or seven core values based on consensus.
- A coach works individually in a dyad relationship with each member of the team to help develop a strategy of value alignment. This can be done in a group if the coach has the skills to do the work with multiple coachees at the same time.
- The team, with the coach, discusses plans to reinforce and preserve the agreed-upon reengineered culture.
- Together they plan future monitoring, benchmarks, and fine-tuning.

The diagnosis based on the two triaxial models presented in Figure 5.3 shows that the dominant personal values are emotional–developmental (60%), followed by ethical–social (40%), with no economic–pragmatic values. The reality in the workplace is remarkable—and is quite different from the values of the team members. There is an 80% domination of economic–pragmatic values, followed by 20% ethical–social values, and *zero* emotional–developmental values. Although the team members individually like and enjoy passion and emotion, they are working in a culture that does not offer opportunities for their expression. **All my research points out that this situation is not sustainable.**

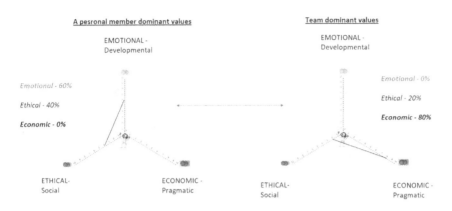

Figure 5.3 An example of work team diagnosis (n = 14 members).

5.3 The Gift of Values: A coaching enrichment module

Have you ever wondered what those gifts that you are either giving or receiving mean? A lot of people may not think about it and just buy anything if they have something to give. But every gift has a meaning, especially to those who are close and value their relationship a lot. Often, the monetary value of the gift is not relevant; it's the meaning that is more important. Christmas cards and birthday cards that you make yourself can be more meaningful than any expensive gifts.

Gifts can convey thoughts, feelings, and sentiments without words. Even cards are sometimes only graphical; they may contain no words, but the meaning behind them is clear. Actions such as helping someone build a garden or bringing soup to a sick friend, can also be gifts. Gifts symbolize expressions or feelings that are sometimes better shown through actions. Some of the expressions that gifts convey are the following:

- expression of love or friendship
- expression of gratitude for a gift received or favor
- expression of piety (in the form of charity)
- expression of solidarity (in the form of mutual aid)

What is the Gift of Values? The Gift of Values is a suggestion made by a coach (or by another person that knows the coachee well) to give/offer a value that they would like to see the coachee adopt in his or her daily life. Obviously the additional value will substitute another value and a new shape of the triaxial model will emerge. Remember, this can become part of a methodology that a coach, a partner, a work team colleague, or any other close person can use as feedback and food for thought; it can solidify the triaxial model, help increase alignment in the long run, and be an important element of the coaching process.

How does it work? After the coachee has built his or her triaxial model, it can be very important for him to understand how another person sees his values in action (behavior) and to understand what the other person expects him to exhibit, given his espoused values.

A coach can ask a person, "Now that I understand your values, will you be willing to accept a gift from me? Here is the value that I am proposing." This new value can change the proportions of the triaxial model. It can be very powerful for a couple when they are attempting to align their values. Because this gift comes from someone that one cares about (e.g., a partner, a colleague, a coach), the recipient will consider it seriously and likely be willing to incorporate the gift into his or her 3Es triaxial model.

I use the Gift of Values very often in my coaching sessions, and the results are outstanding; it makes the coachee aware of personal blind spots and shortcomings. It is one more step in reshaping and aligning the coachee's triaxial model, and the coachee can consider incorporating the gift into his or her final core values.

5.4 The history, validation studies, and co-evolution of the 3E triaxial model of values

Many people ask me when and how the triaxial model of values was born. The fact is that the first version saw the light in the late 1970s, and since then the model has been in constant dynamism and co-evolution: elements like the names of the axes of values have prevailed, but in everything else there have been important significant changes. In this section, I would like to trace this evolution.

The initial idea of the triaxial model of values was born out of a conversation I had with Salvador Garcia in the late 1990s when we prepared a Spanish version of the book *Managing by Values* (*La dirección por valores*). The book was eventually published in Spain by McGraw Hill (1997). At that time, I was still living in Canada and most of my exchanges with Salvador were done via the old internet technology. My own modest contribution was made in English, and Salvador managed the Spanish version of the book. Nonetheless, I understood that this was a breakthrough publication as an original book on management and on values, so I had convinced McGraw Hill to publish it. They dared to, after long hesitation because it was hard to convince the management series editor at McGraw Hill that values are part of management. The book turned out to be a big hit in the Ibero-American market and went through numerous printings.[3] Salvador and I became known in this market, and in the early 1980s I was invited by the government of Cuba (Fidel Castro was also involved) to visit the nation and talk about the concept. When I arrived in Cuba, I realized that our book was being used in all government ministries alongside an accompanying book *Managing by Ideological Values* that was put together by the Castro

regime. You can imagine how I must have felt: first, the original book was pla-
giarized (no royalties) and close to 70,000 copies were printed, and I had been
manipulated to actually push the other ideological book with a similar title. In
any event, as a guest of the Cuban government, I was very well treated. And,
although it has not been in the book, in my conferences in Cuba I talked about
the triaxial model to ensure that it is different from any other ideological model
of values. Having said that, I wish to reiterate that in the Spanish version the
triaxial model of values was not mentioned nor described, although Salvador
and myself started a conversation about such a model.

A few years later, each one of us (Salvador in Spain and myself in Canada)
began to experiment more with the triaxial values model in our workshops
and seminars. Although we did not have any empirically validated support to
our claim, we had noticed, independently, that the executives and participants
of our workshops liked the idea and found it useful. But, empirical validation
to either classify the values or explore the relationships between the axes was
missing.

In 2002, I left Canada and joined the faculty of ESADE Business School
(Barcelona); there, I was appointed to be the scientific director of the Institute
for Labor Studies. I thought that a golden opportunity was presented and had
decided that in addition to traditional labor relations research, I could add a
new line of research connected to work values and their impact on health and
productivity. In parallel in 2003, I negotiated with McGraw Hill to publish the
second edition of *Managing by Values* in Spanish, this time bearing the emblem
of ESADE, which gave more credibility to the book. Only minor editing was
affected. Still, the triaxial model of values was not presented as we thought it
was premature.[4]

That same year, in 2003, I managed to complete the first empirical test of
the triaxial model of values, using ESADE MBA students as my guinea pigs.
An ESADE MBA is very diverse and multicultural, and as I became more
and more interested in the field of Cross-Cultural Management, I wanted to
find out if work values are universal or, on the contrary, have different meanings in different cultures. This was the time that the field of Cross-Cultural
Management was dominated by the theory and framework of the Dutch-born
guru Geert Hofstede. Personally, I was skeptical about his claim that there is
a national model of culture and that in each culture there are some common
universal values; I thought that values are an individual and not a national
phenomenon. Moreover, I thought that in the same country, there are people
with different values, each behaving according to their own values. So, I have
undertaken a comparative study on values (in Catalonia and Andalusia) and
showed empirically what every Spaniard knows: that Catalan culture (shared
values) is different from Andalusian culture (shared values), and thus it is very
hard to talk about national Spanish values, as Hofstede claims. I think that my
assertion was well supported empirically.[5]

So, back to the ESADE MBA study. I developed a survey based on the triaxial model and passed it to a sample of about 120 MBA students; all had several years of work experience. It was the first empirical test of the triaxial model, and the results were encouraging. I published the results in an internal journal of ESADE.[6] The title of the article gave me the idea to reuse it later when we would be ready to publish the first book, *Managing by Values*, in English.

The next step in the development of the triaxial model was when I invited Bonnie Richley to join Salvador and me for an English version of the *Managing by Values* book. At this time Salvador had some health issues, so the synergy with Bonnie turned out to be very productive. Bonnie was a guest lecturer at ESADE and made great strides in her doctoral thesis with data collected in Mondragon (a giant cooperative located in the Basque Country, Spain). Implicitly, many of the concepts of values, including the triaxial model, served as a framework for the completion of her PhD thesis. One day after a conversation with Bonnie about the meaning of the axes, we developed the idea of the complementarity nature of values. That is to say: if the proportion of values is added to each axis, the total of the three axes must add up to 100%. That means that if your values dominate an axis, you have fewer core values than in the others. I always thought that the triaxial model of values is like Einstein's theory of relativity, which we apply to the world of values. The Universe of values has some finite borders, and there is a tradeoff between what is more important and what is relatively less important. The metaphor that came to my mind was a food buffet: Given that you cannot eat all that the buffet is offering, you come up with a configuration of selection that represents things such as what do you like, what is the cost, what is healthy, etc. With Bonnie Richley, we captured this idea in an article published in a Business Strategy handbook edited by Coats and published by Emerald in 2006.[7] I think that this was the first time that we used the words *triaxial model* in an explicit manner.

Thereafter, we have agreed that the time is right to include the new version of the triaxial model in the book that we were preparing in English for Palgrave Macmillan. Curiously, I was so impressed with the re-discovery of the triaxial model power that I had decided to add a subtitle to the book, which represents the mirror for the three axes. In addition, in English, it also sounds very harmonious and inspiring: *Managing by Values: A corporate guide to living (emotional axis), being alive (ethical–social axis) and making a living (economic axis) in the 21st century.*[8] The concept and the book were so successful that we received numerous requests to translate the book into other languages, and today it is available in Hebrew, Portuguese, French, Chinese, and Russian, among others. The triaxial model of values also became the symbol for the Game tool that I developed with my brother Avishai, which was called "the value of values" (see Appendix 3). Our graphic illustrator, Eitan Daniel, converted the triaxial model to the symbol of a juggler who is trying to juggle always three balls.

The concept became so powerful that we also developed over the years the methodology to be used in our card games. We have also used the image of the juggler (a metaphor for the triaxial model) at the beginning of each chapter in this book.

In 2008 I wrote a book with Toni Lingham, a professor from Case Western Reserve University in Cleveland and visiting professor at ESADE, on *International Organizational Behavior*. We have decided to include an entire chapter dealing with culture reengineering and the use of the triaxial model of values as part of the methodology.[9] In the same year, we also published, for the first time, an article with the explicit title Triaxial model.[10]

But, despite all the previous work, I was not yet satisfied. Up to this point, we had not achieved the academic rigor in clearly answering several questions:

• How are values in all three axes classified?
• Are there really some universal values that have similar meanings in different cultures?

- What are the relationships between the axes? Are we talking about zero sum (thereby discussing axes) relationships or are we talking about dimensions or factors where all values have similar meanings and importance?

Again, serendipity took place, and, in 2007, I was appointed the editor-in-chief of Emerald's *Cross Cultural Management: An International Journal*. So, in addition to the normal editorial role, I thought perhaps a great opportunity had been presented to me to undertake serious large-scale cross-cultural research on values. It was also the period that I was supervising numerous doctoral students at ESADE originating from distinct cultures (Israel, Spain, Peru, China, Germany, and more). Being the co-founder of *ISSWOV* (The International Society for the Study of Work and Organizational Values), I had excellent collaborators with value researchers in many countries in the world. So, the mega VAC (Values Across Cultures) project was born. After two years of preparing and creating a global team, we focused on cross-cultural studies, limiting the samples to only public sector employees in each country. The *VAC* study began in 2010–2011. Because of its complexity, size, and many other factors, it took almost two years to complete. For the first time, serious research outcomes were finally published in a special issue of the aforementioned journal (*CCM*) in 2013. I think it was the most rigorous scientific test of the essential elements of the triaxial model of values. If you are interested in knowing more and examining the methodology used for testing the triaxial model of values, I invite you to read the entire special issue.[11]

In parallel, and in 2011, the concept of *Coaching by Values* was born. The main difference in Coaching by Values from Managing by Values is the focus. In Coaching by Values the focus is on the person and his context (family, team, organization). But the flagship of the concept was the triaxial tool and the display of values on its corresponding template.[12] From this point on, we went through various iterations and some fine-tuning. For this purpose, we have invited many more practitioners and researchers to join the development of the model and to help refine it. The model resembles the concept of open innovation.[13] Co-evolution has many advantages as it means inviting people to apply the triaxial model of values in any setting, culture, or profession and share the experience. The Coaching by Values community has created a platform for this type of sharing and the results are astonishing. Throughout this book, we share contributions from professionals certified by us, who belong to the community of *Coaching by Values*, and based on their experience, we have developed methodologies that "hybridize" the triaxial model and adopt it in a precise manner in their corresponding field of specialization (education, family, company, sport, etc.). To see the variety of applications that have emerged from the triaxial model of values, I recommend reading the book that we wrote collectively after the IV Congress of "Coaching by Values," which was held in Barcelona in 2018. Unfortunately, the book is available only in Spanish.[14]

One of the latest empirical tests to substantiate the triaxial model of values was published using state-of-the-art statistical tools in 2019. In all honesty, the methodology is beyond my competence to follow. I provide the reference, in case any of you wish to delve deeper into the triaxial model of values, and into my hypotheses about the interactive effects of the axes, and see their impact on organizations' success.[15]

Since we developed our Star tool, the *value of values* game, we have been improving and refining it in each production. From an initial list of 100 values (first production), we reduced it to 60 cards (second production), and in our last production we noted that with 51 cards we can work very effectively (see Appendix 1). I have also written a tale for children *The Magic Carpet and the Islands of Values* (with my illustrator in India, Niharika Singh), which is based on the triaxial model of values and provides a tool for parents to instill values in their children using story telling.[16] We have translated the tale into about 18 languages with the help of collaborators, but many are only available in the form of an eBook. Finally, we have developed the first app which was released in 2018 called the *Values4kids*.[17] All these are extensions and applications of the triaxial model of values.

The triaxial model does not apply only to values. Over the years, I have learned that if you have a complex model to be presented, it could be of great instrumentality to reduce it to three axes, dimensions, factors, etc. There are those that claim that the so-called *Rhetorical Triangle* is credible, appealing, and logical, and thus determine the persuasiveness of an argument. Consequently, today it has become my favorite way of connecting with people whom I wish to help change or transform. I'm working on different triaxial models.

Throughout the book, you will notice that we are currently developing new triaxial models and applications. One that I have already finished is the triaxial model of trust (the RCH model which we have introduced in chapter 2—**R**eliability, **C**oncern, and **H**armony), where the basis is an investigation that we published jointly with Dr. Shay Tzafrir in 2004 which we have presented in Chapter 2.[18] Also, together with my partners David and Noelia Alonso, we developed in 2019 a tool based on triaxial models for business leaders. It is called "Leadership by Values" and it allows to measure online, in a very sophisticated way, three triaxial models, and all in 360°, which we also presented in more detail in Chapter 2. Just as a recall, leadership by values is a triaxial of the triaxials, hence it analyzes values, trust and leadership competencies (see www.leadershipbyvalues.com).

In 2020 we are planning to launch our newest triaxial tool that will apply to the management of stress, tentatively labeled: *The Stress Map*. The scientific concept and the theoretical basis for this new kit is research that I developed in Minnesota and Montreal, and I am currently following it up with various colleagues in Barcelona. My previous research on occupational stress management was published in tens of scientific journals and also synthesized in my book: *Stress, Self-Esteem, Health and Work*.[19] The tool attempts to make a very complex model parsimonious and converts it into a simple game that will help to discover the three key dimensions connected with the "density" of stress[20]: (a) its symptoms, (b) its origins, and (c) its moderators.

In conclusion, I would like to thank all my collaborators and readers for their interest in the triaxial model of values which is being used by more and more coaches, leaders and other professionals around the globe. I am sure that the co-evolution will continue, and more hybrid models will emerge in the future. I am thankful for the passion that fuels creativity, joy, and happiness and adds value to the quality of our lives. In Box 5.1, you can appreciate how Dr. Kristine Kawamura is working on her own model of values where the focus is on a single value—care, and which she has turned into a core concept for future coaching.

BOX 5.1 THE SYMBIOTIC RELATIONSHIP BETWEEN CARE AND VALUES

Kristine Marin Kawamura, PhD
Founder and CEO
Yoomi Consulting Group, Inc.

The traditional strategic goal of organizational leaders of profit-oriented firms has been to develop sustainable competitive advantage in order to max-imize shareholder wealth. To achieve this end, most leaders have used con-ventional, top-down planning rituals based on macroeconomic forecasting to develop and drive a strategy from goals to measurements; more lately, they have also used competency modeling or real options to determine alterna-tive strategies. Not only are these approaches grounded in a traditional, eco-nomic mindset of traditional business, they are also rooted in the assumption that human beings are rational and linear, emphasizing and valuing the "left-brain" aspects of human nature and behavior in their hierarchical planning processes. Leaders adopting these approaches, however, are ignoring three significant environmental forces:

1) Organizations in the developed world have already shifted from compet-ing within an industrialist-based economy to a *knowledge-service* society/economy, one in which knowledge and the ability to provide quality service to customers and stakeholders are the core resources of most firms. In this era, knowledge may be viewed as the more critical resource of an organization's strategy.[21]

2) Organizations in both the developed and developing worlds are also in the process of shifting to a *relational* society/economy, one in which

people, organizations, and communities are recognized as being not only individual but also relational at their core. Supported by technology, teaming, and cross-border partnerships, organizations in this era are fast-recognizing that their ability to support the development of healthy, productive, and caring relationships can become a significant and distinctive organizational capability.[22]

3) Leaders and organizations around the globe are being challenged by more complex, global, and "wicked problems"[23] such as climate change, migration, terrorism, inequality, and poverty that cannot be solved by traditional models or linear processes or by any individual leader, organization, or institution. Solving these problems requires that leaders use their individual capacities as well as share knowledge and work in relationship with others to begin to address the wicked problems about which they care.

So what is needed for organizations and people to thrive in this new reality?

A new paradigm: Leaders must shift their thinking and adopt a fundamentally new paradigm in how they view organizations and performance. Rather than seeing organizations as purely economic entities that develop product-market positions to compete in their marketplace, exploiting workers to maximize economic outcomes, leaders must first recognize that organizations are comprised of holistic human beings who work, relationally, in human value chains that span the globe. People at every level of an organization are both rational and emotional beings just as they are also spiritual and physical ones. We all thrive on the opportunity to live and work with our paradoxical natures: alone yet relational, competitive and cooperative, and logical and creative. We all want to do well in our work—to perform—yet we all want our contributions to make a difference in the world as well as to provide a sense of personal meaning. We long to find and fulfill our own unique destinies, yet we yearn to be part of something greater than ourselves.

Accordingly, organizations are also both economic and humanistic in nature; comprised of human beings operating in relationships with others, firms, too, are logical and rational as well as emotional and creative in nature. In order to unlock the potential of people and their firm resources, leaders need to expand their methods and toolkits for defining the strategies and resources that deliver sustainable competitive advantage. By adopting both left-brain and right-brain strategies, methods, and tools, they may unlock the fullest potential of the individuals and relationships that comprise organizations.

Values: One avenue for unlocking the right-brain capacity of firms and people is to bring values to the forefront of strategy development, management systems, and hiring and leadership development processes.

Values are usually defined as the enduring beliefs, or principles, that are held most dear to people, individually and collectively, at any given point in time[24]. They describe a personally or socially preferred mode of conduct or state of existence and are the foundation of an organization's culture as well as a primary source of an individual's sense of personal meaning. As such, values are cognitive in nature—structures of thought that develop and become more deeply rooted over years of learning and experience.

Values have been shown to bring value to corporations and individuals.[25] They help firms attract the best talent (people that want to be part of these particular values); align people to organizational purpose and mission; create happier, more engaged employees with higher levels of well-being; and realize higher levels of social responsibility and organizational performance. Values help people guide their thoughts, words, decisions, and actions and help them to grow and develop, to create the future we all want to live, and to define and give meaning to our lives.

We feel good inside about ourselves and our lives when our decisions reflect our values and beliefs. When we feel happier, we have stronger self-esteem, which, in turn, positively affects the attitudes and decision-making processes of those around us. Value congruence, or "value fit," between individual and organizational values is positively related to positive work attitudes, including employee satisfaction, commitment, and involvement as well as perceptions of workplace ethics.[26]

Care: Another essential organizational essential right-brain capacity of people and firms is care. Though care is something that most people recognize as important to them (and which has been studied in numerous disciplines including ethics, sociology, positive organizational psychology, feminism, and economics), it is only recently being studied with respect to leadership, work performance, and organizational strategy.[27]

I've defined care as:

> The heart-based feeling of loving-kindness, concern, and/or nurturing attention given to another person that occurs within a relationship between the one-caring and cared-for in a unique caring moment. This feeling, or emotion, that something or someone matters leads to the

inner feeling of commitment that one must do something—one must act—to nurture, to attend to, and/or to help a person or even an idea grow, actualize or develop. Caring can either be natural (like between a mother and her child) or be consciously generated—a choice to consciously relate to someone. ... When we care, we are fully present with another person; thus we are able to see and to listen to what's important to another person (their identity, values, and meaning model); we gain self-awareness, aware of our own presence, influence, and mirror in the relationship; and, we commit, we act, in the best interest of this person as well as others involved in the situation.[28]

Care, too, has been shown to bring value to individuals and organizations. With caring managers and organizations, employees are more engaged; they experience high levels of well-being and deliver increased performance.[29] In the health care industry, when patients feel cared about by their health care professionals, they have higher levels of emotional–spiritual well-being (dignity, self-control, personhood); enhanced physical healing (lives saved, safety, more energy, less cost, more comfort, less loss); and increased levels of trust in relationships. Nurses who are caring develop a sense of accomplishment, satisfaction, purpose, and gratitude. Through their caring work, they preserve integrity, fulfillment, wholeness, and self-esteem. They are more reflective and develop a love of nursing, a respect for life and death.[30] When working with clients in the Information Technology industry to develop and implement caring- and knowledge-based business, marketing, product, and sales strategies that enhance customer satisfaction, companies have realized up to 65% increases in sales productivity and great improvements in firm profitability. Furthermore, individuals with a history of caring relationships and the ability to foster them have been shown to experience economic success and strong mental and physical health; in other words, they live a flourishing life.[31]

So what is the relationship between values and care?

Both values and care have been studied by philosophers and ethicists in different and distinct traditions. The study of values arises from Western philosophical traditions that are based on moral reasoning and rationality, including Aristotle's notions of intellectual and moral virtues; Kant's ethics of deontology, or duty (acting according to principle); and Mill's utilitarianism. The study of care lies in a "feminine" or relational approach to ethics, where the source of care comes from the fundamental and natural desire for human beings to be and to remain related. Caring may arise from natural caring (such as that experienced between a mother and her child) or from ethical caring, which can be generated by choosing the ethical ideal (i.e., valuing a caring relation over other forms of relatedness).[32] Thus, the study of values and care has been dualistic in nature: reasoning and rationality versus feelings and relationality. This mirrors the traditionally dualistic separation of rationality and feeling—even the negligence of emotion—within the traditional business paradigm and definitions of success.

I believe, however, that there is a non-dualistic, symbiotic, and synergistic relationship between values and care[33] (Figure 5.4).

First, both care and values are related to how we see the world. Values are our cognitive drivers of behavior; they are related to how we *think* about the world. Care, on the other hand, is an emotional driver of behavior; it is related to how we *feel* about the world. Values and care, therefore, are concepts that may be understood individually yet they become more powerful when viewed as synergistic partners—when we, in fact, adopt a holistic view of human beings and organizations. What we most value and what we most care about bring meaning to us, thus the relationship between values and care symbolizes and also actualizes our need for both rational and feeling dimensions within our decision making, our work, and our value-creation processes.

Second, care helps us define what we value. In short, we value (in our minds) what we care about (in our hearts)! Our feelings will draw us toward what is most important to us; they will help us discern a hierarchy of values and will help us identify our level of commitment to each (e.g., low, medium, or high) in relationship to the others. Care also energizes our commitment to, and the actions arising out of, our values. Values or principles that are only mentally identified or verbally expressed will not be as deeply rooted in our lives and behaviors as those we feel and own in our bodies and hearts. When we only espouse the language of values, it will be very difficult to summon the courage needed to live them when "the going gets tough," when choices

Figure 5.4 A metaphor for the infinite relationship between values and care.

are tough. Values describe the ultimate reality in which we want to live. Care-based values fuel us to courageously make the choices, today, that are needed to create the future we want and value—to "present" this future in our current reality.[34]

Third, care lies at the core of healthy relationships. Care, in fact, energizes the development, nurturing, and longevity of relationships, whether between a person with his or her self, a colleague or team mate, a leader and manager, a customer or supplier, an organization, or a community.[35] Care nurtures people, ideas, and values. Care, therefore, can deepen the level of shared values, value congruence, and goal alignment created between a leader and manager, employee and organization, or employee and organizational goal.

Finally, care and values are the "twin sisters" of organizational and human transformation. When leaders want to transform an organization's culture or strategy, they often begin by creating a new vision and mission statement. Then, they articulate a set of core values and attempt to embed them in management practices, which they hope will reinforce those behaviors that will benefit the company and its communities, strengthen its vision and values, and even seek to solve "wicked problems." But how and why will people follow their leaders; why will they participate in the company's transformation process? When they know their organization and its leaders care about them; when all employees, in turn, care about the vision, mission, and values of the company; and when people care about their fellow colleagues, customers, suppliers, partners, and community, viewing their "stakeholders" as human beings. With people being able both to care and to share the values associated with transformation, they will engage, do their best work, and contribute as whole human beings—increasing profits and meaning while working together to solve more complex, "wicked problems" as a result.

Biography

Dr. Kristine Marin Kawamura is the Founder and CEO, Yoomi Consulting Group, Inc. Founded in 2016, Yoomi is a consulting, leadership development, coaching, and training company that helps clients transform their people, culture, and strategies to maximize financial, human, and social wealth and health. Yoomi uses its proprietary HumanNovation™ engagement system of Kawamura, K. to energize the untapped left- and right-brain potential of people, relationships, and firm resources to deliver "wow! value" across their clients' global ecosystems.

Dr. Kawamura was a visiting professor at Esade, Ramon Llull University, Barcelona, Spain; a research fellow and visiting professor at St. George's University, Grenada,

West Indies; and, a lecturer at Loyola Marymount University, Los Angeles, CA. Along with Dr. Simon Dolan, she is the author of *Cross Cultural Competence: A Field Guide for Developing Global Leaders and Managers* (Emerald Group Publishing Limited, 2015).

For more information, please contact kristine@yoomiconsulting.com.///

5.5 CBV processes, methods, and tools for reengineering the life of business

Before presenting the processes and methodologies in this section, I should add that they are likely beyond the knowledge and skill set of a traditional coach. They require an understanding of the dynamics of organizational change, including mechanisms and strategies to overcome resistance to change, so a coach will want to collaborate with an organizational consultant or transformational leader within the organization.

Culture reengineering

To survive in the twenty-first century, companies will have to develop a new way to operate a new culture. But changing the organizational culture is the toughest task managers or any organizational consultant (including a coach) may face. The organizational culture was formed over years of interaction among the participants in the organization. Changing the culture may be a problem either because the leaders of the organization do not see the need to change it or because they do not have the competencies to manage the change.

In the most interesting article published in the *European Business Forum*, J. Sheth and R. Sisodia attribute the increase in organizations that disappear— even those with a history of success are failing in greater numbers—to two principal causes: leadership's inability to change and leadership's unwillingness to do so.[36] Both leaders who do not have the competency and those who do not have the courage to engage in transforming their organizations and adapting to an increasingly complex environment are doomed to create the most stressful situation for their stakeholders: extinction. Figure 5.5 presents the leadership options and the organizational states resulting from their attitudes, as I explain below.

- **Frustrated companies** (and frustrated employees) occur when their leadership is willing to change but does not have the ability to. Usually such leaders do not have the skills and competencies to manage large-scale changes; they do not know how to forge alliances or overcome resistance to change.
- **Arrogant companies** have leaders who can change but are unwilling to because of myopia, orthodoxies based on their past success, and the belief that they, and only they, know what is best for the company. When executives

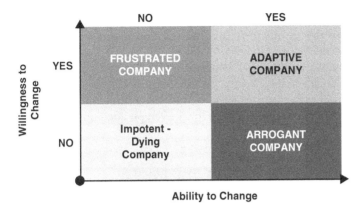

Figure 5.5 Leadership willingness and ability to change.

or organizations succeed by accident, they often become very rigid about their belief system, much more rigid than they were before becoming successful. In a way, they become superstitious. They end up believing that they will succeed forever, and then they become resistant to change. Employees in these types of corporations are highly stressed. Leaders falling into this category must continually identify and battle their own orthodoxies, which are often disguised as strengths but are, in fact, vulnerabilities.

- **Impotent (dying) companies** are those whose leaders are neither willing nor able to change and are therefore doomed to obsolescence.
- **Adaptive companies** are those which their leaders are willing and able to change as needed. These are the companies that will survive and thrive in the long run. These are the type of leaders who may understand the benefits of constantly evaluating their mission, vision, and respective culture and assure an alliance among them.

Consequently, culture reengineering is a top-down approach. In the first step, the coach must make sure that the organization has transformational leaders and that a good value (culture) audit has been carried out so that the current situation is clear. When leaders recognize that their current organizational culture needs to transform to ensure the continuation of the organization's success and progress, change can occur. But change is not pretty, and change is not easy. The good news, however, is that organizational culture change is possible. It requires understanding, commitment, and tools.

Managing the process step by step

This Managing by Values process for organizational change is similar to the process I described earlier for value reengineering for a single person, except many more people are involved and the process is much more complex. Figure 5.6 shows the basic steps of the organizational culture change process.

Pre-phase: Set the conditions for change and conducting value/ culture audit: In the book *Managing by Values*, which I co-authored with Salvador Garcia and Bonnie Richley, we called this "Phase 0" because it is an essential prerequisite, a sine qua non for the whole process.[37] Many projects of strategic revitalization of the ways of thinking and doing things in an organization turn out to be mere intentions—sometimes even pseudo-intentions—not

Pre Phase: conduct value audit

1 Distill the essential values of current culture

2 Collectively visualize the desired future and ensured fit with the vision and mission

3 Build consensus and leadership commitment

4 Put the project team to work; move to action and planning

Design HR Policies based on values 5

Monitor operational values via culture audits 6

Figure 5.6 Step-by-step culture reengineering methodology.

founded on solid arguments or rationale or funded with adequate resources. In other words, *good intentions are not enough for the management of change*. The fate of the initial phase of implementing culture change resides with the answers to the following questions:

- Is the organization serious about a culture change?
- Is the organization ready to engage in a long-term action? How is "long term" defined?
- Does the organization have the right type of leadership to initiate and sustain the process?
- Does the organization have the necessary resources? What resources will be those?

A negative, or even tentative, response to the questions indicates that more thought, time, and discussion should take place before attempting to implement a culture change. The key to a successful change process is dependent on (more than any other factor) the presence of one or more true leaders who can legitimize the process by demonstrating the will, commitment, and capability to deploy all the necessary resources. Regrettably, experience shows that this make-or-break condition is not all that frequently met and is the reason for many culture change failures.

Another component of the pre-change conditions is an organization-wide culture (values) audit. Different culture audits exist and vary depending on the conceptual model used in measuring the culture (see, for example, the vignette in this chapter by Richard Barrett, Box 5.2). The value audit and DOVA are tools for measuring the values of the core stakeholders (employees) and for comparing them with the values of the organization.[38] When an analysis reveals differences between personal values and needs and those of the organization, the need to reengineer the culture becomes critical.

Undertaking culture reengineering is not an easy process. It requires a courageous leader who will lead the process. Not all leaders are brave. Many are afraid to break and leave the comfort zone even though the existing culture does not work. A transformer leader takes the risk and feels a high commitment to act as a change agent. Let's elaborate a bit more about the various phases.

Phase 1: Distill the essential values: Once the political will to change is confirmed as a serious intention, and resources are in place to allocate the resources required, the first phase of work on the culture reengineering consists of reformulating values, with the maximum participation at all levels. There are three basic sequential activities for this first phase of an MBV project:

1. Collective visualization of the kind of future desired, described, and expressed as the final values to be incorporated in the organization's vision and mission.

2. Participation in the diagnosis of the strengths and weaknesses of the organization's current set of values and how these measure up against the opportunities and threats of the organization's environment.
3. Building a consensus on the lines to be followed in the path to change (new operating values to constitute the ruling culture of the organization).

This distillation of propositions, situational analyses, and rules of the game that command common and enthusiastic support may be seen as the generation of a massive dialogue on the basis of the values and shared perspectives of as many as possible of the committed members of the organization, including the associated interest groups such as the main suppliers and customers, trade unions, and professional associations. Involve as many stakeholders as possible. The guidelines to the distillation process will be the framework of the agreed proportion of values in the economic–pragmatic, the ethical–social, and the emotional–developmental dimensions and will be in alliance with the company vision and mission.

The idea of involving as many stakeholders as possible in the design of a new culture may seem totally utopian, but it is logically inescapable if you hope to create an environment based on shared values. Managing by Values recognizes the potential of everyone to contribute based on their knowledge and experience and understands that mutual learning is not constrained by notions of up, down, or sideways, in a dynamic and open organization.

At the beginning of the twenty-first century, some business leaders are timidly beginning to consider a new organizational configuration for thinking and behaving at work: a new culture that breaks with the old, arrogant supposition that only those at the top have "the answers," have the knowledge, experience, and energy to design and implement the strategies for survival and prosperity in the future. It is gradually being accepted that predictions and prescriptions by experts—even internal ones—are not as valid or effective as the creative visions shared by all. The stimulation of entrepreneurial initiative and behavior propounded by writers on "excellent companies" is increasingly recognized as vitally important for competitiveness, and few can muster convincing arguments against it.

A participative process of internal dialogue should begin at the organization at all levels with the aim of reformulating the organization's essential operating values. A task force needs to be created to manage this dialogue. At the end of the process, limited (or distilled) values should be chosen. As a general guide, the company should select and define its values from the CBV triaxial model's three dimensions (as discussed in chapter 3 and earlier in this chapter): (a) economic–pragmatic values; (b) ethical–social values; and (c) emotional–developmental values. If values from all three of these areas are not included, the "new" culture will likely not be very new at all, and the lopsided foundation will result in a failed change effort.

Phase II: We are changing! It's time to put the project teams to work: The work in Phase I began to make changes in the organization's way of thinking and doing things. The inclusive nature of the process alone has likely established a basis for the employees' engagement in the transformed culture, by creating trust and a renewed sense of belonging. Thus, working attitudes have already begun to change. Now the newly defined shared core operating values must be concretely translated into changes in everyday work processes and work tasks. When an organization has an inspiring vision, a meaningful mission, and a workable culture "enshrined" in a good set of agreed-upon operating values, it is ready to define its principal lines of action in terms of a properly thought-out structure for achieving long-, medium-, and short-term objectives. This is best organized through project teams and it should include processes that ensure a flexible, dynamic culture.

Phase III: Design human resource policies based on values: The internal policies related to human resource policies (for example selection, training, promotion, incentives, evaluation, and the like) in most companies normally suffer from two basic characteristics:

1. They are not sufficiently coherent in their relationship to the strategy formally followed by the senior management.
2. They are not appropriately articulated nor are they integrated as a function of any type of model or strong ruling idea.

As a result, they are developed in a fragmented way and thus lose their capacity to reinforce each other. All the values identified by the company as essential for its success should be strengthened by means of training interventions. How is it possible, for example, for any company to adopt a strategy of innovation without establishing a basic training program in techniques of creativity throughout all the functional areas of the organization? Probably, leaders of more than half the companies in any industry in any country would claim to be following a strategy of innovation, but if these strategies do not include effective, inspiring, and energizing training, the leaders will never see the imaginative or ground-breaking innovations they were expecting.

Being effective at modifying and strengthening personal values is one of the most interesting and rewarding training objectives one could aspire to. It is challenging on a professional level because it must be approached with exquisite respect for individual integrity and liberty of thought and expression. It is in this phase that reward systems and promotion criteria should also be evaluated and reinvented.

Phase IV: Monitor operational values via culture audits: The most frequent and regrettable error company leaders can make after they think they have successfully reformulated the vision, mission, and operating values of their company is publishing them in an attractive format—and then *doing absolutely nothing* to evaluate and reward employees' assimilation and compliance with the new culture. In Phase II, I discussed the importance of converting the shared values into action objectives that are directly relevant to everyday work processes. These action objectives not only should be reinforced through rewards and incentives as we discussed in the last step, they should be capable of measurement. The essential architecture of a planned culture change rests on two pillars: the implementation of the change process (i.e., crafting it and putting it into practice) and the maintenance of its sustainability through ongoing evaluation.

The successful adoption of a new culture requires that it be dynamic, with an organization-wide commitment to continuous learning and continuous improvement, periodical reviews of values, mechanisms in place for articulating and instilling the shared values of the vibrant new culture in actions and in words, and procedures for recruiting new employees who are eager to share these values. The continued strength and growth of the new culture requires a process of auditing to monitor progress and to ensure that everyone is actually doing what they have said they will do. This auditing process must be subject to the same conditions as the change process that generated the new culture: It must be all-inclusive, with no levels and no areas free from scrutiny. It must be open. It must be undertaken professionally and sympathetically, not as a threat if deficiencies are revealed but as an opportunity for resolving misunderstandings, compensating for unexpected problems, and allocating more resources if underestimations were made.

Finally, underlying all audits as well as all phases of the change process must be a recognition and acknowledgment that values of the employees need to be aligned with the vision and the mission of the company. The Coaching by Values' triaxial model is an excellent tool to diagnose value gaps and to reengage members at any level of an organization. It can be used at any time—from the start of the change process throughout its implementation and auditing. As I said in chapter 4, leaving an organization is not always a bad thing. When disconnects are detected or suspected, the triaxial model can help determine if adjustment is possible—either by the organization or any member at any level. The process of reengineering is a continuous process, one that can allow an organization to grow and thrive as the world presents evermore complex challenges.

As it progresses, keep in mind the Coaching by Values philosophy: alignment between shared core values, the organization's mission, and its future vision.

The need for culture audit: The case of mergers and acquisitions

Mergers and acquisitions are becoming a normal way to do business and expand in the twenty-first century. The value of global mergers and acquisitions in 2018 was (USD) $3.89 trillion.[39] Between 1985 and 2018, the value of global merger and acquisitions was over ten times more intensive. But despite the time and money invested in merger and acquisition deals, many failed. Recent studies estimate the failure rate of mergers at close to 75%. This statistic raises the question, why do so many mergers and acquisitions fail to achieve their intended results?

The high failure rate has less to do with paying too high a purchase price or making a poor strategic fit than one would think. Rather, many failed organizational marriages are the result of companies having failed to critically examine the possible ramifications of their cultural differences on post-combination success. Just as two individuals with differing values and beliefs will not co-exist for long, unsuitable organizational marriages won't last. Thus, many companies include cultural assessment as part of their due diligence to discern, prior to the altar, if the cultural differences can be managed post-merger.

Because culture represents shared beliefs, assumptions, and values, it is not readily observable. An organization's culture often only becomes obvious when contrasted with the culture of another organization, such as in the case of the merger of two firms. When two organizations unite, the combination inevitably results in some form of culture shock. The extent of culture shock can range from slightly unpleasant to exceptionally distressing, depending on how employees in each organization evaluate the attractiveness of the other culture regarding their own. Generally, the greater the cultural dissimilarity, the greater the culture shock. Culture clashes can be the result of several factors, including ignorance (i.e., lack of understanding of another's culture), disrespect for another company's norms, and arrogance (i.e., a belief that one culture is superior).

Though a seemingly innocent misunderstanding, such occurrences frequently result in failed organizational marriages. Consequently, companies have begun to acknowledge the existence of divergent cultures, identify cultural components that potentially hinder successful combination, and prioritize the cultural dimensions believed to be most important for a successful combination. This process of analyzing the fit between two independent organizations is known as cultural due diligence.

Until very recently, there were no systematic tools for performing cultural due diligence. There was no overall conceptual model, let alone a defined process and analytical tools. The triaxial model and the Managing by Values methodology fill this gap. They can be applied at any stage of the merger or acquisition to provide data that can help managers decide to move forward with a merger, anticipate significant problems as the merger is completed, and deal effectively with problems post-merger.

Cultural audits help to determine the extent to which a company's current culture aligns with the type of culture required for success in the future. When done properly, information from a cultural audit will highlight similarities, and significant differences, between the cultures in question. Cultural disparities, even those that are significant, do not necessarily jeopardize merger and acquisition activities. In many instances it is precisely the cultural difference that attracts companies to one another. Nonetheless, it is imperative that those involved in merger and acquisition discussions have reliable information at their disposal regarding cultural similarities and differences so they can make informed decisions on how to best combine the cultures.

A cultural due diligence technique provides an operational framework for managing cultural differences by uncovering potential pitfalls and their implications prior to completing a deal. Though cultural due diligence often uncovers significant differences in organizational practices among merging companies, the intent of the process is not to discourage integration. Rather, cultural due diligence is meant to alert stakeholders to potential differences in the human side of the merger equation so that plans to manage these disparities can be developed. In some instances, cultural differences may be too intransigent to bridge. However, with information derived from a cultural audit, decision-makers can systematically address potential hazards and take the necessary steps to overcome them before they severely impede the transition.

Implementation of value alignment in a large insurance company

In this section, I will briefly describe a typical process of culture reengineering, or value alignment. This is a real case, but for reasons of confidentiality I cannot reveal the name of the company. The case involves a large insurance company in a former Soviet-bloc Eastern European country. The company went from being state-run to private and struggled to educate its employees about competitive private sector values. It had been private for about 15 years before our intervention, and given its size and market share, the company had been very profitable. Recently, it had gone through structural changes due to its acquisition by a large UK-based insurance company. It is now part of a global operation.

The situation: The management team in the company (we'll call it "the Insurance Company") attempted to develop programs for value sharing and value alignment over the past two years, but results were not satisfactory. Although values were identified, indicators seem to suggest that they were neither shared nor aligned with the vision of the company. A recent survey pointed out that a large percentage of the employees work under stress and feel stressful. As an added difficulty, a large multinational corporation (MNC) based in London had acquired the company. The MNC attempted to standardize its operation worldwide and introduced a management model based on principles of action that did not match the culture and values of the Insurance Company.

Objective of the value alignment intervention: The development and implementation of a hybrid model of value alignment use the MNC head office principles in conjunction with the local values of the insurance company, and moves to set up methodologies, policies, and practices that will facilitate shared and sustainable alignment of the newly developed hybrid model.

Methodology: Project was run jointly by a team of external consultants and a team selected by the Insurance Company. The joint team constituted the culture reengineering task force and was responsible for all phases of the diagnosis, development, and implementation of the project. The methodology is described in Figure 5.7.

Benchmark of principal phases for the implementation included the following:

- creation of a joint task force (training if needed)
- development of an action plan and benchmark timetable
- translation of value questionnaire to local language (validation)
- online questionnaire, data collection, and analysis (production of a report)
- development of alignments plans (hybrid model)
- implementation of plans (division of labor, revising HR policies connected, others)
- behavior audit, monitoring, and adjustment of sustainable plans
- end of the project

After the completion of the process, the Insurance Company was interested in adding an individual change management program. We proposed an expanded Coaching by Values framework, which (see Figure 5.8) included programs for

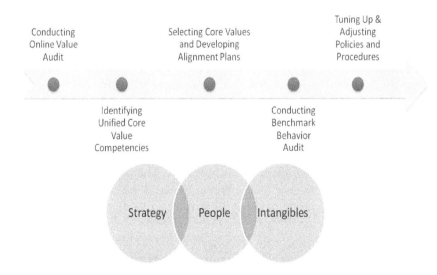

Figure 5.7 Process overview.

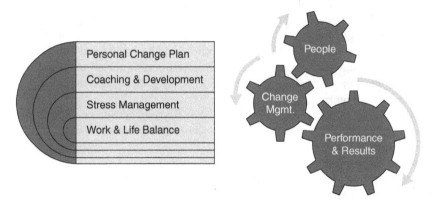

Figure 5.8 Enhanced Coaching by Values model for promoting wellness.

stress management and work–life balance. Coaching can work very well (hand in hand) with these additional modules.

BOX 5.2 TOOLS FOR COACHING:

MEASURING CONSCIOUSNESS BY MAPPING VALUES

Richard Barrett

Values and levels of consciousness

Every value you can think of belongs to a level of consciousness. Therefore, the values that are important to you at any point in your life reflect the state of evolution of your consciousness. By mapping your values, you can determine the levels of consciousness you are operating from.

The model we use at the Barrett Values Centre (www.valuescentre.com) to measure consciousness consists of three stages and seven levels. The first stage, which contains three levels, is about satisfying the needs of the ego by learning how to become viable and independent in your framework of existence. Level 1 is about meeting your basic survival needs. Level 2 is about belonging and meeting your relationship needs. Level 3 is about differentiation and meeting your self-esteem needs. During this stage of evolution, you are primarily focused on satisfying the needs of the ego: values such as financial stability, belonging, respect, recognition, and the like. Whenever the ego gets fearful about being able to get its needs met, you display negative or potentially limiting values, such as jealousy, blame, manipulation, and arrogance.

The second stage, which contains two levels, is about learning to blend the needs of the ego with the needs of the soul so you can become an authentic individual. Level 4 is about individuation, becoming more fully who you are by facing and overcoming your fears. Level 5 is about self-actualization—aligning your work in the world with your passion (soul purpose).

The third stage, which also contains two levels, is about learning how to align and cooperate with other individuals to achieve personal fulfillment. Level 6 is about actualizing your own sense of purpose and at the same time aligning with others who share a similar purpose to make a difference in the world. When you are fully aligned with your purpose and making a difference becomes a way of life, you reach level 7, the level of service.

When you are able to overcome your fears and master each level of consciousness through the display of positive values, you attain full-spectrum consciousness. The *New Leadership Paradigm* book, website, and learning system (www.newleadershipparadigm.com) provide a full account of this process. The learning system includes a downloadable learning module consisting of 43 exercises that can be used by coaches for supporting their clients in learning to lead themselves and become full-spectrum individuals. The learning module also includes a journal and self-evaluation tools whereby individuals can record their progress on their self-leadership journey. In addition to the Leading Self learning module, there are modules for Leading a Team, Leading an Organization, and Leading in Society.

Cultural transformation tools

In addition to the exercises included in the Leading Self learning module, the Barrett Values Centre has developed a series of assessments for measuring the consciousness of individuals, organizations, and nations. Three of these instruments are used extensively by coaches to support their clients in their personal and professional evolution.

The Individual Values Assessment

The Individual Values Assessment is a self-assessment instrument that enables you to measure how aligned you are with the culture and values of your organization; how well you connect with your organization and the work you do; and to what extent you think your organization is on the right track.

The insights gained from this instrument are crucial to understanding to what extent you believe you will be able to find the fulfillment you are looking for in your present job.

The Leadership Values Assessment

Individuals only grow and develop when they get regular feedback. The Leadership Values Assessment compares a leader's perception of his or her operating style with the perception of his or her superiors, peers, and subordinates. It enables you to find out what others appreciate about you; what advice your superiors, peers, and subordinates can offer you to improve your leadership style; what levels of consciousness you operate from; and your level of personal dysfunction—the extent to which you are operating from the fears of your ego. The debrief of the Leadership Values Assessment is rich in feedback and usually takes about two to three hours.

The Leadership Development Report

The Leadership Development Report, like the Leadership Values Assessment, is a powerful coaching tool for promoting self-awareness, personal transformation, and an understanding of the actions a leader needs to take to realize his or her full potential. The Leadership Development Report also compares a leader's perception of his or her operating style with the perception of his or her superiors, peers, and subordinates. Assessors also get the opportunity to indicate how they believe the leader needs to change to help him or her become the best leader he or she can be. Emphasis is placed on a leader's strengths, areas for improvement, and opportunities for growth.

There are three main differences between the Leadership Development Report and the Leadership Values Assessment. First, the Leadership Development Report asks the assessors to rate the leader against a prescribed set of 26 full-spectrum "behaviors" that our research has shown to be significant. The Leadership Values Assessment, on the other hand, allows assessors to write freeform responses to questions about the leader's strengths and areas for improvement. Second, the Leadership Development Report delivers a fully automated report, whereas the Leadership Values Assessment is handwritten by one of our analysts. Third, the Leadership Development Report uses a standard template of values, whereas the Leadership Values Assessment template is customized to reflect the cultural attributes of your organization.

Richard Barrett biography

Richard Barrett is an author, speaker, and internationally recognized thought leader on the evolution of human values in business and society. He is the founder and chairman of the Barrett Values Centre®, a fellow of the World Business Academy, and Former Values Coordinator at the World Bank. He is the creator of the internationally recognized Cultural Transformation Tools® (CTT), which have been used to support more than 6,000 organizations on their transformational journeys. To date, more than 5,000 change agents, consultants, and coaches have been trained by the Barrett Values Centre to use the Cultural Transformation Tools in over 50 countries.

Richard has been a visiting lecturer at the Consulting and Coaching for Change, Leadership Course run by the Saïd Business School at the University of Oxford and HEC in Paris. He has also been an adjunct professor at Royal Roads University, Institute for Values-based Leadership, and a visiting lecturer at the One Planet MBA at Exeter University. Richard is the author of many books. The list is long and we propose that you visit his website to see the full list: www.barrettacademy.com

5.6 Values and ethics in organizations[40]

In 2002 an internal investigation in Ali Baba found that two sales persons were violating the values and paying off. Jack Ma, the funder and legendary CEO, had to make a painful decision. Remember this was in 2002, not now, when his company is worth more than Wells Fargo bank; rather this was at the time when this money was essential for Ali Baba's survival.

Jack Ma said: "If we fire them immediately, the company will not have profit. If we do not kick these two employees out, then what does this signify about us? It would imply that our words are empty." So, we finally decided to let these two employees go. And in a later interview he said: "We focus on the employees and the culture. Everybody is helping each other instead of just making money." Imagine what would have happened if Jack Ma had opted only to pressure employees to meet cross sales quotas? Well, here is another anecdote connected with his value proposition: he dismissed a sales trainer for teaching malpractices. He said: "The training instructor was speaking about how to sell hair combs to monks. After five minutes, I got extremely angry and expelled the instructor. I thought the instructor was a cheat. Monks do not need combs in the first place."

In our work on coaching and managing by value across the globe, with many of the best global organizations, we continually see a crisis of "values in action." For example, we were involved in a process of culture reengineering at SEAT (the largest Volkswagen car manufacturing company in Spain). There was a general feeling in the company that values are not clear, and not shared. While we started to work with top executives on revising the mission, the vision, and the core values, the scamming scandal of tempering with the emission systems in Volkswagen became known. SEAT executives were surprised, astonished, and ashamed but had followed the instructions to stop the culture reengineering process until the head office said something about it. Should the head office of Volkswagen be engaged in such intervention, the likelihood of some engineers fooling around, and cheating would have probably never happened. It is estimated that in addition to a significant dent in the branding the total costs of this scam will cost Volkswagen over $17 billion.

By and large, there is a growing discrepancy between the stated values on the wall and values in action. Here is another example that we had experienced. A few years back, we trained the largest telecommunication company in Spain (Telefonica). Over 50 senior executives (many of them were VPs) had participated in the program. At one point during the training, they were asked to write down the official values of Telefonica. To our surprise, only 2 of the 50 executives listed the complete list of values of the firm. So, imagine that your top managers in your company do not know the core values of your firm. It is said that changes have taken place, and this is no more the case, but we do not have recent evidence. The data that we have accumulated over the years, and across the globe, show that over 75% of companies have a significant gap between the stated values (on the wall—on their website), and the values in action (the one really practiced). The most common current employee training methods largely reinforce values by using a push strategy, which relies heavily on memorizing the official values and retaining them, but not on pull strategy which means incorporating and practicing them proactively on a day-to-day basis.

One reason that companies do not practice values is the difficulties encountered to measure them, and align them with the company's mission and vision. This is the essence of the process of cultural reengineering that we have proposed and described above; an effective way to practice values in action focuses on the process of identifying core values, measuring its practice in the firm, and introducing policies to reinforce it and align it with their mission and vision.

Today, we need to retain and motivate the millennials. The latter are looking not only for values; they want to have a greater sense of purpose and meaning. Learning what their personal values are helps them to connect, to scan for similarities, and to develop respect for diversity. Moreover, our data shows that alliance of values also contributes to greater innovation. Don't you want to have a creative and an innovative workforce in your company? Then, focus on value alignment.

Here is a quick checklist that may help you reflect on the need for alignment between your company culture with your employees' values:

1. Do you practice "hire and fire" for values? Do you emphasize attitude and suitability for your culture and values?

2. Do you tolerate deviation from your culture and values giving concessions and closing one eye when a top performer is needed for your short-term results?
3. Are your policies and processes aligned with your values? Do you create paradoxes by setting unrealistic targets?
4. When was the last time that you conducted a value audit to identify the current gap between the values on your wall and values in practice?
5. With new generations and disruptive technologies and business models, are your values still relevant? Do you need to refresh and update them?
6. Are you at liberty to review and update your existing values? Are you willing to explore a change and solicit wide-based feedback to uplift them or are you forced to live with the words on the wall?
7. Do you provide tools to help teams in your organization understand the values of their team members?
8. How do you teach your values? Do you emphasize only verbal memory retention or do you have procedures in check if values are actually lived? Do you expect role modeling and a sense of ownership?
9. Do you involve many of your employees in your strategic sessions or do you work traditionally top-down?
10. Are the words on the wall empowering, vigorous, and call for action?

Let us conclude, perhaps, with some visionary view for changing the mindset connected with the world of finance but also culture and values. We can't expect the cat to guard over the milk. There seems to be an inherent conflict of interest in the current business model, where public companies appoint both their boards and their auditors. Both are paid by the company and obviously have an inherent personal interest not to lose their position or source of continued revenue. Thus, why would they go against the management of the company when sometimes they should?

In public companies, the role of the auditor is to protect the true owners of the company—the shareholders. We may, perhaps, propose a scenario where auditors are being nominated by the respective stock exchange in which they are traded. This will result in rotation of the audit firms (say every two years), and the auditors will know that they will be audited as well by the incoming auditor firm. Perhaps such a procedure will bring about a higher level of professionalism and prudence. In this scheme, the public companies will pay a fixed fee to the stock exchange for auditing cost accordingly. The stock exchange will be able to get a better price for volume using the RFP system. When the auditors are working for the exchange to represent the public interest, they will be impartial; their duty and loyalty will be to their client; and the audited companies will be transparent. Last but not least, perhaps the time has arrived to consider the undertaking of two types of audits: a financial audit (with the idea expressed above) and also a culture audit. The tools, methodologies, and processes are available nowadays for both, and we hope that in the future we will see more legislation or actions initiated by the firms themselves to offer these new procedures.

BOX 5.3 KEY DRIVERS IN BUILDING A VALUES-BASED CULTURE: AN AUSTRALIAN PERSPECTIVE

By Philip Harrell

Values-based leadership

I have been either practicing, consulting, studying, or teaching leadership in some form for most of my adult working life, and over this lifetime of attempting to make sense of the social process of leadership, I have come to one indisputable fact of life: Leadership cannot be considered in isolation from values and culture. This article draws on my experiences in consulting in values to provide a simple template on how a leader can manage values and culture to achieve organizational success. I believe it complements Simon Dolan's Coaching by Values™ approach very well.

Building a values-based culture

In this template (represented in the diagram on the left), I have outlined three key drivers that are consistently present in exceptional organizations with a strong, aligned values-based culture. These drivers are: direction, clarity, and involvement, consistent, continual, relentless reinforcement; and respect and trust in organizational leadership. With each driver I have provided a couple of examples that I have seen work in organizations that are committed to a values-based culture (Figure 5.9).

Direction, clarity, and involvement

Clarity of direction matters! Time and time again I sadly see organizations that don't necessarily lack direction or goals but rather they lack clarity as to what they stand for. In other words, the organization is not clear on its values. This generally results in a weak culture with employees unclear as to what is expected of them. Conversely, the good news is that I am working with a growing number of exceptional organizations that demonstrate and practice a clear set of values that engage and energize employees.

In my experience, successful organizations are those that have total belief and commitment from the organizational owners/shareholders and senior

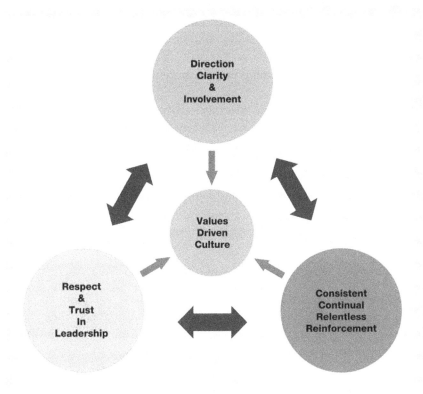

Figure 5.9 The triaxial model of values-driven culture.

leadership team; undertake activities to ensure individuals in the organization are clear on their own values, the organizations' values, and how these align (I recommend Simon Dolan's "value of values"© system to assist here); and the senior team need to continually live the values.

Consistent, continual, relentless reinforcement

Clarity of values requires consistency of work practices. Organizations express their values in the daily actions of leaders, in who they recruit and in workplace policies and procedures. Consider:

- Successful organizations embrace Coaching by Values (CBV). I have found the more widely spread values-based coaching is encouraged and fostered, the stronger values-based practices become embedded.

- Values-based leadership and teambuilding activities provide organizational leaders with the necessary skills and understanding to lead organizational-wide values.
- Integrated Action Learning program in values-based leadership at all hierarchical levels.
- Performance and reward structures designed around consistency of workplace practice with values alignment, for example:
  - Recruit on values (e.g., all job applicant complete values survey)
  - Values-based meeting (i.e., testing managerial decisions against values)
  - "Calling it out"—Anyone in the organization is qualified and encouraged to counsel someone who breaches the values.
  - Behavior aligned to the values is openly rewarded.

Respect and trust in organizational leadership

Trust in leadership is consistently at the top of employee wish lists. People will simply not follow leaders they do not trust. In companies where the leaders act consistently, they are respected by peers and subordinates; also my experience and research have shown employees are more loyal, engaged, and productive.

Leaders train their staff every single work day by their actions alone. My research has highlighted the simple, embarrassingly obvious truth that leaders must consistently "walk the talk."

Making it happen

There is nothing in my dealings with exceptional organizations that cannot be practiced by *any* organization that aims to bring about a strong, values-focused and engaged workforce. It only requires belief in the power of values and commitment from senior management.

Dr. Philip Harrell, BA., M.Litt., MBA., (NE) DBA. (UniSA), is a master coach in "Leading, Managing and Coaching by Values (ICF)." Phil is the executive director of the Leadership Alliance, an Australian-based consulting organization specializing in values-based leadership development, teambuilding, and innovation. www.leadershipalliance.com.au-. Dr. Harrell can be contacted at pharrell@leadershipalliance.com.au

5.7 Conclusion

This chapter is the crystallization of my Leading and Coaching by Values ideas and methodologies to this point. I hope that you are still with me. I know this chapter may have been a bit difficult to read (it was certainly difficult for me to write!), but now that you appreciate the CBV ideas and have a handle on the overall CBV process—that is, you are clear about what each step is, how it arose from the previous step, and how it progresses to the next—there is no limit to where you can go.

A coach can be eclectic. You may want to draw from other coaching schools at various points in an intervention to help achieve your primary goal of effecting change. Follow the steps in the sequence I've described, but within those steps, be creative. Enrich the experience. An example of enrichment that I use is the Gift of Values that I described here. Be imaginative.

This is not the end of the story. In the next chapter, I imagine what might happen to our world and how CBV methods may grow in the future in response to opportunities presenting themselves and challenges confronting us right now.

CLBV Reflection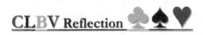

Think of the key message(s) you retained after reading this chapter. Then complete the following sentences:

The principal points I liked in this chapter include

1. _____

2. _____

3. _____

The principal points that I did not like or disagreed with in this chapter include

1. _____

2. _____

3. _____

Notes

1 If you prefer to do something more colorful and playful that is still part of CBV, I propose a card game that I have designed with my brother Avishai, to help convert every father and mother, every teacher, or an educator into a coach—not a professional

coach, but rather one who can serve as a coach for his or her children and other family members. To learn more about it and order it, go to www.learning-about-values. com or https://tiendacoachingporvalores.com/ When you receive it, just follow the enclosed instructions. In addition, we have recently released a new app which can be downloaded free of charge in google-store or apple store and is called "*values4kids.*"

2 See, for example, Dolan, S. L. (2006). *Stress, Self-Esteem, Health and Work.* Palgrave Macmillan; Dolan, S. L., & Moodie, S. (2010). Can becoming a manager be dangerous to your health? Is suicide the new occupational hazard? *Effective Executive, 13*(1), 66–69.

3 Garcia, S., & Dolan, S. L. (1997). *La dirección por valores (DpV): El cambio más allá de la dirección por objetivos.* McGraw Hill.

4 Garcia, S., & Dolan, S. L. (2003). *La dirección por valores (DpV): El cambio más allá de la dirección por objetivos.* Segunda Edición. McGraw Hill.

5 Dolan S.L., Díez Piñol M., Fernández Alles, M., Martín Prius, A., Martínez Fierro, S., (2004) "Exploratory study of within-country differences in work and life values: the case of Spanish business students," *International Journal of Cross-Cultural Management* (SAGE Publication) Vol 4(2):157–180.

6 Dolan, S. L. (2003). Making a life or making a Living: What values are today's Business School Instilling. *Esade Business Review, 1*(1), 8–11.

7 Dolan, S. L., & Richley, B. (2006). Management by Values (MBV): A new philosophy for a new economic order, in Coats P (ed.) *Handbook of Business Strategy, 7*(1), 235–238.

8 Dolan, S. L., Garcia, S., & Richley, B. (2006). *Managing by Values: Corporate Guide to Living, Being Alive and Making a Living in the XXI century.* Palgrave Macmillan.

9 Dolan, S. L., & Lingham, T. (2008). *Fundamentals of International Organizational Behavior.* Sara Books.

10 Dolan, S. L., Richley, B., Garcia, S., & Lingham, T. (2008). A tri-axial model of Managing by Values (MBV): Culture reengineering for managing organizational complexity in a global economy. *European Business Forum,* Spring.

11 Dolan, S. L. y colaboradores (special Issue) (2013, January). 2: Values Across Cultures (VAC) mapping differences and strengths in the public sector. *Cross Cultural Management, An International Journal, 20*(4), 497–501.

12 Dolan, S. L. (2011). *Coaching by Values: How to Succeed in the life of Business and in the Business of Life.* iUniverse Bloomington IND (USA).

13 *Open innovation* is a term used to promote an information age mindset toward innovation that runs counter to the secrecy and silo mentality of traditional corporate research labs. Use of the term *open innovation* in reference to the increasing embrace of external cooperation in a complex world has been promoted in particular by Henry Chesbrough, faculty director of the Center for Open Innovation of the Haas School of Business at the University of California, and visiting professor at Esade Business School.

14 Dolan y colaboradores (2018). *Valores: la brújula para personas y organizaciones de futuro.* Punto Rojo.

15 Fernandez-i-Marin, X. (2019). Extracting configurations of values mixing scores from experts and ignoramus using Bayesian modeling, Frontiers in applied mathematics and statistics, March 4. (www.frontiersin.org/articles/10.3389/fams.2019.00012/full).

16 See short video: https://binged.it/2G4FuKW

17 See short video: https://vimeo.com/225749599

18 Tzafrir, S., & Dolan, S. L. (2004). Trust me: A scale for measuring manager—Employee trust. *Management Research: Journal of the Iberoamerican Academy of Management, 2*(2), 115–132.

19 Dolan, S. L. (2007). *Stress, Self-Esteem, Health and Work.* Palgrave Macmillan.

20 *Density of stress* is a new term that I am proposing that includes a multiplication of the seriousness of a stress sign/symptom and its frequency. So, it is an algorithm that multiplies two important parameters to assess stress.
21 Nonaka, I. (1991). The knowledge creating company. *Harvard Business Review*, November–December, 1–9.
22 Kawamura, K. (2013). Understanding the concept of care in cross cultural settings: Towards a resource definition of care in work organizations. *Cross Cultural Management: An International Journal*, 20(2), 100–123.
23 The term *wicked problems*, originally proposed by Rittel and Weber (1973), is used to describe complex social or cultural problems that are difficult or impossible to solve because of their complexity, expense, size, and interconnection with other problems that are also too big to solve and because of the level of incomplete or contradictory knowledge and number of people and opinions involved. See also: Waddock, S., Meszoely, G.M., Waddell, S., & Dentoni, D. (2015). The complexity of wicked problems in large scale change. *Journal of Organizational Change Management*, 28(6), 993–1012.
24 Rockeach, M. (1973). *The Nature of Human Values*. New York: Palgrave-Macmillan.
25 See Jin and Drozdenko (2010); Peters and Waterman (2006); Barrett Values Centre at www.valuescentre.com/mapping-values/values; and Dolan, Garcia, and Richley, 2006.
26 See: Meglino, B.M., & Ravlin, E.C. (1998). Individual values in organizations: Concepts, controversies, and research. *Journal of Management*, 24, 351–389. [7]Paarlberg, L.E., & Perry, J.L. (2007). Values management: Aligning employee values and organizational goals. *The American Review of Public Administration*, 37(4), 387–407. Posner, B.Z., & Schmidt, W.H. (1993). Value congruence and differences between the interplay of personal and organizational value system. *Journal of Business Ethics*, 12, 341–347.
27 See: Kawamura, K. (2011a, August 12). PDW: Shaping caring cultures and strategies in organizations. Paper Presented at the Academy of Management Meeting: "West Meets East: Enlightening. Balancing. Transcending." San Antonio, TX. Kawamura, K. (2011b, August 13). PDW: Transforming institutions and leaders in support of caring economics principles. Paper Presented at the Academy of Management Meeting: "West Meets East: Enlightening. Balancing. Transcending." San Antonio, TX. Kawamura, K. (2013). op. cit.
28 Kawamura, K. (2016). Care: A resource for energizing the relationship between the coach and the coachee. Paper Presented at the "Leading, Managing, and Coaching by Values" Workshop, ESADE Creapolis, St. Cugat, Barcelona.
29 Ibid.
30 Swanson, K. (1999). What is known about caring in nursing science? In A.S. Hinshaw, S. Fleetham, & J. Shaver (Eds.), *Handbook of Clinical Nursing Research* (pp. 31–60). Thousand Oaks, CA: Sage.
31 Vaillant, G. (2012). *Triumphs of Experience: The Men of the Harvard Grant Study*. Cambridge, MA: Harvard University Press.
32 Noddings, N. (1986). *Caring: A Feminine Approach to Ethics and Moral Education*. Berkeley, CA: University of California Press.
33 Kawamura, K. (2016). op. cit.
34 Scharmer, C.O. (2009). *Theory U: Leading from the Future as it Emerges*. San Francisco, CA: Berrett-Koehler Publishers, Inc.
35 Kawamura, K. (2016). op. cit.
36 Sheth, J., & Sisodia, R. (2005). Why good companies fail? *European Business Forum*, 22, 24–31.
37 Dolan, S. L., Garcia, S., & Richley, B. (2006). *Managing by Values: Corporate Guide to Living, Being Alive and Making a Living in the 21st Century*. Palgrave Macmillan.

38 For a demonstration and more information, go to www.lidershipbyvalues.com. Ask for a demo to be sent to you. The program has several phases, and the first two phases deal with the value audit. Make sure to select "English" (or whichever language you want) from the dropdown menu in the top right-hand corner. In 2020, we hope to complete another audit called DOVA, where the emphasis will be only on the Ethical axis of values. It will be available at: www.managingbyvalues.com

39 Source: www.statista.com/statistics/267369/volume-of-mergers-and-acquisitions-worldwide/

40 This section was inspired by two articles that we have published recently. Liran, A., & Dolan, S. L. (2016). Values, values on the wall, just do business and forget them all: Wells Fargo, Volkswagen and others in the hall. *The European Business Review* (October–November), 13–20; Liran, A., & Dolan, S. L. (2017). United Airlines, Artificial Intelligence, and Donald Trump: Reawakening values in the era of fake service, fake reality, and fake news. *The European Business Review* (June).

Chapter 6

Coaching, values, and the future

New challenges in the new landscape of work

6.1 Introduction

If you have read the first five chapters in this book mindfully—and if I have done my job—you are familiar with the concept, methodology, and tools of Coaching and Leading by Values, and you are equipped to apply them in whatever settings you find suitable. This chapter is a bonus chapter. It is for those who wish to have a go at the future. This chapter is somewhat speculative; more research is needed (and is being carried out) to substantiate some of what I discuss here. Look at it as an appetizer, a few suggestions of what may come to pass (or not) in the future.

In this chapter I will focus on (and sometimes forecast possible future events) in areas ranging from the neurobiology of values to spirituality and values of the new age. I will propose to extend the triaxial model to quadriaxial, with applications for leadership, and imagine how some new age values could help us solve the global challenges facing the world. I do not pretend that my discussion on these issues is exhaustive, because that would require many books from many authors; I just want to share with you some issues that I will certainly address more in depth in future editions of this book and in articles I'm writing, especially for the magazine *The European Business Review*.[1]

Values, Managing by Values, Leading by Values, and Coaching by Values are dynamic concepts and methodologies. They have evolved dramatically since I first began my journey with them in the early 1980s. And they will continue to evolve. It is part of their nature. If you are creative and innovative, you may decide not to wait for the future, but to integrate some of the ideas I speculate about here into the methodology I presented earlier.

6.2 The neurobiology of values

How do humans develop the values that permit us to classify objects as beautiful or ugly and to judge actions as good or evil? In what are good social conduct and ethical principles grounded? We have long been preoccupied with such questions. Some of the answers may be found in our evolution, specifically in our neurobiology. Recent research suggests that the evolution of human values may be imprinted in the human brain, both in its gross anatomy and in the finer details of its physiology, including brain chemistry. Developments in neuroscience indicate that values evolved as the human brain did, with each affecting the other.

Humans have been pondering the origins of their values for centuries. Until recent times, such issues were primarily the province of philosophers, theologians, sociologists, and historians who studied the universality of or variations in specific values across different cultures. Neuroscience and other scientific disciplines are making a more objective and experimental approach possible. The imaging techniques used to display the living brain, for example, allow us to see which areas of the brain are activated when people are manifesting different classes of values. And because the field of neuroscience is expanding to include neurophysiology, neurology, and anatomy, among other areas of science, more tools will likely be available soon to further our understanding of this complicated, vexing, and wonderful issue.

In recent years, several concrete observations have laid the foundation for a neuroscience of values. Brain images of people responding to questionnaires designed to evaluate moral and ethical attitudes show clearly that certain attitudes are associated with certain parts of the brain. We have also learned that specific neurons or neural networks are involved when a person is displaying a sense of empathy. Data from some brain imaging studies suggest not only that there is a cerebral substance connected with values associated with empathy, but also that it developed by evolutionary selection.

One proposed explanation is that the biological blueprint of human values stems from the "life regulation system," which is known as homeostasis. All life forms have systems that permit them to maintain biological processes within a range compatible with life. In complex species (like the human), the regulation of life depends on a close interaction between brain systems and body-proper systems and is controlled in effect by a specific collection of well-coordinated brain regions. Life regulation is not automatic; it involves choices and preferences, but at the most basic levels, those choices and preferences are made subconsciously. The life regulation system, or homeostasis, is built to achieve certain goals, among them the maintenance of health, the prevention of circumstances leading to death, and the procurement of states of life tending toward optimal function rather than merely neutral or defective function.

Homeostasis inherently embodies values in the sense that it rejects certain conditions of operation, those that would lead to disease or death, and seeks conditions that lead to optimal survival. Therefore, one can claim that what we call "good" and "evil" are aligned with categories of actions related to ranges of homeostatic regulation. What we call good actions are, in general, those actions that lead to health and well-being in an individual, a group, or an entire community. What we call evil, on the other hand, pertains to malaise, disease, or death in the individual, the group, or the community.

The same can apply to other values, such as efficiency or inefficiency. The inefficient part of the regulatory spectrum is characterized by higher energy consumption, inadequate performance, impediments, and the like. At the dawn of the human values, we presume, objects that were classified as beautiful were associated with efficient states, either because they occurred in life circumstances in which the homeostatic range was efficient or because the objects themselves can cause efficient homeostatic states.[2]

Throughout this book, I have insisted that social and relational life is strongly linked to beliefs, values, and attitudes, which are themselves governed by an anatomical substance. This has been studied using brain imaging techniques. Davidson[3] found that activity in the ventromedial prefrontal cortices of the brain (VMPEC) is greatest in people who are very compassionate and caring. His work also showed the remarkable heterogeneity among individuals in their affective style and values. Viewing Davidson's work considering the homeostatic theory of values, one can hypothesize that human values evolved along with the species to ensure maximum survival and that these values, in turn, may have caused cerebral modifications. Is there a relationship between changes in the human frontal brain areas and the emergence of values? A variety of scientific evidence confirms the existence of a neural network that is activated during the exercise of some values (moral, ethical). This network links the prefrontal and medial temporal lobes.

Throughout its evolution, the human brain has acquired three components that progressively appeared and grew one on top of the other, similar to strata in an archeological site: the oldest (the archipallium or primitive) is located at the bottom and to the back; the next one (the paleopallium) is in an intermediate position; and the most recent (the neopallium, also known as the superior or rational) is situated on top and to the front. These are like three biological computers that, although interconnected, retain their types of intelligence, subjectivity, sense of time and space, memory, mobility, and other less specific functions.

In 1878, the French neurologist Paul Broca called attention to the fact that, on the medial surface of the mammalian brain, right underneath the cortex, is an area containing several nuclei of gray matter (neurons) that he called the "limbic lobe" (from the Latin word *limbus*, meaning border or edge) because it forms a kind of border around the brain stem. Today the limbic lobe, together with certain adjacent deep structures, including the amygdala, is known as the limbic system. Research suggests that specific affective functions (e.g., some emotions) are developed in this region—such as those which induce females to nurse and protect their toddlers and the playful moods that engender ludic behaviors. Emotions and feelings, like wrath, fright, passion, love, hate, joy, and sadness, which are mammalian inventions, originate in the limbic system.

It is important to stress that all the structures in the brain interconnect intensively. Some contribute more than others to this or that kind of emotion, but no one is by itself responsible for any specific emotional state. The prefrontal area is connected to the limbic region, so when it suffers a lesion, the person loses his or her sense of social responsibility (associated with the limbic system) as well as the capacity for concentration and abstraction (associated with the prefrontal area). When prefrontal lobotomy was used for the treatment of certain psychiatric disturbances, the patients entered a stage of "affective buffer," no longer showing any sign of joy, sadness, hope, or despair. In their words or attitudes, no traces of affection could be detected.

Neuroscience, emotion, and values

What is the relationship between emotions, on the one hand, and values, on the other hand? I claim that emotions are connected to values because they involve appraisals. So, we can even suggest that emotions are correlates of values. The simplest version of this view is the claim that to feel one type of indignation (emotion) is to believe or judge that a situation is unjust—that is, if we believe a situation is unjust, we will become angry when confronted with it. In keeping with this view, one would see a correspondence between the importance a person ascribes to a value and the frequency of his or her emotional experiences related to that value. Therefore, we would expect to find the following:

- Feelings of fear associated with security values (people who frequently feel afraid in daily life ascribe great importance to security values because both fear and security values share the goal of realizing safety).
- Feelings of disgust and contempt negatively related to conformity values.
- Feelings of affection and concern for others related to the values of benevolence and universalism (both express pro-social tendencies).
- Feelings of pride related to achievement and self-direction values (both express the importance of success and goal-attainment).
- Feelings of guilt and shame related to conformity values (whereas pride often involves a positive valuation of the self, shame and guilt involve negative self-evaluation, often following failures to live up to moral or social standards).

Therefore, emotions are triggered by the brain following a sequence involving values. In the triaxial model is an entire axis of emotional values. One of these that has been studied frequently is empathy. Empathy is a value that allows us to relate to the emotional states of others. This value is critical in regulating social interactions as it enables an individual to effect social bonding and exhibit care for others. Interestingly, scientists studying empathy in both children and animals have concluded that it is a major ingredient in explaining human and primate behavior. We see compelling evidence for the strength of the empathic reaction in scientists' findings that rhesus monkeys refuse to pull a chain that delivers food to them if doing so shocks a companion. These monkeys literally starve themselves to avoid inflicting pain on another.

Using values to manage emotions

Can you imagine a world with no emotions? No happiness, no sadness, no anxiety, no love, no pleasure, no pain, no frustration, no urges, and no addiction. Every single one of us simply going about our day, doing whatever it is we are supposed to do (whatever that might be in a world without emotion). Don't just read this and move on. Take a few minutes to really imagine it. Imagine what your life would be like without emotions. Imagine what your soul would be like without emotions. Consider this, without getting too philosophical: Would you even have a soul? It *should* make you think.

Without emotions, you and I would be nothing more than physical bodies and the electrical impulses that produce the energy to run them. All thoughts would be functional. There would be no good or bad. No evil. No hatred. No love. In essence, we would be machines. What makes us human is our emotions. What allows us to experience the wonders of life—as well as the sorrow—is our emotions. Without emotions, not one of us would ever struggle with a single compulsive behavior. There would be no addiction. Life would be ... *wonderful?* Now, take this one step further: If a life without emotions equals a life without certain behaviors, can controlling these behaviors be reduced to the "simple" task of managing our emotions? When we learn to manage our emotions, we have learned to manage our behavior.

There are two types of emotions you need to be aware of in the addictive environment: value-based emotions and behavior-based emotions. Physiologically, they may be identical. Behavior-based emotions are the emotions that are experienced as a result of the triggering stimuli and the compulsive ritualistic behavior that follows. And so that we are clear, the "behavior" can be fantasy, masturbation, pursuing a romantic interest, stalking, smoking, drinking, gambling, eating, or any other action that can alter one's emotions (which can be just about any behavior imaginable—in the right circumstances). Such stimuli and behavior elicit immediate emotional reactions that can overwhelm a person's value system and over a sustained period, progressively destroy values altogether.

Value-based emotions are considerably different. They are based not on the reaction to stimuli, but in the preparation for it. They are based on a foundational commitment to long-term growth and life management. They are based on having developed an open and honest line of communication with oneself. Consider a marathon runner who sprints to the lead in the first couple hundred yards. The sprinting causes the runner to briefly experience the pleasure of winning, but the situation is not sustainable. Soon, his or her body will wear down, and all the tools that he could have used to win the race will no longer be useful. They will have lost their value. His entire race will be reduced to the single action of sprinting and resting, sprinting and resting. Addiction is similar. The behavior-based emotions are the sprint; the value-based emotions are the tools that will keep one in the race for the long haul.

Psychologists, therapists, and other health professionals normally work on altering and changing the negative consequences of behavioral-based emotions. In this book, I showed that by reducing incongruence or enhancing congruence of values, we can lead better lives both at work and off work. When our actions are consistent with our established values, positive emotions result. When our actions are based on spontaneous reaction, instability and chaos may result. The trick to managing the two in unison is being aware that behavior-based emotions can produce overwhelming changes in the here and now. Value-based emotions produce powerful, sustained emotions over time. There is a healthy time for both.

Is there a hereditary, non-genetic basis of values?[4]

A couple of years ago (in 2013), the then UK attorney general, Dominic Grieve, provoked a stir in the media suggesting that some minority communities based in the UK—Pakistan in particular—come from an origin where corruption is endemic: In fact, what he said was that cultural values are inherited.[5]

Experience and science say that observable features (called phenotypes) such as physiology, morphology, skin color, IQ, etc., are based on inherited DNA, and therefore could be applied to different racial groups. But the question persists if factors—such as sociability, mental attitudes, the tendency to crime and corruption (among others)—are also innate and inherited, or simply culturally learned, and will disappear over generations as immigrants assimilate and adapt to other customs and practices.

Recent studies have shown that there is a process called epigenetics (these are inherited changes in gene activity that are not caused by changes in the DNA sequence) in which conditions experienced by previous generations cause subtle changes in the way genes work. In an experiment, researchers have trained mice to fear a cherry-like aroma, and despite not meeting the smell before, their offspring exhibited a more terrifying response to the cherry blossom than the neutral smell. Does it make you wonder why?

There are many similar anecdotes with experience in human beings. Children who have experienced the horrors of wars can go beyond fear of war of other generations; and there are also many stories that lead to a common syndrome called the second-generation syndrome of the Holocaust survivors. Although there is no scientific and rigorous research that clearly shows the mechanism by which phobias, fears, and other extreme experiences are transmitted through generations, through the transmission of the "memory" of experienced ancestral generations, more and more theories about the latter are becoming known. Recent research with animals, which we will talk about later, seems to provide "convincing" evidence of the biological transmission of such "memory," along with associated brain changes, of adult male mice that was evidenced with their children and then grandchildren.

Let's clarify this proposal further. The inheritance is typically associated with the Mendelian genetic laws of transmission of information from parents to offspring by alleles (DNA sequence). However, there are increasing empirical data suggesting that traits (and perhaps some that are value-driven) can be acquired from ancestors by mechanisms that do not imply genetic alleles, referred to as non-genetic inheritance. Information that is not genetically transmitted through the generations includes the traumatic experience of parents and long-term exposure to certain environments (i.e., living within a context of incongruence between important values) that could have effects on parental cell mutations and polymorphisms.[6]

Non-genetic inheritance is not limited to the first generation of the progeny, but it can involve grandchildren and even other generations. Non-genetic inheritance has been observed for multiple traits, including global development, cardiovascular risk, and metabolic symptoms, but this presentation will focus on the inheritance of behavioral patterns related to living through chronic (or long term) periods of value's incongruence. Generational non-genetic inheritance is often interpreted as the transmission of epigenetic marks, such as DNA methylation and chromatin modifications, through gametes (transgenerational epigenetic inheritance). However, the information can be carried through generations by many bioactive substances, including hormones, cytokines, and even microorganisms, without the involvement of the gametes.

Thus, based on experiments with animals and limited anecdotes of empirical data in humans, it is presumed that both acute traumatic experiences and chronic situations such as incongruence of values can trigger diseases, but they can also affect the first and second generations through mechanisms of hereditary processes that are not genetically transmitted. Remember that using the term "epigenetic" to describe processes that are not heritable is controversial. Unlike genetics based on changes to DNA sequencing (genotype), changes in gene expression or cellular phenotype of epigenetics have other causes, thus use of the prefix EPI (Greek: Επque—over, out of, around).

If we are talking about animal experiments, I like to share a classic example. Fearful memories persecute descendants of mice: the genetic footprint of traumatic experiences carries at least two generations.[7] In this experiment, mouse puppies—and even offspring of offspring—may inherit an association fearful of a certain odor with pain, even if they have not experienced pain themselves, and without the need for genetic mutations. Certain fears can be inherited through the generations, as suggested by a provocative study of the behavior of mice. The authors suggest that a similar phenomenon could influence anxiety and addiction in humans. But some researchers are skeptical of the findings because a biological mechanism that explains the phenomenon has not been identified. Researchers propose that DNA methylation, a reversible chemical modification of DNA that typically blocks the transcription of a gene without altering its sequence, explains the inherited effect.

And what about human beings? Studies have hinted that environmental factors can influence biology more rapidly through "epigenetic" modifications, which alter gene expression, but not their actual nucleotide sequence. For example, children who were conceived during a harsh famine in the Netherlands in the 1940s are at increased risk for diabetes, heart disease, and other conditions, possibly due to epigenetic alterations of genes involved in these diseases. A very extensive study of 350 twins (in Minnesota) concluded that for most of the measured traits, more than half of the variation was found to be due to inheritance, leaving less than half determined by the influence of parents, the home environment, and other life experiences.

Based on this evidence, I would like to propose the following hypothesis that occurs for acute reasons (concentration camp, war, etc.) or chronic long-term situations such as living in situations of incongruence of values.

HYPOTHESIS: The ends of the epigenetic changes that can be inherited up to two generations.

If what I have described so far makes sense, I wish to make some tentative conclusions:

- Is it possible that behavioral traits such as corruption, aggression, criminality, non-obedience, violence, disrespect, and other values bearded or exercised by parents pass through two generations of offspring?
- Should we try and intervene and help modify such undesirable traits and if we are effective, will it prevent potential undesirable behaviors to the next two generations?
- What would be the role of future therapists, psychologists, and coaches to reduce unwanted behaviors knowing that they are now aware of the fact

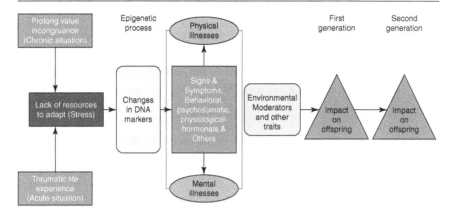

Figure 6.1 Impact of stress and value incongruence on two generations of offspring. This model is a hybrid product of my stress model and combined with the consequences of the epigenetic process. For stress, see Dolan S. L. (2007) *Stress, Self-Esteem, Health and Work.* Palgrave Macmillan. This model also served for the development of the next tool that we are working presently and called: *The Stress Map.*

that they are not only helping the client/coachee (right now), but possibly two more generations?

- And finally, is it possible to reduce the incongruence between values (in time) in order to break the cycle of chronic stress and avoid possible mutations in the DNA that will be passed up to two generations of offspring?

Honestly, my intuition in response to all these questions is Yes. Imagine the consequences for the coaching profession: Now, if you do good work while using the concept, methodology, and tools that we have offered in this book, not only are you helping a coachee/client to overcome their problems and have a better quality of life, but indirectly helping their children and the children of their children. Wow! This is heavy stuff!!!! (See Figure 6.1.)

BOX 6.1 CHILDREN INHERIT THE SUFFERING OF PARENTS

Source: El Pais Digital 21/10/2018 article by Miguel Angel Criado. Free translation of some excerpts.

- For years, animal studies have shown that certain environmental factors cause changes in genetic information that pass from one generation to another. It's like they leave marks that will turn off or alter genes but without altering the DNA. It has been proven that the sugar taken by parents can make their descendants obese or that the bad food of the grandparents would harm the health of their future grandchildren. Despite the great impact it could have on science and health, little is known about these epigenetic mechanisms in humans and knowing more would require experiments that ethics does not allow.

- There is another fact that reinforces the thesis of epigenetic base: within the same family, the children that the prisoners of war had after surviving were up to 2.2 times more likely to die before their siblings at the same age.

- "There is certainly intergenerational transfer of traits in humans, something that can occur by well-known methods, such as genetic inheritance, or cultural heritage, such as learning," recalls professor at the University of New South Wales (Australia), Neil Youngson. "What is special here is that this research shows a different inheritance mechanism, epigenetics, in which an environmental exposure (in this case the hunger or stress, the authors cannot tell which one) induces molecular changes in the gametes which, in turn, affect the health or behavior of their descendants," explains this investigator.

- And, there is one last fact of the study of prisoners of war that intrigues scientists: the trauma of so much suffering was only inherited by the sons; the daughters were not affected as much. Neither the authors nor the experts consulted know for certain the reason for this discrimination by sex. Perhaps a current study in progress might explain the gender variations of the third generation, of the grandchildren and granddaughters of these soldiers.

6.3 Values and spirituality: The inner voyage to coaching

Values, spirituality, and leadership effectiveness

Managers, professionals, and leaders often ask themselves, "Who am I?" and "What am I to do?" Decades ago, the reply to this question depended more on institutional and bureaucratic power, but now it depends on the capacity to articulate and inspire mutually selected values.[8] I mentioned earlier and want to reiterate that values were once considered by business leaders as "too soft" to be included in any serious approach to management, but they have now become a central part of organizational strategy. The concepts "Managing by Values" and "Coaching by Values," which I've introduced in this book are fast becoming the principal drivers for reengineering a sustainable, competitive, and emotional–spiritual culture. A new form of transcendent spiritual leadership is arising from an internal philosophical commitment and is expressed in actions appealing to diverse cultural environments.[9]

The extent to which leaders can obtain sharing and consensus in the configuration of the triaxial model is reflective of their leadership effectiveness. In the recent past, we have witnessed the downfall of leaders in almost every area—business, politics, religion, sports, and more. There might be thousands of reasons for these failures. But I believe that almost all of them are connected by one underlying thread—values.

Therefore, a new leadership framework is needed to enable leaders to understand the true drivers of leadership. The model needs to enable them to stay on track by following their love, passion, and compassion. They need to find the balance between their instrumental values and spiritual values; they need to find the answer to three basic questions: Why did I initially assume leadership? Have those reasons changed? Do I still want to lead?

The triaxial model of values for alignment and realignment has been proposed as the framework for explaining excellence in various fields. In the 2010 world football cup in South Africa, some national teams ended in disaster because of their failure to share values, especially between the leader (the coach) and the followers (the players). In the case of the French team, we can see the incongruence between the coach's values and those of the players. By contrast, excellence (as seen in the Spanish team) can be explained by the degree of harmony and shared values (e.g., competitiveness, hard work, team spirit, collegiality) among team members and leadership. Business leaders should take a note from these experiences in the sports world. Technical competencies alone do not generate success. It requires collective passion and team synergy. The task of an effective leader in the twenty-first century is to build a culture that aligns these values with the corporate core (key organizational values), creating corporate well-being. Corporate well-being is achieved when the core values of an organization are shared and aligned with the mission and vision of the organization.

The missing link: The spiritual values of an inspired leader

Avinash Kaushik identifies three "spires" of great leadership: Aspire, Perspire, Inspire:[10]

- **Aspire:** To have a great ambition or goal; to strive toward an end. Great leaders aspire for greatness—for themselves, for their teams, for their companies, for every individual around them. They are not content with what exists or what is possible. They are long-term thinkers. They have an elevator pitch handy that articulates what their vision is, what they are trying to get done, and how the team they lead can contribute to value for the employees, the customers, and the shareholders. Great leaders are hungry; they want more and are never satisfied with the status quo. They want to change the world (even if the "world" is their little ecosystem) for the benefit of their employees, their companies, and themselves (in that order). An exemplar of such a leadership is the late Akio Morita, the co-founder and chairman of Sony, who was known for the clarity with which he viewed his role as the company's leader: "My most important mission is to create a company where I can satisfy the people who work there, then come the clients, and only after come the shareholders."

- **Perspire:** To work hard, to be industrious, and to sweat. It also means to resist pressures, to perform with great diligence or energy, and to sustain the effort. Great leaders work harder and smarter with every passing day. Great leaders are not necessarily the slave drivers who stay at work until midnight or make people work weekends (which can become stressful and counterproductive[11]); great leaders simply bring 110% of themselves to work during work hours and set an awesome example for all those around them. Great leaders stay focused, and they don't give up easily. Because of their passion for creating meaning, they can get each person around them to bring his or her complete self to work. An exemplary model of such a great leader was John D. Rockefeller, who used to say: "Get up early, work hard, strike oil."

- **Inspire:** To affect, guide, or fill with enlivening or exalting emotion; to stimulate to action. Great leaders' magnificent success (personal and professional) comes from their ability to inspire those around them to contribute to the creation of meaning in this world. Exemplary figures of this type of leader are Nelson Mandela and the late Martin Luther King, who kept their dreams and inspirations intact through years of hardship and in the face of imprisonment, hatred, and all manner of injustices.

Kaushik considers "inspire" to be an essential element of a great leader. Looking at his definition and taking it a bit further, can we define an inspirational leader? There are many ways to view the term *inspirational*, because it means different things to different people. The English *inspire* is derived from the Latin verb *inspirare*: "to breathe into," "breathe upon," or "breathe in." In one of its first uses in English, a use that is now archaic, it literally meant "to infuse with life by breathing." Even though that particular use is now archaic, it has certainly influenced the evolution of the word in all its forms (*inspirational, inspired*, and so on), so we could say that when a person inspires others, he or she breathes in (finds inspiration) and then breathes into (others).

An inspirational leader breathes into others and makes them feel alive, and they, in turn, want to follow. But before inspiring others, a leader must be inspired; he or she must first breathe in inspiration. I think this is the closest I can come to defining spirituality in the context of leadership. Inspiration is personal and specific to each leader. Where one leader will find inspiration, another may not. Some may find inspiration inside themselves, others may find it in the external world, and many leaders will find it in both places. But all are inspired, and all have the ability to engender that inspiration in others.

Internal inspiration emerges from dealing with the most essential aspects of being: What is my core purpose in life? What am I passionate about? What is it, within me, that inspires me to take action? How will I follow and express that inspiration? *External* inspiration emerges from contacts with the external world: Who inspires me? What are the characteristics of the people or things that inspire me? What is it in the external world that inspires me to action?

The most distinguishing characteristic of visionary, effective leaders is their relentless insistence on sticking to their personal values. Visionary leadership is based on a balanced expression of the spiritual, mental, emotional, and physical dimensions. It requires core values, clear vision, empowering relationships, and innovative action. When one or more of these dimensions are missing, leadership cannot manifest a vision.

A commitment to values is an outstanding characteristic of all visionary leaders. They embody a sense of personal integrity and radiate a sense of energy, vitality, and will. Will is standing in a spiritual state of being. Will is a spiritual attribute, which allows a leader to stand for something. Because we have already dealt with ethical, emotional, and economic values (in the triaxial model), in this section, we will explore the connection of visionary leadership to spiritual values.

The category "spiritual values" does not comprise entirely new values. Some of the values in this set might traditionally be considered emotional values or ethical values. The primary reason for differentiating them is that spiritual values come from a beyond-body perspective of life and the universe.[12] The emotional values dimension focuses more on the feelings, attitudes, and traits in individuals: the spiritual values dimension focuses on another level of the individuals, where they create the significance of their being. Unlike other values, spiritual values need not always have the characteristics of direct instrumentality. Spirituality is notoriously hard to define. Giacalone and Jurkiewicz, for example, provide 14 different definitions of spirituality. A sample includes the following:[13]

- A personal life principle that animates a transcendent quality of relationship with God.
- The human striving for the transforming power present in life; the attraction and movement of the human person toward the divine.
- The personal expression of ultimate concern.
- A transcendent dimension within the human experience.

Others describe spirituality according to various characteristics, ranging from the personal to the supreme to interconnectedness to a guiding plan for our lives. In sum, there is no universally accepted definition of spirituality.

Perhaps in the future, the triaxial model of culture will be converted into a quadriaxial model, with the new spiritual dimension providing a place for one to register such values as life purpose, virtue, unity, truth, and hope.

6.4 Toward a new proposed quadriaxial model of values-based leadership

Following the extensive presentation (albeit focus on leadership) of spirituality, the question arises: Should we add a spiritual dimension to the triaxial model to form a fourth axis? Converting the triaxial model to a quadriaxial model? Talking about spirituality and leadership is risky. Business leaders today are usually judged by their results and their ability to create wealth—not by their sense of spirituality and how this has influenced, or led to, their results. However, leadership and even the practice of business always entail risk. Putting any vision into practice is inherently risky, as is selecting the most appropriate leadership role or style for a given situation. Visionary leaders don't shy away from risk or deliberations of risk and return, but rather they assess risk and return from not only an economic perspective but also from human and social ones, asking the question, risk and return for whom?

In a recent "World Congress on Spirituality and Creativity in Management" that was held in Barcelona (April 2015), many respected academic scholars, business practitioners, and CEOs from all over the world very clearly described a strong connection between their spiritual practices of daily life—such as prayer or meditation—and leadership effectiveness. Moreover, they also described many applications of beliefs—emphasized within and by many spiritual traditions (faiths)—as crucial leadership skills, including showing respect for others, demonstrating fair treatment, expressing care and concern, listening responsively, recognizing the contributions of others, and engaging in reflective practice. This suggests: (a) that spiritual values and practices are embedded within the core of humanity—not just within certain cultures or in only part of one's life; (b) that one's personal, reflective spiritual practice has a strong and enduring impact on the people and environments in which people lead and work; and (c) that leaders have a need for reflective practice in order to be universally effective.

Here are a couple of direct quotes from some of the academic leaders who have participated in the Barcelona Spirituality and Creativity in Management Congress:

- "The balance with humanization and spirituality is what matters most" (*Richard Boyatzis*—Distinguished university professor of Organizational Behavior, Psychology, and Cognitive Science at Case Western Reserve University).
- "The quality of a great leader is their spiritual qualities, including the inner freedom to decide" (*Chris Lowney*—Former senior executive at JP

Morgan, prolific author, and chairman of the board of Catholic Health Initiatives).

- "Creativity emerges when we are committed to the expression of our own essence" (*Richard Barrett*—Prolific writer on the evolution of human values in business and society, founder of the Barrett Value Center and the Barrett Academy for the Advancement of Human Values).

- "Future leaders will need to be more humane on one hand and exemplify inspiration on the other hand" (*Jaume Gurt*—Former CEO, InfoJobs, Spain, and member of the board of trustees of the Global Future of Work Foundation).

- "Spiritual people are more daring and thus more creative" (*Simon Dolan*—Former ESADE Business School Future of Work chair, and present president of the Global Future of Work Foundation).

- "We are told that 70 to 80% of what we do comes from accepted and automatic habits, these habits come from our lifestyle DNA that acts as a filter for how we think and act. At the most basic level, 'spirituality' is a filter through which we live" (*Dave Ulrich*—Rensis Likert professor of Business, a partner at the RBL group).

I argue that contemporary leaders need to develop a capacity to embrace and enact all four axes of values of the proposed quadriaxial model: economic–pragmatic, ethical–social, emotional–developmental, and spiritual–universal (see Figure 6.2).

Although spiritual values are not as decisive as those described in the triaxial value model—that is, they do not have a direct impact on organizational effectiveness—they do provide a platform for aligning the instrumental values. In the short term, organizations and leaders can "get by" without spiritual values; in the long term, however, their absence makes their mission, the development of an innovation culture, and the creation of long-term sustainability nearly impossible. Adding spiritual values to leadership practice and the spirituality axis to the triaxial model of values, are therefore essential actions for people exercising leadership in any field. Though no CEO will be around long enough to be judged on whether they have successfully enabled such a culture, or achieved its long-term benefits, they will know from their own sense of inner leadership, meaning, and values that they are nurturing the humanness of people, organizations, and societies and are seeding the fertile soil of flourishing work environments that bring out the potential of people.

Leadership effectiveness, spiritual values, and the paths to happiness

In order to better understand the connection between leadership effectiveness, spirituality, and happiness in relation to the world of work, we need to understand the concept of visionary leadership, which is often equated with the

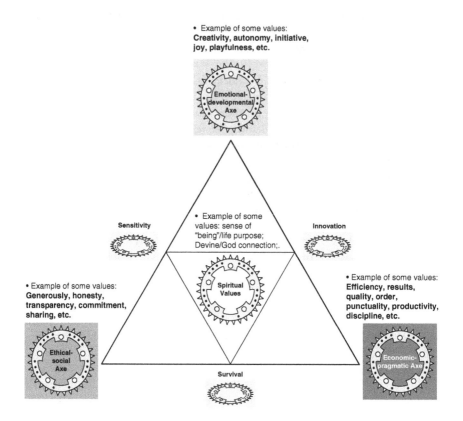

Figure 6.2 A proposed quadriaxial model of value-based leadership.

ability to see higher spiritual forces at work behind the scenes of events. Many visionary leaders seek alignment with these supporting and redemptive forces. Both George Washington and Winston Churchill spoke about the help they received from a "guiding hand." Churchill said, "We have a guardian because we serve a great cause, and we shall have that guardian as long as we serve that cause faithfully." Sojourner Truth, a former slave, was guided by an inner spiritual experience to preach the emancipation of slaves and women's rights all over the country during the U.S. Civil War. President Anwar Sadat of Egypt had a vision in which Mohammed told him to create peace in the Middle East. This is the hidden story behind the Camp David accords. Even Albert Einstein, who considered himself to be nonreligious, turned to the divine and to spirituality, which he saw as complementary to science. Einstein spoke of a "spirit manifest in the laws of the universe" and his sincere belief in a "God who reveals Himself in the harmony of all that exists."

Here are some famous quotes about visionary spiritual business leaders:

> The companies that survive longest are the ones that work out what they uniquely can give to the world—not just growth or money, but their excellence, their respect for others, or their ability to make people happy. Some call those things a soul.
>
> —Charles Handy

> A leader has the vision and conviction that a dream can be achieved. He inspires the power and energy to get it done.
>
> —Ralph Lauren

> A leader's role is to raise people's aspirations for what they can become and to release their energies so they will try to get there.
>
> —David Gergen

Visionary leaders understand that spirit at work is all about finding meaning and purpose, beyond self, through work. It involves profound feelings of well-being, a belief that one's work contributes, a sense of connection to others, and a feeling of common purpose.

Visionary leadership is much more than directing others. It starts from within: from seeing problems to seeing possibilities, from seeing the glass half empty to seeing the glass half full, and from looking outside for answers to finding them within. Leading from within is a shift to focusing on inner knowing and inner strengths. Even if a visionary leader's original inspiration arose from something in the outside world (the "external inspiration" I discussed above), that external phenomenon affected an internal transformation within the leader. The key to understanding this is values.

Times of crisis and times of enlightenment are times with the potential for change and growth. In these times, people often begin to question their values, priorities, and ways of living and working. Significant and painful life events, including the death of a loved one, the break-up of one's family, illness, organizational downsizing, or loss of job can be viewed as opportunities as well as challenges. Sometimes referred to as the "dark night of the soul," these events tend to bring forth the need to create meaning. And the meaning we ascribe to them is central to how we emerge on the other side. Profound spiritual experiences such as near-death experiences or personal epiphany experiences that occur while in a sacred place or being in nature can be similarly transformative.

Visionary leaders who aspire and inspire understand that to engender meaning in themselves and in their followers, they need to show them paths to happiness. Based on growing trends in positive psychology, Seligman proposed three paths to happiness: the life of pleasure, the life of engagement, and the life of meaning.[14] The "pleasurable life" is what we experience when we participate in enjoyable activities like playing games with our children, sharing a good meal, or taking holidays. The "life of engagement" is being wholly involved in, thoroughly understanding, and using our strengths in any activity that we find challenging and rewarding—work, play, or family life, among others. When we experience this deep engagement and total absorption, we are said to be in a state of flow,[15] a state that we discussed briefly in chapter 3. Finally, a "life of meaning" develops when an individual uses his or her strengths for the purpose of something larger than self. A "meaningful life" comes from serving others and may include attending to the family, caring for other people, volunteer activities, or work. The visionary and inspirational leader can help followers move from the life of pleasure to the life of meaning.

A study that reviewed more than 150 research results shows a clear consistency between spiritual values and practices and effective leadership.[16] Values that have long been considered spiritual ideals, such as integrity, honesty, and humility, have been demonstrated to have an effect on leadership success. Practices traditionally associated with spirituality have also been shown to be connected to leadership effectiveness. All the following practices have been emphasized in spiritual teachings, and they have also been found to be critical leadership skills: showing respect for others, demonstrating fair treatment, expressing care and concern, listening responsively, recognizing the contributions of others, and engaging in reflective practice.

Workplace spirituality can be used as a framework of organizational values that promote employees' experience of transcendence through the work process and facilitate their sense of being connected in a way that provides feelings of compassion and joy. Spiritual values do not demonstrate a direct instrumentality like the triaxial values but demonstrate a significant indirect instrumentality by creating a platform on which the other values may be aligned. (If this seems to contradict what I said in the previous section about the future of the triaxial model and the quadriaxial model, read on. I will discuss this in the next section.) Many leadership theories emphasize the need for the leader to articulate an inspiring vision, but as I've emphasized throughout this book, what is most important is not the words but the actions that follow.

6.5 Toward a new universal model of values

In the former section I argue that leaders in the twenty-first century will need to have the capacity to strike a balance between all four sets of values: *economic–pragmatic*, *ethical–social*, *emotional–developmental*, and *spiritual*. I refer to such leaders as "universal" leaders. From our previous discussions, both here and throughout the book, some values suggest themselves as candidates for the proposed fourth axis: cooperation and partnership; appreciation of diversity; respect for life; respect for nature and ecosystems; and a meaningful work and life balance for most of the people in an organization.

The universal values-based leader undertakes the role of identifying and promoting the values—from all dimensions or axes—shared by the stakeholders of the organization. This leader should aspire to become a leader, perspire to achieve goals, and inspire himself or herself to raise the bar for the spiritual contents. The model for this new kind of leader is presented schematically in Figure 6.3.

Leaders who practice this type of leadership will increase organizational well-being. Notice that I say organizational *well-being* rather than organizational *performance*. The three dimensions of values in the triaxial model can be instrumental in enhancing performance or profits if they do not deter from the quality of life and meaning of work. The spiritual values axis, however, should contain non-instrumental properties and need not necessarily be directly linked to organizational performance. This is in accordance with the fundamental paradox of organizational spirituality articulated by Lips-Wiersrma: "Those who practice spirituality in order to achieve better corporate results undermine both its practice and its ultimate benefits."[17]

For use in evaluating leadership and guiding leaders, I propose adding another axis to the model, the axis of spirituality, thus creating a "quadriaxial" model. True leadership requires values from all four axes, or dimensions. The

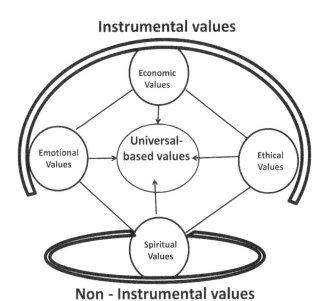

Figure 6.3 A universal values-based leader. Source: Adapted from Raich, M., & Dolan, S. L. (2008) *Beyond*, p. 119. Palgrave Macmillan. Used with authors' permission.

four axes, however, like the three axes of the 3Es triaxial model, need not be symmetrical.

A spiritually friendly workplace respects people's deepest values and belief systems and allows them to incorporate these values in their daily work interactions, bringing meaning to work. At first, some people may feel uneasy about using words such as *spirituality* and *spiritual* when discussing workplace values, but this is often because they are confusing spirituality with religion. Spirituality does not imply adherence to a religion, nor is it defined by an explicit set of religious beliefs or practices. On the contrary, some people are religious without being spiritual, while others are spiritual without being religious. Spirituality is an individual contract that one makes with oneself; it may involve religion, but it doesn't need to. It is a contract about beliefs—often involving a transcendent other, but not always; it may be based on nature, the universe, and its direction (e.g., teleology), or even physics, but it *always* involves how we see and value other human beings and the world. It is how people identify themselves to the outside world, how they view the world, how they interact with others, and on what fundamental basis they make decisions.

Talking about spiritualism and leadership is a risky business. Leaders are normally judged by hard numbers, the added value they might bring, or have brought to wealth creation.[18] The "experiencing of life," an existential agenda, is often missing from the pages of management journals. No matter how broad the range of perceptions of spirituality may be, all definitions in one way or another involve ideas expressed by the word *interconnectedness*. In my experience, the Coaching by Values framework can serve as the link between the instrumental values of the real business world and the spiritual need for experiencing life. Some people call this combination of the body (materialistic drivers) and the soul (spiritual needs) "spiritual intelligence."

Leadership in the twenty-first century needs to go beyond pure pragmatism to encompass a more holistic perception of the world. Coaching by Values using the four-axis (quadriaxial) model can be a benchmark for assessing and understanding a deeper meaning of life. Clearly not all leaders can be described as spiritual leaders, just as not all leaders can act as coaches, but as we enter the Third Millennium, thousands of individuals representing a new breed of visionary leaders in all fields of human endeavor are emerging around the world. They are leading a quiet revolution energized by the power of the soul. Perhaps by embracing and supporting those who lead from their core spiritual values, we can deepen those leadership qualities in ourselves.

As A. Deshpande and S. Shukla have said, "We are all spiritual beings. Unleashing the whole capability of the individual—mind, body, and spirit— gives enormous power to the organization. Spirituality unlocks the real sense of significance of the organization's purpose."[19]

CLBV Reflection

How spiritual are you? A short quiz*

To find out how spiritual you are, take this test, which is adapted from a personality inventory devised by Washington University psychiatrist Robert C. Cloninger, author of *Feeling Good: The Science of Well-Being.*[20]

1.	I often feel so connected to the people around me that it is like there is no separation between us.	True	False
2.	I often do things to help protect animals and plants from extinction.	True	False
3.	I am fascinated by the many things in life that cannot be scientifically explained.	True	False
4.	Often I have unexpected flashes of insight or understanding while relaxing.	True	False
5.	I sometimes feel so connected to nature that everything seems to be part of one living organism.	True	False
6.	I seem to have a "sixth sense" that sometimes allows me to know what is going to happen.	True	False
7.	Sometimes I have felt like I was part of something with no limits or boundaries in time and space.	True	False
8.	I am often called "absent-minded" because I get so wrapped up in what I am doing that I lose track of everything else.	True	False
9.	I often feel a strong sense of unity with all the things around me.	True	False
10.	Even after thinking about something a long time, I have learned to trust my feelings more than my logical reasons.	True	False
11.	I often feel a strong spiritual or emotional connection with all the people around me.	True	False
12.	Often when I am concentrating on something, I lose awareness of the passage of time.	True	False
13.	I have made real personal sacrifices in order to make the world a better place, like trying to prevent war, poverty, and injustice.	True	False
14.	I have had experiences that made my role in life so clear to me that I felt very happy and excited.	True	False
15.	I believe that I have experienced extrasensory perception.	True	False
16.	I have had moments of great joy in which I suddenly had a clear, deep feeling of oneness with all that exists.	True	False
17.	Often when I look at an ordinary thing, something wonderful happens. I get the feeling that I am seeing it fresh for the first time.	True	False
18.	I love the blooming of flowers in the spring as much as seeing an old friend again.	True	False

19. It often seems to other people like I am in another world   True   False
because I am so completely unaware of things going on
around me.
20. I believe that miracles happen.   True   False

Scoring: Give yourself one point for each True and no points for each False.

14–20 points means you are a highly spiritual person, a real mystic

12–13 points means that you have spiritual awareness, that you are easily lost in the moment

8–11 points means that you scored average on the spirituality scale; there is a room for further
spirituality development if you desire to follow this path

6–7 points means that you are a practical, empirical person, lacking self-transcendence

1–5 points means that you are highly skeptical, resistant to developing spiritual awareness

Note: This is a quick-and-dirty test. It is designed to give you a *general* idea about your level of
spirituality.
Source: © Robert C. Cloninger, Sansone Family Center for Well-being, Washington University,
St. Louis, Mo. Used with author's permission.

Our universe is changing as I write. And it is about to change even more. We
are witnessing the birth of global values. A host of nations in the Middle East
are transforming as the masses discover the values of democracy and freedom
and struggle to break from the tyrannical rule (e.g., Egypt, Tunisia, and Libya,
to name a few). These events were predictable, but no one knew exactly when
they would occur.

In our futuristic book, *Beyond*, we argued that there is an urgent need for
humanity to leave its comfort zone before it becomes too late.[21] The world
of tomorrow will be very different from the world of today, or the world of
yesterday. But in what ways will it be different? What will that world look like?
It is up to us.

In *Beyond*, we defined six key areas in which dramatic shifts in basic values are needed immediately if we are to ensure the survival of our species:
society, religion, environment, science and technology, business, and politics.
We drew a roadmap to the future and explored the ways in which previously
unimaginable changes and developments will and are transforming the social
and business landscape of the twenty-first century.

In the new world, the actions of business leaders may well be judged in
regard to their compliance with universal human values, eco-friendliness, and
meaningfulness. Today, we can see customers requesting, and we envision
down the road legislators demanding, eco-friendliness. The millions of eco-
minded organizations could create a powerful alliance of people caring for the
future. The spike in people searching for meaningfulness on the job is an indi-
cation that a significant percentage of the population is already looking beyond

the greed-based economism that has dominated the Western world since the last quarter of the past century.

As we look toward the future, we must also look to indigenous peoples. They have been able to survive longer than any other existing civilizations, in part because of their appreciation for the natural world. They recognize the Earth as a partner whose resources are precious gifts not to be taken for granted and depleted. Their experiences mastering crises that threatened their existence and their appreciation of the systemic connections among all living things have much to teach us. This interconnectedness requires empathy. Scientific research suggests that empathy is the foundation of morality, and many aspects of morality appear to be hard-wired in the brain. In addition, emotions are central to moral thinking. The appreciation that we live in an interconnected system comprising all we can see, hear, and feel requires—and in turn generates—empathy. Indigenous cultures and the stories they tell are an invaluable source of insights (Figure 6.4).

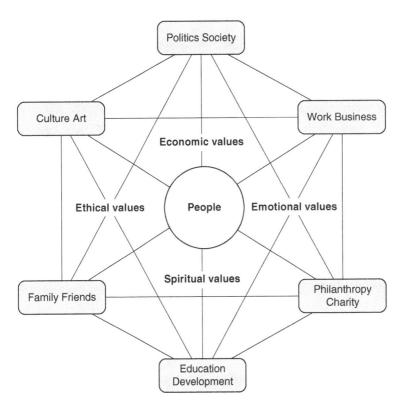

Figure 6.4 Embedded emergent values: A holistic view. Source: Raich, M., & Dolan, S. L. (2008) *Beyond*, p. 89. Palgrave Macmillan. Used with authors' permission.

Figure 6.4 represents a holistic view of people's values and attitudes, which change as a function of changes that occur in the immediate environment, which in this global century may encompass the entire planet. As it shows, *people* (us) are sitting in the center surrounded by several boxes that represent the elements of our environment. At the top of the figure are *politics* and *society*; in the upper-right-hand is the way we *work*, and the way we do *business*. All of these—and all of us—are profoundly influenced by *culture* and the *arts*, by *family* and *friends*. At the base of the figure are the *education* and *development* opportunities open to us. These are one of the most significant determinants of a person's success (or not) and well-being (or lack of it). Finally, the social safety net—whether it is provided by social security or by *philanthropy* and *charity*—is a guarantor of survival if everything else has gone wrong.

As Figure 6.4 shows us, nothing less than models that are systemic and holistic will get us from here to a sustainable future. We need models with which we can co-create holistic and systemic scenarios of the future that encompass all the elements of our environment and consider all four dimensions of values. We need to expand our concept of value-based *management* by embracing the value-based *organization*. We must recognize and appreciate the impact of values on any organization, any system, any culture, and we must craft value creation models and models for determining the impacts of specific values.

The movement to identify and promote the values shared by societies around the world is relatively new but burgeoning, with several initiatives and projects doing just that. The most important is probably the Earth Charter Initiative, with formal endorsements by more than 2,000 organizations, including national and international bodies such as UNESCO (United Nations Educational, Social and Cultural Organization). Its declaration of principles for a just, sustainable, and peaceful world is a call for the shared responsibility of all humanity. It was created during a ten-year grassroots process with input from thousands of people in many countries around the world. This widely recognized, global consensus statement on ethics and values for a sustainable future is based on 16 principles organized into 4 major categories:

- respect and care for the community of life
- ecological integrity
- social and economic justice
- democracy, nonviolence, and peace

This is a step toward filling an urgent need to identify the shared code of ethics and conduct underlying all human societies, defining universal human values, and formalizing them in a global compact.

The creative and spiritual society[22]

With the right values, a creative society can generate real solutions to the existential key issues facing humanity and our planet. At the beginning of Chapter 4, I used the metaphor of a compass to describe an individual's values. Now imagine that compass providing direction for an entire society—and for each of its members. Keeping our eye on it and using it to find the direction again if we start to lose our way, we will be free to imagine and implement solutions at the farthest reaches of the mind. With the support of artificial intelligence entities, we will be able to develop the full potential of our creativity. Virtual reality already gives us the space to explore proposed solutions and test their impact on humanity in ways we never could have foreseen. New and more powerful methods of crafting and testing creative solutions will be developed. But we need to move from searching to finding and from finding to implementing creative solutions.

The first step toward the development of a creative society is overcoming the "gender issue," which has grown into a gender creativity gap. At a time when we need every iota of intellectual and spiritual creativity, we are (willfully at times) ignoring a huge reservoir of it—the "feminine," which resides in every female and, to some extent, in every male. The dominance of reason ("masculine") has come at the expense of intuition and emotional intelligence ("feminine"). The feminine way of thinking, being, and doing is crucial for true partnership and care; it is an essential energizer for the imagination. The demonization of the feminine—and its flip side, the worship of a crabbed and caricatured version of the feminine from afar—has driven the polarization of the masculine and the feminine through the whole population and civilization diminishing not only women but also males with feminine abilities, thus diminishing the entire society.

The resolution of the gender issue requires going much deeper and further than creating gender equality in the workplace, the polling place, and the like. In this regard, we should consider very seriously the framework that Riane Eisler has been developing and her suggestions for its implementation. She has been doing remarkable work over the past 20 years or so through her international Center for Partnership Studies.

In any discussion of developing solutions to the challenges confronting humanity, we should take a moment to consider the concept "innovation." Innovation by its very nature has a lasting impact on the environment. It has led to wonderful advances, but it is a transformative change that disrupts systems and may endanger that which gives our lives value. Some innovations in medicine have saved entire segments of societies around the globe from death. But innovations for the sake of profit in the short term may cause products to be rushed to the market before their effects (on humans or nature) are understood or known. Innovations in farming led to the Dust Bowl in the United States in the 1930s, destroying some of the North American continent's most fertile land.

Depending on the context (and whether one's vision is short term or long term), an innovation may be perceived as negative or positive. Over the long term, an innovation will show whether it in fact represented value creation or value destruction. The value of innovation is contextual in that it depends on what one values. For example, cutting a tree is a transformation, because it is irreversible, but it is a destructive change. Clear-cutting rain forests or old growth forests are large-scale examples of this. In the hands of a carpenter, however, a single felled tree may be the starting point for the creation of something that brings value to people—a chair, an armoire, or a bed. So where do we draw the line between "ethical" and "unethical" innovation?

Capitalism drives unethical innovation. In its rabid search for markets and its need for ever-greater accumulation of capital, it is transforming nature (our ecosystems) and has already resulted in the extinction of some species. It is highly volatile; it goes wherever it encounters the most favorable conditions for itself (safety, security, stability, low taxes, growth potential, and so on) with no regard for the quality of human life or the sanctity of nature, turning all human abilities and natural resources into numbers, churning them up and spitting them out.

All evidence points to the need to go beyond capitalism. If we don't, it will destroy itself—and probably us along with it. Taming, reforming, and reinventing capitalism are not options. It has shown itself to be a wild beast that behaves only behind the bars of a strong authoritarian governmental cage, and even then, only for so long. When freed, it devours everything, transforming it into capital, reifying the imagination, turning all the earth's gifts into products never to be regained, and leaving behind it a wake of death.

Capitalism also damages the mental health of the people who support it. Sound mental health is a universal goal of any human activity, and capitalism is rendering it unattainable.[23] The following are some of the key aspects of the capitalist system that corrode sound mental health:

- greed—for power, position, prestige, and money
- envy—regarding others' achievements, success, rewards
- egotism—about one's own accomplishments
- suspicion, anger, frustration, and paranoia
- anguish—over constant comparisons

We need a new direction for human society. We desperately need alternatives to which we can aspire, and which will provide us with new meaning. At the societal and corporate levels, we need to envision the future and venture into it. We must immediately develop initiatives to create social values and cease activities that forestall the opportunities of future generations. As employees, we can help an organization take society and the future into account. As individuals, we can help the global community through local action. And in everything we do, we can focus on the future. This is the only sure way to avoid unwanted surprises.

We need to strengthen partnership values and leave behind the old programming of conquest and control that has kept us from balanced and harmonious relations with ourselves, with others, and with nature.

BOX 6.2 VALUES INTELLIGENCE AS A WEAPON OF MASS CONSTRUCTION

Salvador García
University of Barcelona

Hyperprosa and hyperpoetry

> *The world lacks philosophy, it lacks poetry and it lacks utopia; a utopia made by responsible men and women.*
>
> Pera Duran Farell, 1921–1999

As Edgar Morin warns, we have been invaded by *"the hyper-economic, techno-bureaucratic."* The old conservative–liberal capitalist paradigm, based on enhancing our individual pragmatic survival impulse, is characterized by understanding money and the market as ends or axes of government, and people, and the rest of the natural ecosystem as resources to be used. This system has been promoting and utilizing our pragmatic Values Intelligence for decades through the formal and informal education system (school, family, and university), orienting us toward short-term material survival.

By achieving individual economic success as a great final value, highly productive individuals are generated that are easily predictable and subject to manipulation. This old capitalist system has made great technological and social advances, but its *chronic lack of a broader Intelligence of Values is beginning to threaten its own pragmatic sustainability due to a lack of ethical and emotional sustainability.* There is too much human and environmental suffering on our Planet Earth.

Under these conditions, good news appears: an awakening of collective consciousness of systemic unity ("everything is connected to everything") and of future viability as a species in the medium and long term is beginning to emerge. This *awakening of strategic consciousness* is enhancing our innate ability to know how to choose the most convenient ethical, pragmatic, and emotional values for our overall personal and collective development.

A eutopic, a realistic and necessary utopia, is emerging: the best technological and social achievements of the current "hyper-prosaic" system, based essentially on the development of our pragmatic Values Intelligence, will drive the development of a "hyperpoetry": a new post-capitalist paradigm, generative and liberating. This new paradigm is based on the connection with our inner source of intuition and wisdom. This internal connection allows the additional deployment of our other two axes of Values: (a) Intelligence, that of ethical values, such as love, authenticity, respect, or dignity, and (b) of emotional-generative or "poietic" values, such as self-confidence, mutual trust, imagination, joy, and enthusiasm.

Values Intelligence

We can define Values Intelligence as the ability to know how to read reality and choose the most convenient values for our overall personal and collective development. *Intellegere*, in Latin, contains the concepts of reading and choosing.

Our ability to understand and choose values depends on our level of *consciousness* (awareness) and *conscience* (consider). These two dimensions constitute the *Full Presence* or stable connection with our Being, the source of our best Intelligence of Values.

When the words-values that must guide our behavior do not arise from the depths of our Being, they tend to remain mere chatter. It is remarkable the superficiality and manipulation with which the subject of "values" is used in many business and political and even religious and educational contexts.

One thing is the final values or goods to have and take care in life (Insert 1) and another are the instrumental values or personal worth to cultivate and manifest to achieve them (Table 6.1).

Insert 1: Goods to have and take care of enabling a happy life (*in alphabetic order*).

Beauty, Clean planet, Culture, Equality, Family, Freedom, Friendship, Fun, Health, Image, Inner peace, Justice, Money, Create, Power, Prestige, Purpose, Recognition, Sense of belonging, Stability, Having time to be useful, Work–life balance.

Source: The ValueSquares Methodology, imagineLab UB -Ethikos 3.0, 2019.

Table 6.1 Triaxial Values Intelligence: Ethical, Emotional, and Pragmatic Values to Manifest and Cultivate in Life

Ethical worth	Emotional worth	Pragmatical worth
Ability to forgive	Adventure	Achievement ambition
Authenticity	Capacity to enjoy	Adaptability
Conscious consumption	Courage	Anticipation
Deep listening	Curiosity	Coherence of action
Empathy	Delusion	Collaboration
Equity	Desire to do and learn	Effort and perseverance
Generosity	Enthusiasm	Mental agility
Gratitude	Have details	Order
Honesty and transparency	Imagination and creativity	Patience
Humility	Inconformity	Persuasive ability
Idealism	Initiative and autonomy	Planning
Integrity of principles	Intuition	Punctuality
Kindness when speaking	Joy and good humor	Realism
Love	Mental opening	Reflection and analysis
Loyalty and commitment	Naturalness and freshness	Resolution
Common good orientation	Optimism	Rigorous
Respect	Overcoming adversity	Security and prudence
Responsibility	Self-confidence	Self-discipline
Service vocation	Trust in others	Simplicity
Tolerance	Warmth	Tolerance of ambiguity

Source: The ValueSquare Methodology© .imagineLab UB-Ethikos 3.0, 2019.

It has been more than 50 years since Milton Rokeach proposed dividing values into final and instrumental values, and these into ethical and competence values.

Competence values can be subdivided into pragmatic values (effort, simplicity, coherence) and into emotional-generative or "poietic" values (joy, imagination, confidence). To the three resulting axes and, honoring the Greek word for "axios," which means the axis, value or worth of a good worthy of being honored, we call them the "Triaxial Model of Values" (*MTV*). As we know, axiology is, precisely, the study of values (Table 6.1).

Following that same model, the concept of Triaxial Values Intelligence (*TVI*) refers to the existence of three axes of intelligence: ethics, pragmatics, and poietics. Its three metavalues are, respectively, love, coherence, and trust.

When three axes move in space in all directions, a sphere is created. In the central nucleus appears the Full Presence. Thus, we can represent the development of the *TVI* in spherical form (Figure 6.1).

Following this analogy of the sphere, the larger the diameter of our axes of values, the greater the axiological journey we will make for Life. On the other hand, when one of the three axes is less developed, distortions are created that make it difficult to roll through it.

Ethical Values Intelligence

The ability to know how to choose ethical values that guide our daily action toward our goals, such as dignity, authenticity, generosity, humility, dialogue, or compassionate love, is strategically essential for our full psychological health and our collective survival and prosperity. It attends to our need for authentic happiness and full existential sense by transcending our immediate egoic interest and orienting ourselves to the well-being of the other and the common good.

Contrary to what one might think, positive ethical intelligence is much more sociobiological than cultural, identifying itself with the modern concept of "neuroethics," that could be defined as the *neurobiological possibility of making the decision to behave lovingly with others so that said behavior can be declared a universal norm for the survival and individual and collective happiness of the majority of human beings* (Figure 6.5).

In other words, the ethical intelligence is a faculty of intelligence that consists of the free strategic choice of values and use of time in order to give full meaning to existence, ensure good coexistence, and ensure the survival of the species in the planet. In fact, these are the main problems we face as human beings and our ignorance is more than evident to solve them.

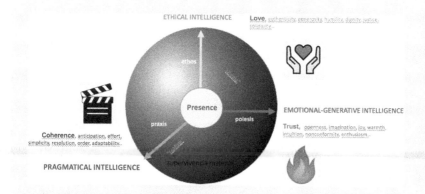

Figure 6.5 Triaxial Values Intelligence Sphere.

Poietic Values Intelligence

The Poietic Values Intelligence constitutes a second axis of the Triaxial Values Intelligence. It can be defined as the talent of going through Life releasing and helping to release emotional values that generate positive energy and creativity to do things. Therefore, it can also be called generative emotional intelligence or, simply, creative intelligence. Its meta-value is trust, related to others such as imagination, enthusiasm, openness, warmth, intuition, initiative, or joy.

Poiesis is a Greek word whose meaning is associated with generating, engendering, giving birth, but which is also linked with making, manufacturing, and building. Thus, poiesis also refers to imagine, create, or innovate. From this word is derived *poiema* (poem), which comes to mean from "creation from the spirit" to poetry or verse writing. In fact, classical philosophers speak of "poetry" as of creative activity in general.

Deciding to have time for poetry, in balance with ethics and pragmatism, demonstrates a high level of intelligence for Life well lived, to undertake projects with full meaning, and to lead them successfully. What is Life without poetry, without illusion, without details, without dreams, without surprise, and without courage? Of course, it is an extinguished life, without spark, without fire.

Unlike machine or cybernetic systems, such as an appliance or a computer, living systems have the *autopoietic* (self-organizing and generative) ability to self-generate by maintaining their own organization, which gives them identity and the ability to reproduce. In medicine, hematopoiesis is the generative capacity of blood cells to self-fabricate and multiply, just as it happens with the ability of human groups to self-organize with shared values.

Insofar as it deals with mental functions related to creativity, intuition, and emotional and artistic capacity in general, poietic intelligence is processed fundamentally in the frontal area of the right hemisphere of the brain, and its synergistic balance with those of the brain is highly recommended, logical and analytical functions supported by the left hemisphere.

The intelligence of especially generative emotional values, such as spontaneity, imagination, confidence, and joy, is often drowned in cultural contexts oriented to the maintenance of vertical power. In these vertical contexts, there is an excess of control structures, such as the army, the public administration, religious institutions and, of course, the vast majority of companies and educational institutions that are still based on rigid and bureaucratic paradigms, while the organizational metaphor is that of machine functioning.

The political power of the dominant socio-economic and cultural paradigm shows historical signs of being very interested in amputating highly poietic values such as imagination, trust, creativity, and the spontaneity of citizens through the educational system. And we must recognize with some sadness that the result is excellent for their interests of social control.

Pragmatic Values Intelligence

As we said at the beginning, the Pragmatic Intelligence is the Values Intelligence more reinforced by the educational system at the service of the system in general, and is the predominant one in the conventional business discourse. It is the perfect complement of the other two values intelligences: the Ethical Intelligence and the Poietic Intelligence, because without it both would remain mere ideal abstractions.

It is undeniable the utility of prose to make dreams come true and manage reality effectively, efficiently and, therefore, effectively. Having pragmatic intelligence means being able to choose good practical values to apply good theories and realize the "eutopia" that the world can one day be truly governed by ethical and poietic values.

Pragmatic intelligence is essential to face and solve challenges realistically, logically, "economically," and coherently in any activity of life, whether in the paid work environment, in voluntary work, or in daily tasks and domestic affairs.

This operational capacity serves no more than to survive, to succeed professionally in conventional environments, to manage organizations profitably and efficiently, not to leave things to do throughout life and, colloquially, not to "stay in clouds." As we have commented elsewhere when talking about the neuroscientific bases of the Triaxial Model of Values, the prefrontal lobe of the left hemisphere is the one that processes the most rational and analytical logic of pragmatic intelligence, which takes advantage of what is in the immediate perceived reality.

Other conceptualizations close to the instrumental values of pragmatic intelligence are those of talents, abilities, strengths, or, as they are usually called, "competencies." For the typically pragmatic and rationalist mentality, ethical and poietic values such as spontaneity, gratitude, authenticity, love, generosity, dignity, fantasy, or joy are not formally considered as talents that can lead to success and "practically" are never included in the lists of competencies usually used at the business or academic level.

However, from a strategic coherence perspective, a Value Intelligence that is genuinely pragmatic and survival-oriented is interested not only in short-term behavior, but in the long-term consequences of this behavior. For this, the Pragmatic Intelligence of Values must overcome deviations such as technocracy, efficiency, materialism, and, of course, human greed without limit, cause and effect of the state of ethical, emotional, and environmental decline of the currently dominant political and socio-economic paradigm.

The personal and collective deployment of our *Values Intelligence has to promote the massive construction of new microworlds* (classrooms, families, companies, cities, or entire countries) that, when resonating among them, favor the emergence of another possible world.

Note

1. *Eutopia* is a word invented by Tomas Moro, the author of *The Island of Utopia*, in the middle of the European Renaissance period. It means "good place" to live in the generative boundaries between the utopia or dream of an ideally necessary world and the pragmatic realism that can make it possible.

Salvador Garcia is the author of the first book in Spanish on "Management by Values," which was published in 1997 (McGraw Hill), 20 years ago, with the inestimable collaboration of Simon Dolan and later adapted to multiple other languages. His latest proposal is "Values Intelligence: a good step into oneself and three steps forward." In it, he exposes the foundations of his initial vision of the Triaxial Model of Values: ethical, pragmatic, and emotional-generative or "poietic."

Trained as a medical doctor. Obtained a diploma in Management Training and Development from Harvard University. Professor of Personal Development, Entrepreneurship, and Social Innovation at the Faculty of Psychology of the University of Barcelona (UB). Founder of the "imagineLab" a UB laboratory of "Intelligence of Values for the transition towards the new emerging post-capitalist paradigm."

6.6 Change and transformation as a value[24]

As mentioned before, in the last several years I have been researching and writing about the future of work. While I do not have a crystal ball neither am I a prophet, and nobody can talk with high certainty about the future, one conclusion that is certain is that "we are experiencing a profound paradigm shift from which there is no turning back." In other words, we are witnessing all over around us and especially in business and education a transformation. Remember, a transformation is not a change; hence there is no going back. That is why the leaders, in business and in the social and political sphere, need to acquire and deploy a set of skills of the type called "soft," as well as a significant change of attitude that will prepare them for them the future. The principal attitude that is needed from the new breed of leaders is to "open up," to "unlearn and relearn." The second set of attitudes requires one to forget the successes of yesterday and even today, and to focus on the new landscape. Leadership in all fields and sectors should be able to produce thoughts and actions aimed at understanding the future, which is no doubt Volatile, Uncertain Complex, and Ambiguous (VUCA). Getting out of the comfort zone is not an easy task, and many leaders may need the help of a good coach.[25]

Often, decisions taken at the organizational and/or individual level may trigger the demolition of solid companies and their reputation. From the bankruptcy of Lehman Brothers to the scandals at Enron that swept Arthur Andersen; from Wells Fargo Bank's bogus accounts to the latest Volkswagen scandals, a common factor seems to be at the root of these falls: people become incapable of acting in line with their level of responsibility, juggling simultaneously company values and their own values.[26]

This occurs because of a misguided sense of what is valuable. It may produce an altered scale of values where people base their decisions on unsustainable ideas and attitudes about themselves and their organization or even the environment. For a long time, the idea of leadership has focused on the idea of secular authority and power. It was believed that these were the characteristics necessary to make people want to follow the leader. Today we know that leadership depends on values. For example, if I asked you to think of someone who represents your icon of the best leader and to describe what determines that a leader be worthy of your trust, you would surely describe values.

Many leadership training programs believe that "soft skills" are too emotional to be included in any serious approach. However, studies and research on these topics consistently indicate that factors such as integrity, honesty, the ability to inspire or motivate others are at the top of the scale of importance when employees and peers evaluate their leaders.

In a context marked by VUCA, nations, communities, and businesses need to deploy their best talents. Values-based skills have become a central part of the organizational strategy today because rules, instructions, and procedures are not enough to awaken people to the kind of emotional bond and motivation that guarantee creativity, innovation, and teamwork. When the organization and individuals also face the uncertainty of transformation, the only way out of the comfort zone starts from the inside, where leaders wonder "who I am" and "what is the meaning of what I am doing."

The concepts of Managing and Coaching by Values sustain cultural reengineering that goes in the opposite direction to what we know as Hubris syndrome, which Sir David Owen described as "two intertwined features: diminished empathy and intuition unbridled." When intelligent people act driven by ego and overwhelming self-confidence and contempt for others, they end up exhibiting a form of incompetence that can culminate in catastrophic leadership failures. Some see the Hubris syndrome as nothing more than the extreme manifestation of normal behavior along a spectrum of narcissism. Others simply dismiss Hubris as an occupational hazard of powerful leaders, politicians, or leaders in business, the military, and academia; an unattractive but understandable aspect of those who crave power. The key concept is that Hubris syndrome is a disorder of the possession of power, particularly power, which has been associated with overwhelming success, held for a period of years, and with minimal constraint on the leader.[27]

Remember, values are not good or bad in themselves. The configuration of the main values is what defines and predicts people's willingness to act in one way or another. The implementation of the models by values (leading, managing, or coaching by values) applies to individuals, teams, and managers, and opens the door to the understanding of leadership from a truly holistic point of view, which recognizes change as a value for revitalizing cultures in life and business and inspires a base of collective commitment.

6.7 Values, expectations, and conducts of the Y generation

Parents, leaders, and managers must have the skills to manage different generations. I cannot finish this chapter without giving reference to the workforce of tomorrow. The coach must know that changing his pace, vocabulary, and conduit depends on the age of the client. Technology, the internet, cable television, social networks, and the globalized world give power to today's young people who did not exist before. Today, a 15-year-old boy knows a lot more than a baby boomer did at the age of 30. Until recently there were lots of talks about the millennia, but we must talk more and more about generation Y and Z. These generations think that they can challenge anyone, not because they have or will have academic degrees, but because they are raised with knowledge that keeps on changing, and they know how to "fish" the latest and that gives them power (Table 6.2).

If you read the characteristics of generation Y, you might think that it will be a real challenge to manage them. Among many existing companies, generation Y is getting a bad reputation for being difficult to both hire and manage. True, they're time-consuming, demanding, and they want to be both pushed and coddled. As a coach, you should only become sensitive that generation Y clients have different needs and expectations than your other coachees and may respond to you well if you show that you understand them. So, here are five coaching tips for managing generation Y:

1. Push them to become leaders themselves—Generation Y is used to having a strong role model. This generation grew up being told that there were no stupid questions. They will ask, and you must be ready to deliver.

Table 6.2 The Ten Values that Characterize Generation Y

Value	Meaning
Self-reliant	Their lifestyle and sense of liberty affects their learning style but also their relationships with their parents, friends, and potential employers. They think that they are self-sufficient. The value of liberty is cherished, but many times collide with reality, as 20 to 40% of this generation at some point will return to their parents' home safety net after not being able to economically support themselves.
Short-term orientation	They do not usually think of staying with the same company for more than a couple of years, and that these values inevitably lead to this other value that is the termism. The generation has short-term sights and objectives, knowing that if they will be even well-formed academically, it will serve only for a short while due to the speed of changes in business and society.
Personal branding	They want personal projects and want to develop a personal brand above and beyond what the company wants. For this reason, they understand the value added of being creative, which enables them to eventually be mobile and move elsewhere.
Individualist	Individualism should not be confused with selfishness; they are people who are committed and aware of social causes; but although it seems a countersense—some studies show that many young people of this generation live isolated in their world of internet and social networks and outside of the normal frame of social relations.
Scattered	Over-reporting, disruption, and lack of serious reflection or analysis contribute to dispersion. The desire to cover everything and to know everything in the shortest possible time leads this generation to be dispersed.
Flexible and virtual	They look for more flexible working hours and more relaxed workspaces. Their relations with the environment and with the world of work are based on this flexibility. They think that virtual relationships are enough to keep their privacy and independence.
Limited thoughtfulness and impatient	Impatience leads them to give less laps to things and think less about the consequences they may have; they are driven and act more by what they like. Their common motto/phrase is: "I don't live to work, I work to live, and if possible, I really want to settle in work that makes me happy, whatever time it lasts."
Dynamic and opportunist	They do not seek a long-term contractual relationship; they are more inclined to the freedom of being able to decide without ties, changing of work, or the place of residence always looking for the best opportunities.

(Continued)

Table 6.2 (Continued)

Value	Meaning
Disruptive	It is a term that is frequently used to denote a sudden rupture; thus, they are not satisfied with the traditional models of labor relations or work in general, and seek to break from past dogmatic schemes that their parents or grandparents performed labor. They want more open and direct communication with their bosses as well as the balance between family life and work.
Global	In a globalized world and with easy access to all new technologies and the use of fast and instant communication, this generation does not think so much about settling in a specific place of work but aspires to be able to work in any part of the world. This is often referred to as the triple A: work can be performed from **A**nyone, **A**nywhere, **A**nytime.

Don't forget that they will try to lead by example too. Generation Y is happy to get their hands dirty.

2. Ensure that they get specific training—Generation X was happy to be shown their desk and left alone. Generation Y might have a heart attack under those circumstances. Don't throw them in the deep-end either. Give them training wheels for a while. They will appreciate it, and you will receive superior work.

3. Ensure that the work is challenging—Boredom at the workplace was endemic for previous generations, but it will not work with this generation. They crave stimuli. They were brought up during the technology boom and their attention span is short. They will do so best when challenged. And remember, these fresh faces are **multitaskers**.

4. Keep technology current—An iPhone may not seem like a good coaching technique, but it will help you connect with a Generation Y worker. Without the proper technology, Generation Y will feel out of the loop. While they are not expecting everything to be state-of-the-art, if they know that there is an easier way to accomplish a task using technology, they will quickly become frustrated without it.

5. Respect generational differences—Generation Y is bursting with new ideas and a desire to share them. Don't assume that just because they are young that they are incapable. A good Generation Y coach will show them how to bring out the best in their ideas. This does not mean that Generation Y always has respect for older generations. Frequently one of the biggest clashes in the workplace has to do with a lack of respect for generational differences. Veterans, Baby Boomers, Generation X, and Generation Y all have different work techniques. As a coach you need to show how to manage them well together.

6.8 Conclusion

This chapter began with an interesting way to look at the neurobiology of values. Who could have ever imagined that values can be inherited? The discovery of epigenetic mechanisms allows us to trace values through three generations. While more research is needed, it seems that there is new recent evidence to support the claim that values indeed can be inherited.

Human beings are endowed with spiritual capacities. Sages, philosophers, poets, and artists, the founders of all the world's religions, and other thinkers, explorers, and seekers have shown this throughout history. An understanding of the positive virtues and values that reside in the spiritual gives individuals and societies the moral accountability that is the basis of human integrity. But even though values clarification is essential, so too is values education. This goes a step beyond critical analysis and intellectual appreciation and moves values into the realm of volition, stimulating the desire for improvement in ourselves, our families, our communities, and the world. Knowledge is impotent if not realized in action. We must translate our most precious principles and deeply held ideals into behaviors, individually and collectively.

The children of today will be the leaders of tomorrow. That's why we have dedicated this relevant section to understand the particular values and expectations of generation Y, and perhaps generation Z. If they are to hold and embody the values and the awareness that will transition our world to a healthy future, we need to demonstrate these ourselves through our behaviors and give voice to them with our words. This is a task for parents, for educators, for managers, and for politicians.

We live in a world that is every day more interconnected and more interdependent, and there is no place to escape. Universal values are more acutely needed in this age of globalization than ever before. Every society needs to be bound together by common values, so its members know what to expect of each other and are equipped with shared principles for managing their differences nonviolently, respectfully, and imaginatively. This is true across all cultures, from the smallest tribal body to the largest nation. And now, as our lives are affected almost instantly by things that people say and do on the far side of the world, it is increasingly true for us as a global community.

We must have global values in action that bind us together. In the end, history will judge us not by what we say but by what we do. Those who preach certain values loudest—values such as freedom, ethics, and morality, the rule of law and equality before the law—have a special obligation to live by those values in their own lives and their own societies, and to apply them to those they consider their enemies as well as their friends.

CLBV Reflection

Think of the key message(s) you retained after reading this chapter. Then complete the following sentences:

The principal points I liked in this chapter include

1. _____

2. _____

3. _____

The principal points that I did not like or disagreed with in this chapter include

1. _____

2. _____

3. _____

Notes

1 If you undertake a google search and place my name and the *European Business Review*, you will encounter a dozen articles that I have published (with colleagues) and they are all dealing with the future. As I have an agreement with this journal to publish two articles per year, I am pretty much sticking to this agreement. There is no need to provide the full list (some articles have been referred to in various chapters), but other may have become already obsolete given the pace of change. For example, here is a paper that was recently published (February 2019): Raich et al. Rethinking Future of Higher Education, *The European Business Review*, (www.europeanbusinessreview.com/rethinking-future-higher-education/).

2 See Damasio, A. (pp. 47–56) in: Changeux, J. P., Damasio, A., & Singer, W. J. (Eds.). (2005). *Neurobiology of Human Values*. Springer.

3 See Davidson, R. J. (pp. 67–90) in: Changeux, J. P., Damasio, A., & Singer, W. J. (Eds.). (2005). *Neurobiology of Human Values*. Springer.

4 This section is quite speculative. It is a synthesis of my talk at the expo-coaching in Madrid in 2016. Please remember that my suggestions represent only plausible hypotheses, and these have not been studied sufficiently or supported by rigorous empirical a research. At the same time, while I presented my thesis, the reaction of the audience in Expo-Coaching was very enthusiastic, hence the message is strong. Thus, I have decided to include this subsection in this book.

5 See: www.bnp.org.uk/news/national/apologies-all-round.

6 The important terms to understand are **non-genetic inheritance**—occurs when bioactive substances, including hormones, cytokines, and even parental mutations of microorganisms, have an impact on the next generation. It is also called a non-Mendelian inheritance (https://en.wikipedia.org/wiki/Non-Mendelian_inheritance); **polymorphism**—the occurrence of two or more distinctly different morphs or forms; **the genetic transmission**—Mendelian-is inheritance of biological characteristics following the laws proposed by Gregor Johann Mendel in 1865 and 1866 and rediscovered

in 1900; **genetic alleles**—one of several alternative forms of the same gene or same genetic locus.

7 See: www.nature.com/news/fearful-memories-haunt-mouse-descendants-1.14272, December 2013.

8 For more, see Ulrich, D., & Ulrich, W. (2010). *The Why of Work*. McGraw Hill.

9 For more, see Dolan, S. L., & Altman, Y. (2012). Managing by values: The leadership spirituality connection. *People and Strategy, 35*(4), 20–25; Dolan, S. L. (2015). Values, spirituality and organizational culture. *Developing Leaders* (21). Full paper can be download free at: www.researchgate.net/profile/Simon_Dolan/publication/283210564_Va lues_Spirituality_and_Organizational_Culture_The_Challenges_of_Leadership_in_ Tomorrowland/links/563348fc08aefa44c369dd30/Values-Spirituality-and-Organizati onal-Culture-The-Challenges-of-Leadership-in-Tomorrowland.pdf?origin=public ation_detail.

10 Kaushik, A. (2006). Three "Spires" of great leadership (www.kaushik.net/avinash/ 2006/08/three-spires-of-great-leadership.html).

11 For more on this, see: Moodie, S., Dolan, S. L., & Arsenault, A. (2011, February 24–27). *Exploring the Multiple Linkages between Metabolic Syndrome and Stress: An Empirical Analysis of the Relationships between Stress, Health, and Metabolic Syndrome among Catalan Nurses.* Paper presented at International Conference on Prehypertension & Cardio-Metabolic Syndrome, Vienna, Austria.

12 For more on this, see Garcia-Zamor, J. C. (2003). Workplace spirituality and organizational performance. *Public Administration Review, 63*(3), 355–364; Coetzer, G., Biberman, J., & Tischler, L. (2008). Transcending belief: A non-theistic model for operationalizing spiritual values, practices and states, and their relationship to workplace behavior. *Interbeing, 2*(1), 19–30; Veer, P. van der. (2009). Spirituality in modern society. *Social Research, 76*(4), 1097–1120.

13 Giacalone, R. A., & Jurkiewicz, C. L. (2003). Toward a science of workplace spirituality. In *Handbook of Workplace Spirituality and Organizational Performance*, pp. 3–28. M. E. Sharpe.

14 Seligman, M. E. P. (2008, July). Positive health [Issue supplement]. *Applied Psychology, 57*, 3–18.

15 Gardner, H., Csikszentmihalyi, M., & Damon, W. (2002). *Good Business: Leadership, Flow, and the Making of Meaning*. Basic Books.

16 Reave, L. (2005). Spiritual values and practices related to leadership effectiveness. *The Leadership Quarterly, 16*(5), 655–687.

17 Lips-Wiersma, M. (2007, June). *Practical Compassion: Toward a Critical Spiritual Foundation for Corporate Responsibility*. Paper presented at the Academy of Management meeting.

18 Hess and Cameron have written an extraordinary book arguing that leading by values, including spiritual values, can convert organizations into high-performing organizations. See: Hess, E. D., & Cameron, K. S. (2006). *Leading with Values*. Cambridge University Press.

19 Deshpande, A., & Shukla, S., (2010, August 11–13). Spirituality at workplace. *Proceedings of the AIMS International Conference on Value-Based Management*, p. 848.

20 For more information, see: Cloninger, R. (2004). *Feeling Good: The Science of Well-Being*. Oxford University Press.

21 See: Raich, M., & Dolan, S. L. (2008). *Beyond: Business and Society in Transformation*. Palgrave Macmillan.

22 This section is based on: Raich, M., & Dolan, S. L. (2009). Managing in the new landscape. *Effective Executive, 12*(10), 48–56.

23 For more information, read: Dolan, S. L. (2006). *Stress, Self-Esteem, Health and Work*. Palgrave Macmillan.

24 This section is based on an interview that was done with me by Paola Valeri in 2018. See: www.other-news.info/noticias/2017/07/el-cambio-como-valor/.

25 By the way, our book *Beyond: Business and Society in transformation* (Palgrave Macmillan 2009), when it was published in German, had its title changed to: "Out of the Comfort Zone" (see: Raich, M., & Dolan, S. L. (2010). Jenseits der Komfortzone: Wirtschaft und Gesellschaft übermorgen. www.amazon.de/Jenseits-Komfortzone-Wirtschaft-Gesellschaft-%C3%BCbermorgen/dp/3525403526/ref=sr_1_1?ie=UTF8&qid=1551089174&sr=8-1&keywords=Raich+Dolan).

26 Really good article about these scandals, see: Liran, A., & Dolan, S. L. (2016). Values, values on the wall, just do business and forget them all: Wells Fargo, Volkswagen and others in the Hall. *The European Business Review*, November–December (http://simondolan.com/wp-content/uploads/2018/12/TEBR-NovDecember-2016-Values-Values-on-the-wall-Just-do-business-and-forget-them-all-Wells-Fargo-Volkswagen-and-others-in-the-hall.pdf).

27 To read more about the Hubris syndrome, see: Owe, D., & Davidson, J. (2009). Hubris syndrome: An acquired personality disorder? A study of U.S. Presidents and UK Prime Ministers over the last 100 years. *Brain*, *132*(5), 1 May, 1396–1406 (https://academic.oup.com/brain/article/132/5/1396/354862).

Chapter 7

Let's practice

Sharing practical applications

David Alonso

7.1 Introduction
7.2 The six-step method for aligning personal values
7.3 Method for aligning values with your partner or in any relationship
7.4 Antecedent step: Validating the core value—Trust
7.5 V×O method: Practical application for achieving objectives
7.6 Examples of other applications of the triaxial model of values
  in different sectors
7.7 Conclusion

7.1 Introduction

I (David Alonso) discovered the game *Value of Values* in one of the very early training sessions that I participated in back in 2010. I wanted to become a better coach and for life circumstances, I stumbled across the game during a training session that I had attended; I fell in love with the game's little green card box, even before opening it. And upon opening it, I was overwhelmed with emotions and instantly decided to get 48 units for my coaching practice with our clients.

  The magic happened when we opened the game box. On the one hand, it made it easier for us to work as coaches. on the other hand, it helped our clients connect with what they really cared about. That is one of the reasons why people came—and still come—to us: they don't know what's wrong with them. They have lost the illusion and motivation to continue do whatever they are doing, and they do not know what else to do to recover it.

  In the middle of 2011, we ran out of games. Even though we needed more, the person who sold them to us was no longer involved. So, we checked the game box in order to find the name of its creator. Looking for it on the internet, we discovered that he worked at the ESADE Business School in Barcelona. It was very close to our offices. So, we contacted the game developer and he attended us immediately.

This gentleman was *Simon Dolan*

While visiting him at his office, we explained how we were using the game. At that moment something unexpected happened again: he gave us 64 units more and, honoring the value of values—Trust—he told us to come back when we had run out of stock. Only then would we have to pay him! This was an astonishing experience of trust and his compassion to have partners that really believed in values and wanted to spread the message.

That's how our relationship began. Whenever we saw him again, we asked him about the methodology, and he gave us a brief explanation, but this was not enough. Remember that at that time the *Coaching by Values* book was not yet available. Things dramatically changed when one day he invited us to one of his workshops in the neighboring country, Portugal.

During the workshop we were very impressed. We understood why that game helped us so much and what motivated and generated effectiveness and happiness with the people we coached. We also had the opportunity to learn about his research and about the triaxial model of values—which underlies the game. Our passion for the methodology was already unstoppable.

On our return to Spain, we began to offer workshops on values using the card game tool and the methodology acquired in various cities in Spain including Madrid, Barcelona, Zaragoza, and Valencia, among others, with the aim of promoting the tool and making it known to all colleagues in our coaching profession. We noticed that peers were delighted and wanted more, so we decided to create different levels of training and certifications which included a basic training (2.5 days approved by the International Coaching Federation), an expert training of 9 days, and a "trainer" certification that was spread over 1 year. The breadth, depth and scope of each program was different and ever since this we have continuously expanded as the collective experience of the trained coaches reaches us via a platform that we have created. The enthusiasm for the use of the concept, methodology and the tool was hard to imagine.

So, this was our early experience in Spain, and we knew that Simon Dolan offered additional training in other parts of the world and in other languages. But back to Spain and the Ibero-American community—today, March 2020, we have run more than 43 programs of the international certification in coaching by values (in Spanish: CoachingxValores), reaching countries such as Spain, Peru, Chile, Colombia, Ecuador, Puerto Rico, Argentina, Chile, Guatemala, Honduras, Mexico, Costa Rica, Uruguay, and Italy. And with our allies in Israel, Australia, Singapore, France, Portugal, Morocco, Canada, and other countries, the number is significantly higher. Additionally, as of today, we have added more than 16 online training sessions and the numbers are growing. In the Ibero-American market alone, we estimate a total of 1,600 participants certified in the use of the concept, methodology, and tools. Some of the trainees have become our new business partners, and thus we are certain that growth is inevitable.

Our dream is that in every house in the world there will be the game *Value of Values*, so people can truly connect with what they care about and really understand what is important, thus leading them to achieve fuller and more satisfying lives. In this chapter we will contribute to this by sharing some of the ways in which you can apply the methodology that has given us so much.

7.2 The six-step method for aligning personal values

As in real life, the key value underpinning the model is trust, which must be reciprocal when we are working with a client. On the one hand, he/she trusts me as a professional and sets out to share intimate aspects of his/her life that would probably otherwise be kept secret. On the other hand, I trust that the client can achieve the objective posed, because otherwise there would be no coaching relationship. Only then do we work with their fundamental values, those that are inalienable and must be present in their lives regardless of whether they are being fulfilled or not today. We will address that issue later.

7.2.1 Step 1: Detect your values

The objective in this first step is to ensure that, in the end, you have selected your five core values. You pick them from the deck of cards offered in the "Value of Values" game tool, and when you've been through all of the 51 of them, you select only the five that are relatively most important to you.[1]

Follow this scheme with each value you choose:

BOX 7.1 ABOUT MY MOST IMPORTANT VALUE

1. My chosen value is ___.
2. Define the meaning of the value for you.
3. Why is it fundamental to you?

It is essential that you devote the time needed to reflect on why you have selected or discarded certain values. That information will help you detect a myriad of beliefs that explain how you see the world.

7.2.2 Step 2: Prioritize your values

Once your five core values are detected, it is a matter of placing them in order of priority so as to attach relative importance to them, reflecting on your understanding of them at this moment of your life. Assign values from 1 to 5, where 1 represents the most important value. You can do it using Figure 7.1.

ORDER	VALUE
1	
2	
3	
4	
5	

Figure 7.1 Rank order of core values.

7.2.3 Step 3: Clarify the current degree of satisfaction with each value

Once you're clear on what your core values are, analyze how much they're currently being fulfilled in your life. In order to align values, it is essential to know where you are today, in relation to each value.

To get to know just that, answer the following question: on a scale of 1 to 10, what is your degree of satisfaction with each of these values at this point in your life? Assign 1 to represent the minimum degree of satisfaction and 10, for the maximum.

Use Figure 7.2—this is an extension of Figure 7.1.

7.2.4 Step 4: Detect what value or values are out of alignment

We will then detect what value or values are not aligned or at least which ones are currently less aligned. The unaligned values will be the foci of the next steps that follow. We consider that alignment exists when the scores are higher than 7 or 8. However, it is important that you ask yourself if you really think so. Obviously, the greater the misalignment, the lower the score. So, now you know, and become aware of why a value or values need to be aligned. The journey towards alignment (alone or with the help of a coach) begins here.

ORDER	VALUE	LEVEL OF SATISFACTION TODAY
1		
2		
3		
4		
5		

Figure 7.2 Core values and their fulfillment in daily life.

7.2.5 Step 5: Set an action plan

Choose one or two values based on the lowest scores and build a list of options or actions you can take to live a fuller life. From this list you must extract an action plan that follows the following structure:

1. Of these options, which one do you want to start on first?
2. When do you want to start? Set a deadline.
3. Is anyone else involved? Are you going to need someone else?
4. How will you know that your action plan is working?
5. On a scale of 1 to 10, what is your level of commitment to each action plan?

Remember that they must be specific actions. They should include:

- What are you going to do?
- How are you going to do it?
- When are you going to do it?
- Whom are you going to do it with?
- Is anyone else involved?

An example of what is not correct: "I'm going to lead a healthier life." This type of action plan is not specific, but rather a desire that may or may not be fulfilled in terms of whether, in the end and by chance, the necessary actions are fulfilled. If you want to align the value of health through physical exercise, a well-constructed action plan would be "to leave one hour to walk on Tuesdays and Thursdays after work."

Step 6: Set a follow-up for the plan

Establish a plan of action, but also prepare a contingency plan, something like "see plan B just in case." Imagine that you define the actions, and, for whatever reason, you cannot put them into motion because unforeseen circumstances kick in. If you consider this option, you make sure you are more likely to carry through with the action plan. The solution is to ask yourself: *Is there anything that prevents me from doing action A?* It is a matter of reflecting and thinking in detail about possible contingencies and unforeseen situations. If they happen, ask again: *When can I then do what I initially proposed? What other day or hour?* Once you have clarified it, it shows how you will monitor whether you have completed the action.

In short, here are the steps for the full session:

1. Select the five core values.
2. Assign them an order of importance from 1 to 5.
3. Clarify the current level of satisfaction for each value on a scale of 1 to 10.
4. Detect what value or values are misaligned (or less aligned).
5. Establish an action plan.
6. Define follow-up and monitoring for that plan.

BOX 7.2 STORYTELLING ABOUT THE *VALUE OF VALUES* CARD GAME:

THUMBS UP FOR THIS POWERFUL GAMIFICATION TOOL

By Avishai Landau

Abstract

In this short vignette I wish to trace the development and application of the *Value of Values* card game in Israel, from its naïve infancy in 2008 until today. After all, a small production made in Israel has become today a global tool. The ten editions have been made available in 19 languages; over 30,000 cards have been sold worldwide; and it is used by professional coaches in more than 44 countries. As a co-developer of the game, I wish not only to trace its history, but to share my story to highlight places, sectors, and events that have contributed to its co-evolution.

You can discover more about a person in an hour of play than in a year of conversation

Plato

Many years ago, I participated in a conference delivered by my big brother (today my partner) to a large Israeli firm. While presenting he suddenly challenged them by asking: "Can you imagine a company where people will not come to work but rather come to play? And in addition, they really feel like they are at home." I observed their facial expressions—they were mesmerized. From there he spent the entire conference explaining the why and how of the culture reengineering process in order to get to this "utopian" stage. Obviously, some were cynical and others thought that this was wishful thinking, but they all understood that in order to succeed in a sustainable manner in the future, they should aim to apply the "Managing by Values" concept. This was perhaps the first time that it also affected me. I would not have thought about this possibility without this provocative idea of my brother—**Simon**.

I had spent most of my professional career working in senior executive positions in some of the leading companies in Israel. Afterward I worked as a management consultant specializing in HR. During all these years I did not have time to read my big brothers' books on managing people or on managing by values. Until one day it happened. When I read *Managing by Values* which he co-wrote with Salvador Garcia and Bonnie Richley, I had an instant flash of inspiration and suddenly understood the importance of values in our life, at work, and from then on, have adopted his assessment tool (found in the book) to examine the fitness of employees for different positions in companies. Reading the book was also the impetus of my decision to be trained as a professional coach. Years later, this combined experience helped me see even clearer how values can help a coachee, a manager, a parent, or an educator to become a better, happier person, and more productive in whatever they do.

One day I met a lady who showed me a card game that did not target values but was fun to play. And, another thought crossed my mind: we adults spend too much time massaging the left hemisphere of the brain (logical, rational, and unemotional), and we neglect using the right hemisphere (fun, creative, emotional). This was certainly my case, but observing my colleagues, I noted the same. But, after playing the card game, I felt a big joy; I felt the power of using the right side of my brain.

The result led to the joint development of a value-based game for children, in Hebrew and English. We really thought of developing something fun for limited application. To our great surprise (and contentment), the game was highly appreciated, and super positive feedback came from the coaches, educators, and parents who used it. Mind you, the first prototype version of the game had no underlying base in the triaxial model; values were described via some naïve sentences, but nonetheless, the reaction was amazing. Following my departure from corporate life, and becoming a full-time coach and consultant, I noticed that I have a unique tool that helps me a lot in my new career path. At that time, I was a very eclectic coach and worked with families, educators, and later with executives. I also started offering seminars to executives and professionals always accompanied by the card game, and success was almost guaranteed, not to mention that the cards were illustrated by a super talented and creative designer and this added value. In retrospect, I realize today that the principal weakness of the game was that we failed to upscale it for becoming a real professional tool; hence the linkages to the source—the value questionnaire found in Dolan et al.'s *Managing by Values*— were not established in a systemic manner. One day I shared this observation with my big brother and values mentor, Professor Simon Dolan, and the rest is history, as the real development of the professional game then began.

You need to know that Professor Dolan was a typical academic who had been studying values from a research angle for many years. He even co-founded in the 1980s a scientific association that studied values in organizations (ISSWOV—The International Society for the Study of Work and Organizational Values). Following many years of conducting research on values, tons of published articles, and testing his model of values in over 20 countries, we have jointly decided to embed his version of "the triaxial model of values," also known as the "Dolan 3Es Triaxial model of values," into a new production of a card game. The three axes that are at the heart of the game/tool are: **e**conomical–**e**thical–**e**motional. The first production of the card game included 60 values (20 for each axis). This version of the card game included two languages for the Israeli market (Hebrew and English), four languages for Europe (English, French, Spanish, and Portuguese), and a special version (which included some mini cases of resolving conflicts between values for Costa Rica). Over the years, and following more validation studies, we have decided to reduce the number of cards to 51 universal values (almost culture free), 17 values for each of the group axes. In the latest production of the game more languages were added and today we have a total of 19 languages available in various continents.

Regardless of the version of the cards, one conclusion emerged and reinforced my activity as a coach and as a consultant: gamification is desirable; it provides good results in either coaching sessions or workshops and seminars. Now that the game is supported by a clear conceptual model, and participants have a tangible template of a triaxial model to take away, the effects are greater and faster. So, in the next couple of paragraphs I wish to share experiences and anecdotes from applying the *Value of Values* card game in different sectors in Israel.

Application of the card game in the military

The Israeli army had adopted a very important document named "The spirit of Zahal," which was guided by one of Israel's leading army ethics scholar, Professor Asa Kacher, and which was derived from very philosophic principles and led to an attempt to instill a values-based culture in the army. We all know that the military is involved in wars and bloodshed, but still, it is a place for experiencing values. The army is a big machine and a huge bureaucratic organization. Upon hearing about our concept of values and the tools used, the education unit of the army decided to conduct workshops and seminars using our card game. I do not have official statistics, but we estimate that over the years hundreds (if not thousands) of soldiers across units and ranks have participated in the workshops. These included important units, like the air force, the intelligence corps, and others. Most of our activities in the army were focused on the gap between personal core values and professional core values, the current leadership style of the officer and his/her expectations of himself/herself, and of course the core values of his/her unit presently and his/her expectations for the shared values in the future.

Application of the card game in educational systems

The card game has been used in many classrooms to create core values among youngsters, to facilitate one-on-one interactions between teachers and pupils, and to determine the areas about which a pupil is enthusiastic, thus allowing the pupil to trust and move forward with the teacher.

As I write this text, there is an ongoing ambitious project aimed at children that is part of the "Rona-Ramon Foundation," which attempts to connect children that were elected from 27 educational systems to an elite air force unit. All individuals involved play the card game, complete the triaxial template, and discuss how to fit into a future air force position. Kids follow a guide and can learn which of their values might need to be changed in order to come closer to the air force culture.

Our activities in kindergartens with the game are based mainly on the use of the illustrations. The kids select what they like and are asked to tell a story based on their selection. Some of the kindergarten teachers select a single value each week which becomes the subject of presentation and conversation during the week. Pupils draw their own images, and some of the activities also involve the parents.

Application of the card game in ethnic communities

Naturally, we apply the card game to all kinds of communities, including all types of nonprofit organizations. I wish to share three examples. The first, and to our great astonishment, was when we used the game in some of our training in orthodox religious communities. The experience was great, and gratitude kept pouring in.

Remember that the last production of the card game included values (and instructions) in Arabic, Russian, and Amharic in addition to the original Hebrew and English. Since then, demands originating from the Arabic Educational authorities have been growing for seminars and workshops on values. We have accumulated a lot of positive experience in applying the game in the Arab community. Shortly before passing away, the former president of Israel, Shimon Peres, wrote us a short letter thanking us for bringing the Jewish and Arab communities closer via the language and the game of values. We keep and cherish this recognition. Actually, we are also receiving messages from Arab participants that the card games lead to family closure, a greater sense of belonging, and other positive feelings, and all this is due to a greater extent when they can use the game in Arabic.

In Israel there is a large community of Russian immigrants. Like any immigrants in other parts of the world, using a tool in your native language makes it more user-friendly. Since the Russian version was made available, large segments of this population have been experimenting with the card game either in the context of coaching (i.e., with a Russian speaking coach) or in educational institutions where the language is used as an additional tool for recently arrived immigrants.

And finally, the last large flock of immigrants to Israel are black. These are the black Jews from Ethiopia-Eritrea. There are hundreds of stories of their suffering and difficulties in integrating into the Israeli fabric, including sporadic cases of violent behavior. Thus, for a purely altruistic reason, I decided to help them weave faster into the main stream, by enabling them to understand the core values which they have brought and the core values of the Israeli society with which they interact daily. There was a substantial investment in time, talent, and money to translate and offer the card game also in Amharic, but personally I think that the effort was well worth it. Today, many of the members of the Eritrean community use the game, and it has become very popular also with couples and families within this community. I work myself with some leaders of the community, and I noticed that several difficult issues had been resolved. I am getting messages (and physical gifts) showing the gratitude of this effort on our behalf. See, for example, a traditional Ethiopian music tool that was given to me as a gift from one of the Ethiopian coachees that I voluntarily coached (Figure 7.3).

Anecdotes steaming from personal coaching experiences using the game

Just like the community of Coaching by Values worldwide, we offer certification training for coaches. Certification is in its infancy but seems to be growing. The early reaction of certified coaches in "Coaching by Values" is very

Figure 7.3 Amharic traditional instrument: A gift from a cochee.

positive and encouraging, and most likely we will continue to certify coaches in Israel in the future. The content is very similar to the flagship certification developed by the CoachingxValores in Spain.

Anecdote 1: One day I got a call from a man who wanted to surprise his wife with a unique gift for their wedding anniversary. A week later he called again and explained what had happened. They started to play the game during breakfast with the hope of spending one to two hours and then doing other things afterward. But after the initial identification of five core values (each), and then identifying five as a couple, they realized a gap that led to a serious conversation. Time was flying, and without noticing it they had ended in the middle of the day when they reached a consensus about their triaxial model of values. The man told me that it was one of the most significant events that had happened to both of them in many years, and the results would increase harmony and would serve them for many years to come. He thanked me for co-inventing the game and the methodology.

Anecdote 2: A coachee had arrived to meet me for the first time. Even without hearing his case and the reason for him coming, I proposed that we play a card game. Obviously, this was risky; hence I gambled on the fact that he will collaborate simply because he heard about me and trusted me. During the play, the cards showed that this man lived through a significane incongruence among his core values. I sent him home to think about it and proposed that we discuss his reflections in the next session. When he came to the second meeting, he already had a very detailed analysis, and his request was to continue the coaching by focusing on "what was really important in his life," and how to narrow the incongruence. So, without knowing the initial reason that he wanted to meet with me, the coaching took its turn and ended up to his complete satisfaction in record time.

Anecdote 3: The story I am sharing here was told by a psychologist friend who had recently learned about the card game and the triaxial model. She had a generic understanding of it but was far from being convinced that the tool could serve in therapy. So, one day, she decided to experiment with one of her patients, and here is her account:

One evening, parents of a 14-year-old boy contacted me. They were concerned about their son's changing patterns of behavior following a move to a new school; they noticed that he had become a different child, often absent from school and in general in a bad mood. So, I decided to suggest the parents use the card game while I listened carefully to the conversation. Finally, each of them selected five core values and explained the "why." It was not connected to the issue of the child, but for the first time I noted that neither of the parents had selected a single "economical" (red color in the card game) in their triaxial model. It was strange to observe, and thus the conversation started around this issue. They told me that they have a very average salary and that they spend the money as need arises. Interestingly, towards the end of the month, they had to curb expenses; hence the remaining balance is very low or even negative. A week before the child started the new school, the bank stopped activities in their account and canceled their credit cards. Consequently, they bought their teenage child cheap "non-brand" Gym shoes, instead of a famous brand (like Nike) that he had before. The boy was embarrassed and felt ashamed to tell his parents, so he preferred to be absent and withdraw from social activities and isolate himself in his room. Of course, this revelation led me to recommend a coaching session focused on economic matters. Naturally, the child did not need any therapy or treatment.

Immediately after the parents left (it was late evening), the child psychologist phoned me, very excited, to inform me that she finally understood how powerful the "3Es triaxial model tool card" was and enthusiastically committed to use it and the respective methodology and tools in the future. The name of this psychologist is Anat Garti, who later became my professional partner.

Anecdote 4: In my work with companies, I have developed many alternative versions of playing the card game. But the most important new idea is to take an important subject that concerns the organization, start thinking about it using the three axes of the triaxial model, and recognize gaps between the current situation and the desired situation.

Having this focus in mind, I wish to share another anecdote. A friend was recently nominated as VP R&D in his firm. He has asked me for advice on the best way to get to know quickly his new team without disproportional expenses or engaging outside consultants. So, he took the card game and used it to facilitate a discussion based on the selection of the values of each member of the team. This was followed by five hours of diagnosis and conversation. It is worth mentioning that he himself was also part of the game and he exposed his core values to the team. The feedback was instant and revealing, and mutual trust was achieved in record time. He told me that he saved lots of time by not needing to undertake a personal interview with each member of the team, avoiding reading lengthy reports, etc. Using the card game was super instrumental for him. In addition, mutual trust and group effectiveness were achieved.

Conclusion

In January 2019 I had the pleasure of participating at the international congress on *Coaching by Values* that was held in Barcelona. About 150 participants came from many corners of the world to share how they were working with the tools in different sectors/countries and how they co-developed their own hybrid model. I then understood the power of co-evolution, a dynamic that is encouraged by Professor Dolan and the *Coaching by Values* community.

This conference also became part of the repertory of my learning experience. The conference was organized around 12–15 themes and applications of the *CLBV*. Each presenter was asked prior to the conference to describe himself/herself in a short sentence, to provide a standard photo, and to select one value (card) that he/she would describe as being the most typical of them. During the presentation, this single slide had a powerful impact, hence regardless of the theme presented, regardless of the length of the presentation, you had the sensation that just by focusing on a single card you had known the person for a long time. I was in this meeting for the first time, so I did not know anybody apart from three to four people, and the feeling of bonding was amazing. While flying back from Barcelona to Israel, I reflected upon this experience, and I finally understood that my dear brother, myself, and the promoters of the *Coaching by Values* community really succeeded in creating *a new language* using the *Value of Values* game and the Dolan 3Es *triaxial model of values*.

Today I would not be exaggerating if I said that this is a powerful tool, which is complemented by a powerful methodology, which is complemented by a powerful triaxial concept of values, which is complemented by a select group of enthusiastic coaches that make the whole thing very cohesive and sustainable. While I am writing these lines, I notice a sense of pride and satisfaction. Let me end by toasting to the community of *Coaching by Values* and by saying that I am looking forward to many years of productive innovations and sustained amicable interactions.

Avishai Landau is the co-founder of the *Value of Values* card game. He is the founder and principal partner of "The Israel Values Center" a leading management consulting company based in Israel that specializes in leading, managing, and coaching by values. He is the co-author of *Managing by Values* (in Hebrew) and *Coaching by Values* (in Hebrew). He is a coach, consultant, and promoter of the *Coaching by Values* and *Leadership by Values* certification in Israel. For more information: www.values-center.co.il

7.3 Method for aligning values with your partner or in any relationship

At this point, we want to share the methodology we apply with couples to help them get reconnected. Films and society transmit a fanciful image of relationships that, in many cases, make us feel disappointed or frustrated. On the other hand, we do not get tired of repeating that the couples we work with are dynamic. Now then, what does that mean? Let's examine it using a concrete example.

- indicate your favorite book or song from ten years ago: _____
- indicate your favorite book or song this year: _____

Do they match? Probably not—most likely they have changed.

The same is true for couples: either the two members have changed, or one continues to maintain the same attitudes, life perspectives, and concerns and the other does not. One of the key points for couples to evolve and stay together is their mutual satisfaction, something that is achieved by knowing at what point of evolution and growth they are; in other words, revising their common couple project. The common project is what unites the couple, the path they want to share, and the destiny they want to reach. It is a question of revising and communicating because most likely their illusions, goals, and projects might have changed.

The evolution of a relationship happens for many reasons, which include day-to-day struggles and routines, the environment, circumstances that we cannot control, growth, and the experiences of each member of the couple. Thus, we must review if the common project remains the same or needs adjustments in order to avoid feeling trapped or miserable in the relationship. This is precisely the issue we will address, showing how we can plan a step-by-step revitalizing of the "common project" so that both members feel that they own and share it. Naturally, this procedure works for couples who look for a methodology that will enable them to continue the common project with a higher level of satisfaction.

The methodology we use for couples is based on Coaching by Values and on shared values. When we talk about a common project, we find the values that bind us to the other person and that we decide that it should be present in the relationship. Shared values are the rules of the game that the couple establishes. So, we propose that you follow the steps that we were talking about in the former section and apply it to a couple. Look at the gap, look at the common triaxial model, and together make a plan of action for the couple. Our experience, based on coaching hundreds of couples, is that you can revitalize a relationship using this methodology. It is clear, it is fast, and it is very constructive. But, let's demonstrate this again with some more detail.

7.4 Antecedent step: Validating the core value—Trust

Do you trust your relationship? Do you trust your partner? Do you think that trust needs to be recuperated? These are elementary questions to discuss before you apply the methodology of Coaching by Values to a couple. If there is no trust, the focus should first and foremost be focused on building (or rebuilding) trust. Hence without it, the methodology that we are discussing will not work. Having said that, the first step in the process of coaching is to expose the reasons that have diminished trust and to learn how partners feel about it.

7.4.1 Step 1: Choose five core values for yourself and also five values you think your partner would have selected.

Individually, each member of the couple will select their five most important values at this time of their life, defining the meaning of each value and assigning a score according to their degree of satisfaction on a scale of 1 to 10. At the same time, point out what actions you can put in place to increase the level of satisfaction with the chosen values.

Then, select the five values that you think your partner has and define what you think each one of them means from their point of view. One way to do this is to imagine that you are your partner and you express the values that you think your partner will select; this is a key point to undertake, to the extent that it helps to become aware of how each of us perceives the other. Similarly, it provides a concrete content to the joint session (with a coach) where clear communication is established around shared values.

7.4.2 Step 2: Selecting shared values

In this second step we need to work together. You're already present side by side with your partner. One of the purposes of the session is to contrast the information, check if the values you have chosen by your partner coincide with those selected by him/her. It is a consciousness-raising point that helps us to understand why we act the way we act, and what the consequences of these assumptions are in the day-to-day relationship. After opening the space of awareness and communication, it is time to continue to agree on the five shared values.

Again, a space for reflection and dialogue must be created, for only then can you hear what matters are important to the other person. From there, you can reach an agreement on the five values to be shared in the relationship. This means that you must be complacent. Here there is no place for impositions; you can't simply select values at random. Doing so will cause the entire process to be irrelevant while the desires of the relationship are lost along the way, engendering only a feeling of emptiness or a high level of dissatisfaction. Agreeing on the five core values to share is really the key to the next step.

In short, choose a value from each group of values and assign to each value your own shared definition. It will ensure that the values have the same meaning to both of you. Then, if you want to make a change, you may add a value from another group or one that has not appeared in the list of values provided in the *Value of Values* card game. We have offered wild cards in the game, so that you can add any shared value using this wild card. Just make sure that you attribute to the card/value the same meaning. The only rule is that you must end up with five values. Place the selected shared five values on the template offered in Figure 7.4.

7.4.3 Step 3: Prioritizing shared values

Now, put the five most important values for you in the relationship in order. That allows you to have a focus and really know what to consider the relatively most important. Again, consensus must be reached (Figure 7.5).

7.4.4 Step 4: Assess the satisfaction status

In this step you must rate each of the values already selected and prioritized. On the one hand, you tell us how satisfied you are with each value on a scale of 1 to 10 in accordance with the definition you have drawn up (this is what

COUPLE SHARED VALUES	COUPLE SHARED MEANING

Figure 7.4 List of shared values of a couple.

ORDER	SHARED VALUES	SHARED MEANING
1		
2		
3		
4		
5		

Figure 7.5 Ordering shared values.

we will call the current state of satisfaction), and on the other hand, note the degree of satisfaction that you want to achieve in each value within a 3- to 6-month period (we will refer to this indicator as a desired state of satisfaction). Just try to be realistic. If expectations are not realistic, they will cause a sense of frustration or failure because they have not been achieved (Figure 7.6).

7.4.5 Step 5: Detect possible misaligned values

The scores enable an interesting observation and show the couple's values in a relatively simple manner. As you have learned from this book, values are considered aligned when their current degree of satisfaction is equal to or greater than seven or eight points. From there, the lower the score and the higher the desired satisfaction status, the more misalignment will be present. Please be aware that this need will not be interpreted dogmatically in all relationships. We usually recommend starting to work on the two most misaligned values or at least the ones that are most interesting to prioritize. Now we'll see how to do it.

7.4.6 Step 6: Creating an action plan

The objective of the present step is to agree on what actions will be carried out to be consistent with the five shared values. It is advisable to start from the information you have extracted in the previous steps and the level of

ORDER	SHARED COUPLE VALUES	JOINT MEANING	PRESENT LEVEL OF SATISFACTION	DESIRED LEVEL OF SATISFACTION
1				
2				
3				
4				
5				

Figure 7.6 Actual and desired levels of satisfaction with value attainment.

satisfaction noted in each value. If we have reviewed the above, we begin to work on one or two values determining what is going to happen, so you know for sure that you have achieved what you proposed. By supporting yourself in defining the value in question, create specific actions that address the following questions:

- What will you do?
- How are you going to do it?
- When are you going to do it?
- Whom are you going to do it with?
- Should anyone else be involved?

Here is a poor example (not worth pursuing): "I will communicate better with my partner."

If you want to align the value of communication, a well-built action would be "every day from Monday to Friday, after the children have gone to sleep, we will talk, the two of us alone, for 15 minutes about how the day has gone and how we feel."

7.4.7 Step 7: Creating an action plan/follow-up

It is good that both agendas leave space dedicated to the revision and modification of the established plan. This is the way in which you can maintain the motivation and overcome contingencies that may threaten the viability of the plan. Make a simple but powerful question: Is there a situation or person that can prevent the action plan from being achieved?

Step 8: Develop a sort of "collage of values"

There are many couples who enjoy creating a space for rapprochement, communication, and knowledge, working with their shared values and, ultimately, with their common project. An excellent footprint is to elaborate the "collage of the five shared values"; a sort of "special events" in the life of the couple represents and reinforces the most important events that have transpired in the relationship. It's about collecting images that you feel representative of those values. Later, you can frame it and place it in a visible area of the house in a way that will help you remember what is important for the couple.

Here is a short summary of the principal coaching session for couples:

1. Validate the presence of the mega key value—Trust.
2. Choose five core values for yourself and the five values you think your partner has.
3. Select and agree on shared values.
4. Prioritize the shared values in order of importance from 1 to 5.
5. Rate the current satisfaction status and desired satisfaction status.
6. Detect the possible unaligned values and work on them; select the five shared values.
7. Establish a concrete action plan.
8. Create a monitoring—tracking—plan.
9. Develop your "collage of values" and celebrate these moments.

7.5 V×O method: Practical application for achieving objectives

V×O stands for Values × Objectives. It is a method for achieving objectives and is based on the goals set up during the coaching sessions. The application helps you to achieve positive results when you have set a very clear goal you want to reach. From there we will walk you step by step to make it happen.

7.5.1 Step 1: Apply the SMACET principles for defining a goal or an objective

The first step is to have a clear goal for the next three or six months. We recommend that you comply with the "SMACET" guidelines, because if it is not well defined, the work you do will lose meaning. It is therefore important to devote the necessary time to the formulation of the goal in accordance with SMACET:

S—Specific
M—Measurable
A—Achievable
C—Challenging
E—Ecologic
T—Time bounded

Example. Let's see if you can complete an objective that meets all the SMACET criteria:

_____

_____

7.5.2 Step 2: Identify five values to be used in order to achieve the goal

When you already have a goal or an objective, the next step is to select what five values you need to apply in order to meet the goal. It does not mean that you must use all five values, but that the chosen ones are the essential ones for being connected to the goal; otherwise the goal will not be met.

As an example, let's say that your goal is to open a bakery in your neighborhood in the next six months. One of your values is "to have money," because you think you need money to cover all the expenses (licenses, rent, equipment, personnel, purchase of raw materials, etc.). Following this reasoning, if that value is not fulfilled, you will not reach the goal. Having already defined the five values you need, define what they mean to you depending on the target you have marked. In order to do the assessment, use the template in Figure 7.7

7.5.3 Step 3: Know where you are with respect to the values you need

It's about measuring where you are with respect to the values needed to achieve the goal. Again, we will assess the satisfaction status with each value on a scale of 1 to 10. Subsequently, we repeat the exercise by writing down what level of satisfaction is required in the next three or six months, so that we can reach the goal (Figure 7.8).

7.5.4 Step 4: Compare your triaxial model configuration with your definition that is connected to your objectives.

Based on Dolan's 3Es triaxial model, draw the value diagram for your objective. We invite you to compare it with your core values, so it will give you

ORDER OF VALUES	VAL USES REQUIRED TO ACHIEVE THE GOAL	THE MEANING OF THE VALUES
1		
2		
3		
4		
5		

Figure 7.7 Values instrumental to achieve goal(s).

	VALUES NEEDED ACHIEVE GOAL	MEANING	CURRENT LEVEL OF SATISFACTION	DESIRED LEVEL OF SATISFACTION
1				
2				
3				
4				
5				

Figure 7.8 Assessing values, goals, and levels of satisfaction.

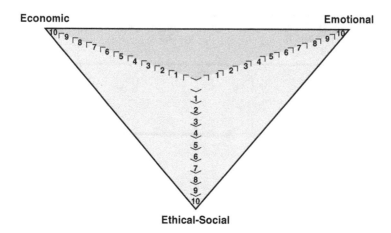

Figure 7.9 Template for charting your selected values on the Dolan 3Es triaxial model.

information on what model you are moving and what you need to change in order to meet your goal. Consciousness-raising sometimes leads to adjustment, identifying difficulties that may be blocking you or even giving you some early warning of reasons that may prevent you from advancing as originally planned. That information will be essential, and you can rethink the goal or leave it as it is. A template is offered in Figure 7.9.

7.5.5 Step 5: Detect what value or values are out of alignment

Simply analyze the difference between the degree of current satisfaction and the degree of desired satisfaction. The greater the difference, the greater the misalignment. Remember that a misaligned value is generally considered to be a score greater than 7 or 8.

7.5.6 Step 6: Chart an action plan

In the same way as in the formerly described methods, construct an action plan. Draw up concrete actions that allow you to align those values that you need considering the starting point. You can start working on one or two values that you consider the most important.

7.5.7 Step 7: Monitoring and follow-up

Repeat the procedure already discussed. You must establish how you will know that you are fulfilling the actions derived from the action plans. Thanks to this habit, you will be able to make adjustments that will keep the plan alive and your motivation high.

In sum, here are the steps for the full coaching session:

1. Define the goal or goals with the SMACET criteria.
2. Select the five values you need in order to reach the goal.
3. Clarify the current and desired degree of satisfaction for each value.
4. Draw the value diagram for the objective in the template provided (the Dolan 3Es triaxial model) and compare it with the diagram of the fundamental values you have done before.
5. Detect which value or values are misaligned.
6. Design your action plan.
7. Create your tracking plan.

7.6 Examples of other applications of the triaxial model of values in different sectors[2]

In 2018 during the annual congress of certified coaches by values, we heard of some amazing applications of the Dolan 3Es triaxial model of values in various sectors. So, we have invited 17 selected coaches to share their hybrid experience in a book. This was a spinoff of this congress. The book, for the moment, is only available in Spanish. The title, if we translate it to English reads: "Values: A Compass for People and Organizations of the Future." The book is a clear example of the process of "co-evolution" and group effort. While we do not intend to translate and offer the content of the entire book hereafter, we thought that sharing the titles of the chapters and indicating the names of the contributors could be instrumental so that you can look them up on social networks, and perhaps some of them can offer a version of their contribution to you in English. Obviously, if you read Spanish, we recommend that you read the entire book.

CLBV Reflection

Author (a)	Brief title or content of the chapter
Raquel Sánchez de Benito	Explains how the triaxial model of values is applied in highly sensitive people
Beatriz Ballesteros	Explains how to apply your own values to boost your self-confidence and self-esteem

(Continued)

(*Continued*)

Author (a)	Brief title or content of the chapter
Encarna Medina	Explains her concept of #optimal day (#diaÓptimo), where values are served as a mathematical formula to optimize activities
Laura Moncho	Explains how to apply Coaching by Values and the 3Es triaxial model in coaching couples
Viviane Gamerro, Alfredo Julià, and Liliana Lucero	Explain how to apply the triaxial model of the values in any relationship and how it can serve as an effective GPS
Ani Páez	Explains how values can serve as soft skills to help educators
Pedro Frean Pérez	Connects the world of values with neuroscience in the teaching sector
Miguel Ángel Palenzuela	Shares experience in the application of the triaxial model of values in the sports industry
Beatriz Calvo	Explains how to improve the household allocation of money using the triaxial model of values as a reference
Carlos Gil	Explains how values can help entrepreneurs develop a sustainable business model
Guzmán Martinez Griñán	Explains how you can apply the triaxial model of the values in the selection of personnel, and thus achieve the creation of a cohesive and productive team
Roberto Páez	Discusses the use of the mega value—"trust" and explains why "with trust" you cannot fool around"
Paola Valeri	Shows a hybrid model of combining the triaxial model of values with the systemic model in applying it with executives
Noelia Alonso	Explains the new leadership by values model in the development of organizational leaders
Nacho Plans	Explains the application of the values within a team with the integration of the client's emotional experience to create a cohesive team

7.7 Conclusion

As you can see, there are numerous applications offered in this chapter. In this chapter, an attempt was made to demonstrate a small part of everything that connects values, the Dolan 3Es triaxial model and the card game that is used as a coaching tool—"*The value of values.*"

If you want to know more, you may contact us and perhaps you will consider joining one of the next training certifications which are also offered online. Log into our website and follow the development in this area: www.coachingxvalores.com or www.leadershipbyvalues.com. If you wish to comment or make suggestions about the applications presented in this chapter write to: laura@coachingxvalores.com or to Noelia@leadershipbyvalues.com.

We hope that this chapter has been revealing to you; at least this is what our coaches are telling us. We have adopted a very nice moto for all that we do which years ago could be considered utopia or at least a dream: "let's change the world through values." And with this in mind we wish to conclude this chapter by citing Eduardo Galeano, who said: "ordinary people from unknown small places around the globe doing small things can change the world."

Can we count on you?

CLBV Reflection ♣ ♠ ♥

Think of the most important information you remember after reading this chapter and then fill in the following phrases:

The main points that I liked about this chapter are …

1. _____
2. _____
3. _____

The main points that I have not liked or with which I disagree with this chapter are …

1. _____
2. _____
3. _____

Notes

1 If you read Spanish and if you wish to use the complete template with the list of values, as well as a guide to carry out the exercise, download the instructions at the following address: www.coachingxvalores.com/plantilla-metodo-6-pasos. Otherwise, get the list of values, and the template at the appendices in this book.

2 The source for this section is the book entitled: *Values: A Compass for People and Organizations of the Future*, published in Spanish by Punto Rojo in 2018. Used with permission of the authors. https://tiendacoachingporvalores.com/libros/46-libro-la-brujula-para-personas-y-organizaciones-de-futuro.html

Postscript*

The following article was published digitally in the *European Business Review* on April 6, 2020, by Dolan, Raich, Garti and Landau (experts on Coaching and leading by values). The full link is at: https://www.europeanbusinessreview. com/the-covid-19-crisis-as-an-opportunity-for-introspection/

The article has been reproduced here with permission by Elenora Elroy, Editor at *The European Business Review*. The article was incorporated into this book, as the insights are highly relevant at this critical time. It complements the core messages of the book and, while it wasn't planned, one can clearly see how the various concepts discussed and tools presented can be applied during a time of crisis, like the COVID 19 pandemic, that the entire world is experiencing in 2020. Ordinary people, business people, politicians and even professional health employees are relearning and re-examining their values in order to make sense and align their conduct in times of uncertainty, chaos and high ambiguity. Above all else, values provide a guide. It is this internal compass that is so needed. The article shows this working at different levels: it is one thing to sense, react and assess during a crisis, but another to plant the seeds for the future. What have we learnt about ourselves? What kind of society do we wish to be part of in the future? By including this article within the book, we hope to provide some answers to these critical questions.

"The COVID-19 Crisis" as an opportunity for introspection: A multi-level reflection on values, needs, trust and leadership in the future

April 6, 2020

By Simon L. Dolan, Mario Raich, Anat Garti and Avishai Landau

The current period of misery and even despair surround us. It is perhaps an opportune moment to reflect on our lives and conduct as individuals, families, organizations and society in general. This short reflection has been written by

★   This article has been reproduced here with kind permission from *The European Business Review*. This book is printed in black and white but the full **color** article can be found at: https://www. europeanbusinessreview.com/the-covid-19-crisis-as-an-opportunity-for-introspection/.

practitioners and researchers who are concerned about values throughout the phases of our lives. Over the years, we have developed a concept, a methodology and tools to help people understand what is really important in their lives. It is a mirror of the hierarchy of their core values and helps these people align the latter with their day to day activities, and ultimately leads to having a more meaningful and satisfying life. When the 3E model of values was developed, it was not intended to be applied to an acute, emergency or life-threatening pandemic like we are witnessing nowadays. Based on years of research, the proposal advanced in all our books, articles and speeches around the globe is based on the following assertion: *values (and specifically core values) are a far better predictor of our behavior than our needs*. Still, we always state that in an emergency context, the understanding of needs (or perceived needs such as survival), will be more impactful to understanding our behavior then values.   This short paper is a first time attempt to examine the applicability of values in conjunction with our needs, to explain behavior and actions of ourselves and our leaders. We also reiterate the important role of the construct of trust, which we often label "*the Value of Values*" in the etiology of behavior.

In order to do this, the underlying presentation is based on the authors' previous writings such as Dolan's 3Es model of the three axes of values, complemented by Garti and Landau's usage in Families, and Raich et al's vision of the future. It allows to observe the proactive leadership style and behaviors at different levels ranging from micro settings (individuals, couples, families) to macro settings (organizations, communities-societies and even countries). The Coronavirus pandemic enables introspection across levels, across sectors and across cultures. No doubt that its implications will remain with us for a very long time. So, let's see what we observe and the lessons that we can already learn.

Let's begin with understanding the underlying model of values. The triaxial model of values was first introduced in 1997 (*Garcia and Dolan, 1997*), refined in 2006 (*Dolan, Garcia & Richley, 2006*) and fully developed and described in 2011 (*Dolan, 2011*). The model was articulated over the years based on rigorous empirical research and validation in over 20 countries (*Dolan et al, 2013*). Since then, the model was coined Dolan's 3Es triaxial model of values (hereafter 3Es). Multiple scientific papers and thousands of workshops as well as certifications world-wide, lend support to the concept, the methodology and the tools proposed (see recent books: *Dolan, 2019, 2020*). The essence of the 3Es triaxial model divides the entire universe of values, into three Axes (which are interrelated in a specific configuration).

- **The Economic-Pragmatic** Axis (called the **Red Axis,** illustrated hereafter as a proxy in the top right corner of the triangle template) embeds values that connect values important to our achievement of specific goals be they individual, couple, family, organization or societal. This axis includes values such as: influence, planning, consistency, resilience, flexibility, productivity, efficiency and the like. The key question is to what extent we know our core values in a conscious manner (as a person) and to what extent we share them as a couple, a family, an organization or a society.

- **The Social-Ethical** Axis (called the **Blue Axis,** illustrated hereafter as a proxy in the top left corner of the triangle template) embeds values that connect values important to our relationships as individual or as a collective. This axis includes values such as: friendship, honesty, collaboration, family relationships, and the like.
- **The Emotional-Developmental** Axis (called the **Green Axis,** illustrated hereafter as a proxy in the bottom center corner of the triangle template) embeds values that connect what is important to us as humans or as a collective who seek to keep on learning and developing as well as self-actualizing during our lifetime. This axis includes values such as: initiative, creativity, open-mindedness, joy and the like.

"Values are people's motivators. For most people they are unconscious motivators. However, in highly successful organizations, or healthy families, each member is aware of their personal values and how these relate to the organization/family value system"
    – Garti & Dolan (*The European Business Review*, 2019)

Based on values, culture reengineering processes were developed in organizations and communities and tested in several countries. Since 2010, and following certification of consultants, coaches and leaders, the applications were used in various sectors and contexts ranging from families, sport teams, virtual teams, high tech companies, military organizations, educational settings and many more via a process that we call co-evolution (see for example: *Dolan et al., 2018*). The accumulated wisdom suggests three sets of conclusions:

1) That the 3Es model of values, and more specifically when we focus on core values, is an asymmetrical model; this means that some axes are more important to individuals or a collective of individuals than other axes.
2) In order to successfully and sustainably navigate throughout the stages of our lives, we need to have a minimum percentage of core values of each of the 3 axes; an absence of a value on any of the axes will not allow us to function well across time as individuals or as a collective.
3) The model can be applied equally to any type of setting or relationship, be it a couple, a family, a team, an organization or a society. The key to having an enjoyable, healthy and productive life depends on our understanding of what is important to us (bring it from the unconscious level or the implicit level to the conscious and explicit level). We must ensure that it is aligned with our definition of "success" and the audience for whom we function (family, team, organization) as well as the extent to which we are aligned and share values with the others with whom we interact (more detail in *Dolan, 2020*).

Having explained the generic part of the 3Es model, let's place the Coronavirus event in the middle of the Triaxial model, and examine it from the three angles. This will allow us to introspect on where are we today and how it will affect our lives in the aftermath of the Coronavirus.

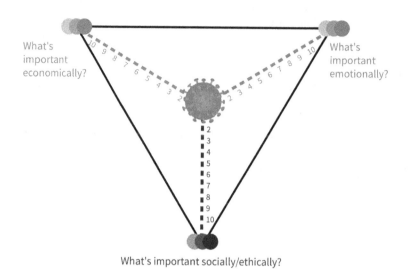

Figure C.1 The Generic Triaxial model of Values and the Coronavirus crisis.

Most people are so busy running so many errands that they have no time to stop and think whether they are doing the right things. We are so used to doing whatever we do, that we really don't think twice about the "why". This is especially the case when we are in our comfort zone (*Raich & Dolan 2008*), or perhaps think that we are eternal. The real reflection occurs when we are in crisis. Crisis at the individual level (i.e. serious disease, serious accident, sudden loss of a job, marital and/or family breakage, romantic or terrible disappointment and the like). This can also happen at the organizational level (i.e. being denied a top position, closing of a company due to mergers or acquisition or simply declaring bankruptcy). Now it is occurring at the societal level; in fact, it is occurring at the global level. The Coronavirus is by all accounts the greatest threat to societal order (economic, emotional and ethical) and to personal life in the last 300 years.

Let's delve a bit more into the world of values and the Coronavirus but let's examine it one level at a time.

At the personal level

The Coronavirus crisis is an opportunity for personal soul searching, for analysis and reflection: what have I done today? Did I succeed in whatever I did? What is the true meaning of success to me? How can I strengthen the areas where I feel I am succeeding? What do I want to do differently?

Examine these points through the three axes. What do I want to achieve in my life and how (the Red axis)? Why is it important for me to achieve these things? Is it for emotional-personal reasons? If the answer is yes, then perhaps the leading axis is the **green one**. Will achieving these things help me with my self-image? If this is the case, it's important to ask myself why I need to achieve them to reinforce my image. Is it important for me to achieve these things for my own development? Does it fulfill me? If so, the green axis is even more dominant.   By contrast if my reflections center on what is the extent to which I become independent financially or economically so that I will not have to worry about economic survival it´s another angle. Do these goals align with my relationship, with the **blue axis**, or maybe they are in conflict with them? I should check which axis is more important to me and why. What are the relationships that matter to me and what values lead me when managing them? Am I satisfied with the way I run them? Do I want to do something different?

During this crisis we recommend personal observation which will allow you to accurately understand the core values in each axis and the relationship between the axes. Is one axis intended to help fulfill the values in another? Are the axes in conflict? If so, how can things be managed differently? We recommend using all tools developed to work with the triaxial model to allow this observation (Dolan, 2011, 2020; Garti & Dolan, 2019).

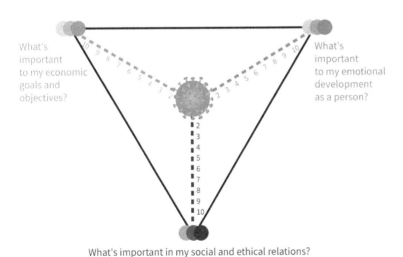

Figure C.2 The Coronavirus and the hierarchy of values at the individual level.

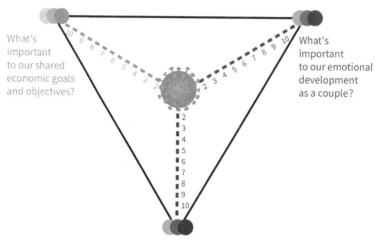

What's important to our shared economic goals and objectives?

What's important to our emotional development as a couple?

What's important in our social and ethical relations?

Figure C.3 The Coronavirus and the hierarchy of values at the couple level.

At the couple level

The Coronavirus crisis can be an opportunity to examine whether we succeed as a couple. What are the common areas, conversations, mutual support and collaboration that make our couple relationship successful? Where do we succeed and how can it be strengthened? How do we survive as a couple?

In addition, it is an opportunity to examine the values in our relationship that we would like to preserve. What values in the **blue axis** enhance our relationship and what values are missing? Does our relationship have compassion and cooperation? Do we feel affectionate in our relationship? Is our relationship managed by the value of competitiveness?

On the **green axis** we will try to examine what are the core values. Are they passion, development, creativity? Are we satisfied with the values in this axis or want to change them?

On the **red axis**, we recommend exploring how we, as a couple, manage to achieve our marital goals. Are we aligned with our marital goals and the way we achieve them?

At the family level

The Coronavirus crisis is also an opportunity to examine the family's strength, and how and where to strengthen it further. What tools and practices are needed to do that or perhaps create new tools and a more refined-shared family culture. How do we survive as a family?

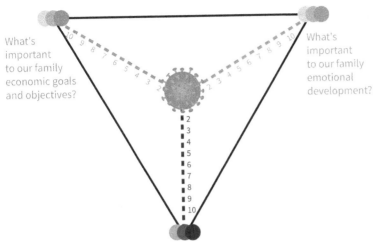

What's important to our family economic goals and objectives?

What's important to our family emotional development?

What's important to our family social and ethical conduct and relations?

Figure C.4 The Coronavirus and the hierarchy of values at the family level.

Let us look at our family culture through the three axes. In the **red axis**, look at the values that lead us to achieve results. Are we a family whose core values are ordered, perhaps saving? Maybe we are flexible? Do we persevere in what we decide?

In the **blue axis**, look at how we manage our relationships in the family. Are we patient with each other? Do we tolerate each other? Are we honest? Do we function well and do things together as a family? At the same time, do we allow each family member to preserve and manifest their own uniqueness?

On the **green axis** look at whether each member feels appreciated in the family. Does everyone feel psychologically safe in the family?

Nowadays, the whole family spends hours together. We recommend sitting down as a family activity and building the family values map. Look at what the family needs to do to make changes and turn the map into a roadmap through which we live as a family. This is a great gift for every family.

At the organizational level

Corporations (in the private sector) are there to provide products, services, or solutions, with an end goal to also make money. This is embedded in the mission and vision of the vast majority of all companies. But the question becomes: how much profit do you wish to amass and why? The old paradigm (before the Coronavirus crisis) was that the more the better. It guarantees financial wellbeing to all stakeholders and probably wealth guarantees the long-term survival of the company. The Coronavirus crisis shows us clearly that this is not the case. When the entire supply chain changes, your past or present economic success does not guarantee survival. The Coronavirus crisis may stimulate a philosophical reflection on why we need organizations/corporations. Do we need organizations to serve people and society, or do we need society (with its capitalistic rules and regulations as practiced today) to serve organizations? The Coronavirus shows, perhaps, for the first time, that other values seem to be by far more important than economic values; in a crisis situation, health, for example, is by far more important than wealth. Additionally, it is the first time in history (perhaps) that agents in the health profession need to make terrible and difficult decisions about which patients they will try to save and which they will let die given the scarcity of resources. A terrible decision to make. It reflects societal, organizational and individual values that are tied to this most difficult decision. On the positive side, we see a chain of philanthropic activity with a magnitude that would have never occurred prior to the Coronavirus crisis. In this situation, economic considerations are placed lower on the hierarchy. The contribution to the common need by some of the wealthy people/organizations in the world, shows care, camaraderie and compassion as core values (centered along the **social-ethical axis**). Money and resources are channeled towards purchasing protective gear, accelerating research, and providing emergency shelters to the needy. True, it is done in certain geographic areas where rich corporations operate, but the medium-term benefits will be to society at large. Every day, we hear stories of people like Bill Gates, Jack Ma, Mark Zuckerberg, and Amancio Ortega to name a few, who get on the bandwagon with their personal wealth. It is also a time to reflect on issues such as: what is our corporate social responsibility today, and which will we follow after the crisis. Medtronic, with headquarters in Israel, has decided for example, to give away its patent for producing respirators as a solidary act to enable the production of these devices worldwide. This is one of many examples that are being shared daily. Having business policies as usual is not accepted, and more and more organizations attempt to show that they are sensitive to the human needs. They are attempting to be more ethical, equitable, environmentally conscious, gender sensitive, and even more sensitive towards the poor, the sick, the old, the oppressed, etc. Similar considerations can be asked for a societal level which we summarized in Table C.1.

Table C.1 A Synoptic Table for the Societal Level

Value Axis	Key Question
Economic-pragmatic	What's important to our society's economic goals and objectives?
Social-ethical	What's important to our society's social fabric and ethical conduct?
Emotional-developmental	What's important to our society's emotional and creative development?

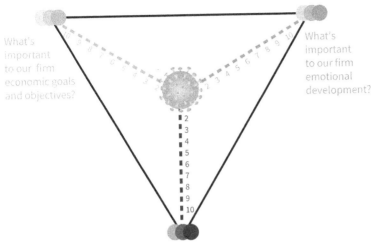

What's important to our firm social and ethical conduct and relations?

Figure C.5 The Coronavirus and the hierarchy of values at the firm/organizational level.

On leadership, values and the embedment Spiritual axis

The Coronavirus crisis is also a real test to see how our political leaders manage the crisis. Leadership is all about followership.   The Coronavirus crisis shows the kind of leaders we trust and are willing to follow, and others we are not. It also shows the level of collegiality and the level of obedience. The Coronavirus crisis shows how the state manages the delicate balance between achieving efficient results (avoiding high rate of mortality) and intruding on personal privacy. It establishes the tradeoffs between what is more important: health or economy. To what extent leaders respect core democratic values, and what is permitted in the name of a health crisis. The Coronavirus crisis shows the many faces of good and evil governance. At the societal level, the Coronavirus crisis has been a real test to values such as brotherhood, voluntarism and other cherished values that are badly needed in times of crisis. We have already mentioned in former writing that spiritual values surface much stronger during times of crisis. A leader who does not have the capacity to embed some of these values cannot inspire (Dolan, 2015, Dolan and Altman, 2012). The heart of society as well as the organization is the values that the leader instills. In fact, we argue that culture is nothing more than shared values. Our values are acquired during our education and become our invisible guides. They define the direction for our desires, behavior and actions. We should not forget, nonetheless, that values are contextual. The same value can have contradictory meanings in different contexts. For example, for some people "love" is considered a very important value (although we think it is more a need). Nevertheless, possession can be manifested in the name of love. It can be extremely negative and even dangerous, having little in common with the concept of unconditional love. Similarly, blind trust can be a recipe for disaster. History is full of examples of people trusting a leader blindly. We must be careful because we are good at fooling ourselves.

Culture is the soul of the organization or society in general. At the foundation of culture are system relevant paradigms: social, political, worldview, business, economy, and work. Culture is driven by strong beliefs and assumptions built on those paradigms. They are also strongly linked to the dominant world view and religion. They permeate the way of life, community, politics, education and even science.

Values come in next because real values are born of underlying basic assumptions and beliefs. They "ride" on them. Otherwise they are either wishful thinking or fake values. Values are in their essence, neutral. The context defines whether they are good or bad. Again, the message is that values are contextual.

People tend to respect the values which have direct consequences on their life, their wellbeing, or career. If the propagated values are in contradiction with their inner values, people tend to make trade-offs. The propagated values have to be confirmed and corroborated by the behavior of the leaders. On the other hand, if the values are aligned with their inner values it can generate incredible amounts of energy and lead to peak performance (Dolan, 2020).

Today the wrapping seems to be more important than the content. We like nice looking wrapping, but once we purchase it, we throw it away creating environmental problems. It has a mainly aesthetic purpose. Buying a wrapped object; its function is advertising, promotion and publicity. Most of the nice and impressive statements about vision, mission and values have the same purpose. They come from the same kitchen be it for organizations, corporations, politicians, or even individuals. We live in a world of reality shows and false promises, where impression is more important than truth. We are addicted to a superficial glittering world. This leads to fake democracies and wrong education. Maybe crossing the "**danger zone**" (such as the Coronavirus) can help create a more human, sincere and honest civilization, where people will no longer accept all the falsehood and fake around them. Liran and Dolan talked about this corporate phenomenon in their paper entitled: *Values, values on the wall, just do business and forget them all* (Liran & Dolan TEBR 2016).

The expected paradigm shifts of economy and business have a big impact on our culture as well. Our culture will partially shift into the Virtual Reality (VR). The Coronavirus is having an unprecedented impact on the events scene, but the virus doesn't have to bring the industry to a halt. Virtual reality (VR) seems to offer a solution to the travel bans companies all over the world are facing and the restrictions on large gatherings that are being imposed by governments.

The impact on culture and quality of life is immense, in both directions: positive and negative. Part of our comfort zone is already and will be transferred more intensely to the VR. New forms of culture will be developed. For example, fictions can be experienced like real in the VR; we can have active parts in novels, movies etc. We will be able to dive into any historical period and observe it directly. Education will be free or at very low cost and accessible for all already in the digital form. Later on, in global virtual "schools" learners will drive learning, and the teachers will become guides, tutors, coaches and trusted experts in learning. Learning will be complemented by individual development of core competencies enhancing talent development. Education will encompass learning, deliberate skills training, and practice focused on talents[i]. Students will be able to explore how the chosen domain of expertise may affect their life and try different options to find the most suitable in VR.

All these dramatic changes affect our comfort-zone. The "growth and greed" capitalism seems to be coming to an end. Because of the claim that free markets are tightly linked to democracy, our democracies are also affected. Democratic systems are running out of steam. Global economic crash is constantly looming because of the astronomic debt of all economies. All this leads people to yearn for past greatness. Maybe it is also a symptom of the aging populations in the leading countries.

We argue that the next 20 to 30 years will lead the world out of the historical comfort zone towards a future still widely unknown. As this will lead to economic, political and social turbulence and increased anxiety in people. We hope that the terrible experience of the Coronavirus pandemic will alert political leaders to carefully consider the path to mere economic growth. It will be a real challenge for governments, business, education and all of us. It requires a multidisciplinary and systemic approach with a view towards the future. We need to write, and dream about a positive state of the future which considers the three axes of values as the underlying paradigms and contrary of the past, not allow the economic axis to dominate all actions (Raich et al 2014).

> Culture is the way we see the world and behave accordingly. Culture is the soul of the civilization, the society and the organizations.

Spiritual values may be an interesting bridge to connect all classes of values. A hybrid of need and spiritual value; perhaps the concept advocated by all spiritual gurus in all religions and spiritual movements is the concept of love. We refer to love in form of a universal and unconditional state. Likewise, we argue that another meta value is the concept of trust.   Think about it. If at any society, at any organization, in any family there is a real sharing of unconditional love and unconditional trust, what else do we really need in order to feel part of something important? On the top of it, if we are conscious of our triaxial model of economic, emotional and ethical values, we become part of the universe and our daily conduct is hyper aligned (Dolan, 2020).

Some believe that nature as a whole can be considered as spiritual values. The Universe contains intricate organization at every level from the atom to the galaxy. The biosphere of our earth contains countless organized entities, and every day there is something new under the sun. From the womb of Nature has come sentient creatures who care, who value. Around these creatures is this rich world capable of meeting needs and desires. Is all this an accident, per the physicalist or the result of design, per the theist, or the result of something quite different than those polar positions have imagined? Nature is seen as an essential part of the universe and thus should not be interfered with. In an interesting blog, Schenk suggests that "Whatever "value" is, it arises from and is a part of Nature's ability to self-organize and to create complexity, including conscious, intentional, and valuing beings such as our selves. Ultimately, Nature is responsible for creating both the being that values and the things that satisfy the wants and desires of this being. From this fact, we can deduce that this "creative" activity of Nature is the progenitor of all value. Nature is the origin of value – and thus finding value in Nature is not merely a matter of taste, but a matter of fact" (Schenk 2020). In this sense, futurologists and other scientists claim that the Coronavirus, might have occurred because the advanced technological society is really interfering with natural ecosystem. They call our attention to the fundamental need to shift paradigms in the Cyber-Age economy in order to restore the universal values-order. This includes the following shifts:

- From focus on (infinite) growth towards sustainable transformation and innovation
- From focus on profit towards a balance of profit, life quality and social good
- From fear of technology towards collaborative intelligence
- From having towards becoming and being
- From representative democracy towards authoritarian regimes
- From control towards mutual tolerance, trust and respect
- From strategy towards TrAction, which is a new concept to replace the traditional strategy (Raich et al, 2020 -forthcoming)

The Coronavirus crisis: Needs vs. values

Needs and values are indeed highly interconnected. Both are connected to the things we care about. There will be times, in your process of gaining a deeper understanding of another person, when it won't be important to distinguish whether you're exploring a need or a value. But there is an important distinction between the two: *needs tend to be very similar for all people, whereas values tend to be highly individualized.* However, needs might have some sort of hierarchy for which when our survival is at stake; they supersede our values. Needs, nonetheless are mostly chosen for us by the physical environment (breathing, eating, drinking for survival). Values, by contrast are chosen by us. Needs and values show themselves in a variety of ways. Each has some characteristic patterns that make it possible to distinguish one from the other, even in an acute situation as the Coronavirus crisis.

Why trust is the "value of Values" and more specifically during the Coronavirus crisis?

"Trust takes time to build, it can be lost in a fraction of a second and is very difficult to restore!"

Trust is the mother of all values. All relationships are based on mutual trust. Trust is the fundamental condition for cooperation, collaboration and partnership. Trust may also be dangerous, because not all people we trust are trustworthy and may deceive and betray us. Thus, one should be careful who we want to trust.

Trust is the belief we have in another person or in an institution. It is the core of the relationship. Experience can reinforce trust, but false promises not only undermine, but destroy trust. Lost trust is difficult to restore and sometimes even impossible. Therefore, it is the highest social good. Genuine trust must be earned. People trust leaders more by their actions than their words.

There is no doubt that we live in times of high uncertainty. This is the time that we need to follow our leaders be they our family leaders (at home -family), our corporate leaders or of political leaders. This is the time when we need to change (or even transform attitudes, behavior, and daily activities) to the extent that we have never seen before. We do it as followers only when we have trustworthy leaders. Trusting parents will provide the safety and security that children need, trusting our health professionals will provide the confidence in placing our bodies in their competent hands, and trusting our political leaders is critical in changing behaviors such as social distancing, having a protective mask, or staying at home. Trust, as we have mentioned in all our writing is a process that takes times to build but could be lost in a fraction of a second. This is the real moment to examine who we trust in times of uncertainty, who we are we willing to follow. We are not certain that we trust our leadership in handling the Coronavirus crisis (except perhaps the ones in China, Korea and other odd countries), which takes a huge toll on our physical and emotional wellbeing.

We place our trust (and hope) in our scientists and in our collective intelligence that is manifested across borders and frontiers. We are certain that a real solution to the Coronavirus crisis will be found. History indicates that real breakthrough innovation comes from the sharing of trustworthy and reliable scientific information and from global solidarity. The value of solidarity is the key to true collaboration. When one country is struck by an epidemic, it should be willing to honestly share information about the outbreak without fear of economic catastrophe – while other countries should be able to trust that information and should be willing to extend a helping hand rather than ostracize the victim. Today, China can teach countries all over the world many important lessons about Coronavirus, but this demands a high level of international trust and cooperation. Recently, an amazing collaboration was set up between doctors in Spain and doctors in China (all work is in real-time with the help of volunteers that translate back and forth on a platform that was created see: https://covid19alliances.com/). Early results seem to be very promising. Perhaps the best manner to conclude this paper is by paraphrasing to say:

IN TRUST WE TRUST.

Conclusions

"The world before Coronavirus and after cannot be the same"
– Goldin & Muggah (2020)

Values act as a compass to follow the direction we have chosen. If we want to have a chance to cross the *'danger zone'* we need to initiate a value shift. We need to move from growth towards care and responsibility; from confrontation, egocentrism and conflict towards empathy and partnership; from profit towards the quality of life. We also need to redefine the quality of life as allowing a decent life and making it accessible to everybody worldwide. The overall shift needs to convert a path from the materialistic towards spiritual values. Here are a few interesting points for reflection:

- Care and responsibility for nature and the eco-system becomes a must if we wish to stay alive on this planet. It will require sustainability, a zero-waste attitude, and a shift away from cheap mass production and the throw-away mentality.
- We will need to deploy all the creativity and entrepreneurship we can get to implement creative solutions developed globally for the threats in the 'danger zone'.
- Once we have crossed the danger zone, the next direction will be the development of the Meta-Mind-Society leveraging cyber technology for the good of humanity. For this purpose, we will have to focus on futurizing thinking and humanizing work while fostering collaborative intelligence (Raich et al, 2019). We will need to create concurrent direction and action. Similar to the creation of the UN following WWII, perhaps we will need to establish a Global Ethical Council to act as a 'global conscience' for the direction and progress of our journey across the danger zone and later on our progress towards the Meta-Mind-Society. This council will also have the task of developing recommendations and policies to prevent

the abuse of future advanced cyber technology by powerful lords, organizations and cyber criminals, as well as cyber entities based on advanced AI getting out of control. A cyber virus can become indirectly as vicious and deadly as the Coronavirus.

- The arts and the special media have to play a particularly important role in our journey across the danger zone and later on towards the Meta-Mind Society, spreading the message and creating role models to follow.
- Education will have to raise the awareness of the young generation and leverage their creativity to get creative solutions.

It is time to look forward to the emerging future. To the time after the peak of COVID 19 infections i.e. the time of de-escalation of the harsh protection measures. It will take some time before we will be out of the state of emergency. We still don't really know what the new "normal" will look like. This pandemic has shaken the foundations of the globalized world. We cannot exclude the possibility that we will be in completely different economic, social and even political circumstance. Therefore, it is also time to start preparing for a new world.

It appears that the Coronavirus pandemic may return next fall. We hope that an effective vaccine (and treatment) will be found before. None of us (individuals, couples, families, organizations and societies) wish to re-live it. This pandemic is a proxy for other disasters and threats that will most likely come up.

- In the next decade over a billion young people will enter the labor market and many of them be will be trained but unemployed. Large numbers of young people face a future of irregular and informal employment according to several predictions (see for example – *Trading economics Forecast* 2020–2022). At the same time technology development, in particular automation, robotics and AI will affect many professional activities and reduce the number of jobs requested.
- Climate change will force hundreds of millions of people out of their homes worldwide.
- Polarizations across most countries will continue to rise leading to a weakening of social cohesion and the creation of dangerous tensions and conflicts. The number of armed conflicts, and the arms race between the countries, in particular if the global and regional power continues to grow. In hindsight, the Coronavirus pandemic may look like a dress rehearsal for the management of multiple simultaneous global crises.

Whilst several Asian countries have managed the Coronavirus pandemic quite well, most of the affected countries struggle, and the international institutions failed to manage the downside risks generated by the globalization. The world is forced to find a vaccine for COVID 19 to avoid massive disruptions for years.

The Coronavirus pandemic is a comprehensive crisis encompassing health, financial-economic, social and human crisis.

Final note: The lessons learned

At the micro level (Individuals, couples, and family)
- We need to have r values in place and test the extent to which we share them way before a terrible crisis emerges.
- This way contingency and proactive plans can be prepared in advance at all these levels. We can see a surge in coaching that help people, couples and families reexamine their goals and objectives, challenging if the latter are realistic, and helping them set up plans to align daily behavior with the objectives, and easily switch behavior in case of a severe crisis. It is a worthwhile investment. The end results of this type on introspection is a way to develop life more consistent with what is really important.
- Three things will be changed forever following the pandemic: the way they think, the way they relate to each other and the way they think about what they value (Kruglanski, 2020)

At the macro level (Organizational, community, state or the world)
- We need to loosen the dense global connectivity on all levels to reduce the number and intensity of dangerous systemic risks. At the same time, we need to reinforce the role of international institutions in global risk management.
- Countries need to be better prepared for big and global crises. Priority of sustainability over infinite growth.
- Life sustaining production needs to have a back-up in the country and not rely only on the global value chain.
- The healthcare industry needs to be re-evaluated in view of global disasters and pandemics. Shift priority from profit towards real life saving.
- In a national or global crisis people turn to strong leaders. Autocratic countries seem to deal with crises better. Democratic countries need to develop ways to enable temporary strong but trustworthy leaders to take over, without invading the freedom and privacy of individuals.
- We need to get prepared to cope with a dramatic economic crisis due to a disaster like the pandemic, which can lead to a reduction of more than 10% of the global GDP. Basic income in some form may be part of the solution. Maybe we need a global Marshall Plan?
- Global risks require global solutions to get a comprehensive response. Globalization can transform global opportunities to global risks and threats. The way we deal with the threat created by the Coronavirus pandemic shows whether we are ready and able to handle a global threat.

The collateral disruptions created by the Coronavirus pandemic will shape the world for the next decades. They are manifold, life losses, disrupted partnerships and families, vanished jobs, bankrupt businesses, structural disruption and weakening of social cohesion, and last but not least failed trustworthy leaders. Future post Coronavirus leaders will face two critical challenges: futurizing and humanizing (Morgan, 2020).

Despite the many negative effects of the Coronavirus virus on our current and future lives, there are also some positive effects. Ism & Leyre, (2020) proposed in their article "16 ways Coronavirus may change the way we look at the world, and Fortwengel (2020) insist on 3 ways the crisis will have permanent effects: (1) Business travel considered critical before will significantly diminish (2) Flexible working arrangements and virtual work will become more habitual (who says that we need to go to a place called work), and industry will start to seriously prepare for disruption pressures that will come from both the demand and supply side. At the risk of being a bit naïve yet based on data we have accumulated at the Global Future of Work Foundation over the past several years (www.globalfutureofwork.com) , we wish to conclude this paper with some positive predictions in the aftermath of the pandemic :

- There will be a marked shift towards digital technologies in business and education, e.g. virtual conferencing, workshops, and home office for work and home-based education.
- There will be an accelerated push forward towards intelligent collaboration of humans with smart machines in order to come up with rapid solutions to pandemics and other crises.
- It seems that there is a re-discovery of direct human contact and communication on the phone or over the digital channels.
- There will be more production on-site, on-demand customized using 3D printing and related technologies.
- There will be an expansion in the creation of digital ownership, i.e. algorithm-based recipes and solutions.
- There will be a concentrated global effort to cope with the highly uncertain future.
- There will be many more scholars, visionaries and even political leaders who will start to seriously consider future oriented thinking and action in an uncertain environment.

According to Sneader and Singhal (2020), in a paper published in the Mckinsey & company, the Coronavirus is not only a health crisis of immense proportion – it's also an imminent restructuring of the global economic order. The Coronavirus disrupting effect may constitute shock transformation that will have a permanent (we hope) effect on our core values, on our definition of success and happiness, on our enhanced global concerns (the ecosystem, poverty, immigration, or others) and on the search for a better global solution that will protect us all.

(*The authors wish to thank Mrs. Keren Dolan for a speedy quality copyediting as well as insightful comments made on an earlier version of this paper.*)

About the authors

Simon L. Dolan is currently the president of the Global Future of Work Foundation (www.globalfutureofwork.com). Prof. Dolan used to be the Future of Work Chair at ESADE Business School in Barcelona, and before that he taught for many years at McGill and Montreal Universities (Canada), Boston and University of Colorado (U.S.). He is a prolific author with over 75 books on themes connected with managing people, culture reengineering, values and coaching. His full bio can be seen at: www.simondolan.com Contact him: Simon@globalfutureofwork.com or simon.dolan@esade.edu

Mario Raich is a Swiss futurist, book author and global management consultant. He was a Senior Executive in several global financial organisations, and Invited Professor to some leading business schools like ESADE (Barcelona). He is the co-founder and Chairman of e-Merit Academy www.emeritacademy.com), and Managing Director for the Innovation Services at Frei+Raich Ltd. in Zurich. In addition he is a member of the advisory board of the Global Future of Work Foundation in Barcelona. Currently he is researching the impact of Cyber-Reality and Artificial Intelligence on society, education, business and work. Contact: Mario@emeritacademy.com

Anat Garti is a social psychologist, couple and family therapist, management consultant, and a coach. She has recently obtained her doctorate from the University of Haifa. She is the chief psychologist of the Israel Values Center: (www.values-center.co.il). Contact her: anatgarti@gmail.com

Avishai Landau is a certified coach and trainer in "Leading and coaching by values". He is the founder and CEO of the Israel Values Center (www.values-center.co.il). He has over 30 years of experience in various senior executive positions at some of the leading corporations in Israel. Co-author of several books on leading and coaching in Hebrew. Contact him at: mbv.org @gmail.com

References

Dolan, S.L. (2020). *The Secrets of Coaching and Leading by Values*. London: Routledge.
Dolan, S.L. (2019). *Más coaching por valores*. Madrid: Lid Editorial.
Dolan, S.L. (2018). *Valores, la brújula para personas y organizaciones de futuro*. Madrid: Punto Rojo.
Dolan, S.L. (2015). Values, spirituality and organizational culture. *Developing Leaders*, 21, 22–25.

Dolan, S.L. (2011). *Coaching by Values: A Guide to Success in the Life of Business and the Business of Life*. Bloomington: iUniverse.

Dolan, S.L., & Altman Y. (2012) Managing by values: The leadership spirituality connection. *People and Strategy*, 35(4), 20–26.

Dolan, S.L., Garcia S., & Richley B. (2006). *Managing by Values: Corporate Guide to Living, being Alive and Making a Living in the XXI Century*. London: Palgrave-Macmillan.

Dolan, S.L. et al. (2013). *Mapping differences and strengths in the public sector*. Cross Cultural Management: An International Journal, *20(3)*.

Fortwengel, J. (2020). Coronavirus: Three ways the crisis may permanently change our lives. *The Conversation*, March 19 (https://theconversation.com/Coronavirusvirus-three-ways-the-crisis-may-permanently-change-our-lives-133954).

Garcia, S., & Dolan, S.L. (1997). *Dirección por Valores*. Madrid: McGraw Hill.

Garti, A., & Dolan, S.L. (2019). Managing by values (MBV): Innovative tools for successful micro behavioural conduct. *The European Business Review*.

Goldin, I., & Muggah, R. (2020). The world before this Coronavirus and after cannot be the same (https://theconversation.com/the-world-before-this-Coronavirusvirus-and-after-cannot-be-the-same-134905?utm_medium=email&utm_campaign=Latest%20from%20The%20Conversation%20for%20March%2030%202020%20-%2015782 15106&utm_content=Latest%20from%20The%20Conversation%20for%20March %2030%202020%20-%201578215106+CID_cd9964cbdc42c3c9352c53bab3eb9907 &utm_source=campaign_monitor_uk&utm_term=how%20different%20the%20world %20after%20COVID-19%20might%20look).

Ism, C., & Leyre, J. (2020. 16 ways coronavirus may change the way we look at the world. *Singularity Hub* (https://singularityhub.com/2020/03/25/16-ways-Coronavirusvirus -may-change-the-way-we-look-at-the-world/?utm_medium=email&utm_content =16-ways-Coronavirusvirus-may-change-the-way-we-look-at-the-world&utm_source =newsletter&utm_campaign=fy18-hub-daily-rss-newsletter&mkt_tok=eyJpIjoiWkdG a09HVXdOVEk1TlRCCaSIsInQiOiJwdnFcL082bVRqNDIzZjZHTmwyRWNcLzJy ZW5QNEt0VEFZVjlYdEh4VjBCCTk1kQTJGNVBZNE9kVkl1RThRQkZzUTVTd ib0ZpMmlRVHN4bSswbXXliSm9a ZHZQT1NNUGZxWDJTMDJWQWRRR zhNNEZFRDBWbUdVZHp2N2hFWlFuU3U0QU9WIn0%3D).

Kruglanski, A. (2020) 3 ways the coronavirus pandemic is changing who we are (https:// theconversation.com/3-ways-the-coronavirus-pandemic-is-changing-who-we-are-133876).

Liran, A., & Dolan, S.L. (2016) Values, values on the wall, just do business and forget them all: Wells Fargo, Volkswagen and others in the hall. *The European Business Review*, October-November.

Morgan, J., (2020) Leaders of the future will face these 2 types of challenges. *The European Business Review*, January 23.

Raich, M., Krzeminski, T., Cisullo, C., & Richley, B. (2020). *The Emerging Concept of TrAction* (forthcoming).

Raich, M., Dolan, S.L., Cisullo, C., & Richley, B. (2019). Beyond collaborative intelligence we can see a meta-mind society surfacing and we can dream of a Ω-mind? *The European Business Review*, September-October.

Raich, M., Eisler, R., & Dolan, S.L (2014) *Cyberness: The Future Reinvented* (https://www .amazon.es/Cyberness-Future-Reinvented-Mario-Raich/dp/1500673382).

Raich, M., & Dolan, S.L. (2008) *Beyond: Business and Society in Transformation*. London: Palgrave MacMillan.

Schenk, T. (2020). Nature-based spirituality and our sense of value, spiritual naturalist society (https://www.snsociety.org/nature-based-spirituality-and-our-sense-of-value/).

Sneader, K., & Singhal S. (2020) Beyond coronavirus: The path to the next normal (https://www.mckinsey.com/industries/healthcare-systems-and-services/our-insights/beyond-coronavirus-the-path-to-the-next-normal).

Trading Economics (2020). Youth unemployment rate – forecast 2020–2022 (https://tradingeconomics.com/forecast/youth-unemployment-rate).

Appendix 1: List of the 51 values of the triaxial model

Affection	Initiative
Austerity (savings)	Innovativeness
Calmness	Integrity
Compassion	Justice
Concern for the environment	Leadership
Communication	Loyalty
Contribution (adding value)	Maintain traditions
Cooperation	Open mind
Creativity	Optimism
Determination	Organization - order
Empathy	Patience
Equality	Perseverance
Fairness	Planning
Family relationships	Playfulness
Flexibility	Pragmatism
Forgiveness	Privacy
Freedom	Professional success
Friendship	Punctuality
Generosity	Respect
Harmony	Security
Healthiness (well-being)	Self-control
Happiness	Self-esteem
Having money	Simplification
Honour	Supportiveness
Industrious	Transparency
Influence	

Note: Originally, each value is expressed in color. But, given that this book is not offered in color, we use different shades of gray to parallel the colors that are found in the "Value of values" card game:

- Dark black is red (the economic–pragmatic axis)
- Gray is blue (the social–ethical axis)
- White is green (the emotional–developmental axis)

Appendix 2: Dolan 3Es Triaxial Template

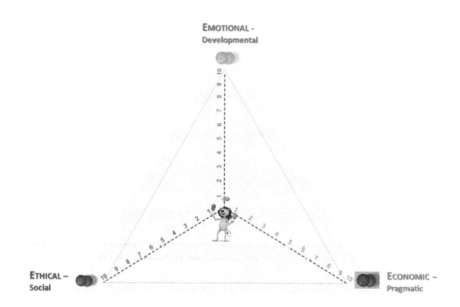

EMOTIONAL -
Developmental

ETHICAL –
Social

ECONOMIC –
Pragmatic

Appendix 3: The card game "the value of values" in all available languages

English - Spanish - French - Portuguese - German - Italian - Hebrew - Arabic - Russian - Amharic
Vietnamese - Thai - chinese - (Taiwan) Behasa Malaysia - Behasa Indonesia - Burmese - Cambodian - Tegalo Philippines

Appendix 4: Recommended videos and links

Simon Dolan shares a brief history about himself as well as the birth of leading, managing, and coaching by values—www.youtube.com/watch?v=6z-rhrS1fVI

The value of values in brief—www.youtube.com/watch?v=dbrrsYSG-wo

It's a matter of values—Documentary (use the CC option for subtitles in English whenever the audio is in Spanish or Catalan)—www.youtube.com/watch?v=AFXPXMCV4bc

Dolan about the future of work—Conference in Poland (note: very long speech)—www.bing.com/videos/search?q=Simon+Dolan+video+future+of+work&src=IE-TopResult&conversationid=&ru=%2fsearch%3fq%3dSimon%2bDolan%2bvideo%2bfuture%2bof%2bwork%26src%3dIE-TopResult%26FORM%3dIETR02%26conversationid%3d&view=detail&mmscn=vwrc&mid=B34D6F41D5565E9C49F3B34D6F41D5565E9C49F3&FORM=WRVORC

Interview by Liza-Maria Norlin—www.youtube.com/watch?v=4cYIaydoeHE

Kaleidoscope of conference images about values and about the future—www.youtube.com/watch?v=awP9VAticRE&index=3&list=PLgXk7ExUvlf1suRd2syA3tlzWHeWm1i-e

The future of work—by Esade—www.bing.com/videos/search?q=Simon+Dolan+video+future+of+work&ru=%2fsearch%3fq%3dSimon%2bDolan%2bvideo%2bfuture%2bof%2bwork%26src%3dIE-TopResult%26FORM%3dIETR02%26conversationid%3d&view=detail&mid=BC0175B42FBDB3511780BC0175B42FBDB3511780&&mmscn=vwrc&FORM=VDRVRV

Dolan on motivating people—www.bing.com/videos/search?q=Simon+Dolan+video+future+of+work&ru=%2fsearch%3fq%3dSimon%2bDolan%2bvideo%2bfuture%2bof%2bwork%26src%3dIE-TopResult%26FORM%3dIETR02%26conversationid%3d&view=detail&mid=86503EB21C211DA2001C86503EB21C211DA2001C&&mmscn=vwrc&FORM=VDRVRV

Simon Dolan on the value of values and culture reengineering—www.bing.com/videos/search?q=Simon+Dolan+video+future+of+work&ru=%2fsearch%3fq%3dSimon%2bDolan%2bvideo%2bfuture%2bof%2bwork%26src%3dIE-TopResult%26FORM%3dIETR02%26conversationid%3d&view=detail&mid=A9A9F4C787FBBE9695D8A9A9F4C787FBBE9695D8&&mmscn=vwrc&FORM=VDRVRV

Simon Dolan on leadership—www.bing.com/videos/search?q=Simon+Dolan+video+future+of+work&ru=%2fsearch%3fq%3dSimon%2bDolan%2bvideo%2bfuture%2bof%2bwork%26src%3dIE-TopResult%26FORM%3dIETR02%26conversationid%3d&mmscn=vwrc&view=detail&mid=0BA1E7F99BB1358EF6700BA1E7F99BB1358EF670&rvsmid=BC0175B42FBDB3511780BC0175B42FBDB3511780&FORM=VDRVRV

Values4kids—www.b ing.c om/vi deos/ searc h?q = S imon + D olan + VIME
   O&&view=detail&mid=2 1A3EB 0C0B4 8AE3B 62FB2 1A3EB 0C0B4 8AE3B
   62FB&&FORM=VDRVRV

The magic carpet and the islands of values—www.bing.com/videos/search?q=Simon+
   Dolan + VIMEO&&view=detail&mid=8 1933D 11759 AA6EB F4168 1933D 11759
   AA6EBF416&&FORM=VDRVRV

Index